REVISUALIZING VISUAL CULTURE

Digital Research in the Arts and Humanities

Series Editors
Marilyn Deegan, Lorna Hughes and Harold Short

Digital technologies are becoming increasingly important to arts and humanities research, expanding the horizons of research methods in all aspects of data capture, investigation, analysis, modelling, presentation and dissemination. This important series will cover a wide range of disciplines with each volume focusing on a particular area, identifying the ways in which technology impacts on specific subjects. The aim is to provide an authoritative reflection of the 'state of the art' in the application of computing and technology. The series will be critical reading for experts in digital humanities and technology issues, and it will also be of wide interest to all scholars working in humanities and arts research.

Other titles in the series

Interfaces of Performance
Edited by Maria Chatzichristodoulou,
Janis Jefferies and Rachel Zerihan
ISBN 978 0 7546 7576 1

Modern Methods for Musicology
Prospects, Proposals, and Realities
Edited by Tim Crawford and Lorna Gibson
ISBN 978 0 7546 7302 6

Revisualizing Visual Culture

Edited by
CHRIS BAILEY
Leeds Metropolitan University, UK

HAZEL GARDINER
King's College London, UK

Routledge
Taylor & Francis Group

LONDON AND NEW YORK

First published 2010 by Ashgate Publishing

Published 2016 by Routledge
2 Park Square, Milton Park, Abingdon, Oxfordshire OX14 4RN
711 Third Avenue, New York, NY 10017, USA

First issued in paperback 2016

Routledge is an imprint of the Taylor & Francis Group, an informa business

British Library Cataloguing in Publication Data
Revisualizing visual culture. -- (Digital research in the
   arts and humanities)
   1. Art--Digital libraries. 2. Art--History--Data
   processing.
   I. Series II. Bailey, Chris. III. Gardiner, Hazel.
   025'.06-dc22

Library of Congress Cataloging-in-Publication Data
Revisualizing visual culture / edited by Chris Bailey and Hazel Gardiner.
      p. cm.
   Includes bibliographical references and index.
   ISBN 978-0-7546-7568-6 (hardback) 1. Art--Historiography--Data
processing. 2. Historic preservation--Data processing. 3. Historic
preservation--Documentation. 4. Cultural property--Protection. 5. Information
storage and retrieval systems--Art. 6. Information technology. 7. Technological
innovations. 8. Knowledge management. I. Bailey, Chris. II. Gardiner, Hazel.

   N380.R48 2010
   701'.18--dc22

                                                                              2009030233

   ISBN 13: 978-1-138-26991-0 (pbk)
   ISBN 13: 978-0-7546-7568-6 (hbk)

Contents

List of Figures

List of Tables

List of Plates

Notes on Contributors

Chris Bailey is Professor of Cultural History and Dean of the Faculty of Arts and Society at Leeds Metropolitan University. He has been active as a member of the CHArt committee for a number of years, was a member and latterly chair of the Advisory Committee of AHDS Visual Arts, and before that of the Art, Design Architecture and Media (ADAM) Information Gateway and its successor service, the Visual Arts Data Service (VADS). While at Northumbria University he helped to set up the interdisciplinary Institute for Image Data Research, establishing its programme of research into content-based image retrieval, digital image user studies and a range of theoretical projects. He has served on the boards of many arts organizations including a period as Chair of West Midlands Arts and as Vice Chair of Culture North East, for which he helped to establish a regional cultural observatory. He has worked as an adviser and consultant for the European Union on culture and social cohesion, on music policy in Cyprus, on regeneration and cultural management in South Africa and on visual arts provision in the Republic of Ireland.

Sue Breakell is head of Tate Archive, which collects archives relating to British art and art in Britain since 1900. The Archive is located at Tate Britain with the Tate Library. She leads a team working on all aspects of the archive's work, including acquisitions, cataloguing, research services, preservation and access. She began her career at Tate, working on the large archives of Cedric Morris and Kenneth Clark, among others. Subsequently she worked as Company Archivist at Marks and Spencer, and as War Artists Archivist and Museum Archivist at the Imperial War Museum, before returning to Tate in her present role in 2004. As well as the Archive's collecting area, Sue's recent research has focused on the nature and meaning of archives, and the relationship between archives and memory. She co-organized the ARLIS/Tate event 'The Archival Impulse: Artists and Archives', at Tate Britain in November 2007.

Charlotte Frost is a PhD candidate at Birkbeck, University of London. Her thesis demonstrates how emergent technologies impact the archivization and thereby the experience of art, through an analysis of the way in which online platforms for art reception develop the Net art encounter. She is a writer/researcher in the field of new media art, and is currently one of four writers involved in Media Mates, an art organization and journalism partnership scheme co-managed by Digital North and Audiences Yorkshire, where she covers the activities of a number of new media arts organizations in the North of England. Prior to this she was the commissioning editor of Furtherfield.org the sister-site of Furthertxt.org.

Hazel Gardiner was Senior Project Officer for the AHRC ICT Methods Network, based at the Centre for Computing in the Humanities (CCH) at King's College London, from 2005 to 2008. She is joint-editor of the CHArt (the Computers and the History of Art group) Yearbook and a member of the CHArt Committee. She is Editor for the British Academy research project The Corpus of Romanesque Sculpture in Britain and Ireland (CRSBI), and a researcher for this project and the Corpus Vitrearum Medii Aevi (CVMA), another British Academy research project. She contributes to the Material Culture module of the Digital Humanities MA programme at CCH.

Charlie Gere is Head of Department and Reader in New Media Research in the Institute for Cultural Research, Lancaster University and Chair of CHArt. Prior to this he was Programme Director for the MA Digital Art History programme at Birkbeck, University of London where he was also Director of Computer Arts, Contexts, Histories, etc. ... (CACHe), a three-year AHRC-funded research project looking at the history of early British computer art. He is the author of *Digital Culture* (Reaktion Books, 2002), and *Art, Time and Technology* (Berg, 2006) and co-editor of *White Heat Cold Logic* (MIT Press, 2009), as well as many papers on questions of technology, media and art.

Leif Isaksen specializes in the application of IT to analyse the use and conception of space in the ancient world. He was formerly Senior IT Development Officer at Oxford Archaeology where he worked on methodologies to map maritime heritage, amongst other projects. He moderates the Antiquist IT and Cultural Heritage community and co-organized the AHRC ICT Methods Network workshop 'Space and Time: Methods in Geospatial Computing for Mapping the Past'. He has an MSc in Archaeological Computing and is currently studying for a PhD developing an assistive research framework to integrate information across multiple excavation data repositories.

Stuart Jeffrey is User Services Manager with the Archaeology Data Service (ADS). With the ADS, he is responsible for ensuring the usability and the reuse of ADS resources as well as the project management of a number of UK and European-funded research projects in digital archaeology. Before working with the ADS he was a senior archaeologist with the West of Scotland Archaeology Service with particular responsibility for the Sites and Monuments Record in that area. He graduated from the University of Glasgow with a BSc in computer science and archaeology in 1997 and later returned to Glasgow to undertake a PhD in Three Dimensional Modelling of Medieval Sculpted Stones.

Kirk Martinez is a Senior Lecturer in Electronics and Computer Science at the University of Southampton. Previously he was Arts-Computing Lecturer at University College London and Birkbeck, University of London. He has been involved in nine major European projects relating to technology for cultural heritage. These range from the VASARI project where he helped design the world's first high-resolution colorimetric imager for paintings, along with other internationally important imaging projects, to Artiste, which developed a system for retrieving art images based on their content and allowed cross-collection searching through web services. More recently SCULPTEUR moved this forward to using ontologies enabling searches for 3D objects by similarity in shape, and eCHASE aims to expand this technology for commercial use by picture libraries. Publications include a summary of his imaging research in the *Transactions of the IEEE*. He holds a BSc in Physics from the University of Reading and a PhD in Image Processing in the department of Electronic Systems Engineering at the University of Essex.

James MacDevitt is currently Assistant Professor of Art History at Cerritos College, Norwalk, California and Adjunct Professor of Photography at Chaffey College, California. He has previously served as the Assistant Director to the Sweeney Art Gallery and the Digital Media Associate at the California Museum of Photography, both at the University of California, Riverside. He has also previously taught courses at both California State University San Bernardino and Whittier College, California. He has an MA in the History of Art from University of California, Riverside.

Mike Pringle is Director of the Swindon Cultural Partnership. Prior to this he was Director of the Visual Arts Data Service (VADS) and AHDS Visual Arts, a leading advisory service and repository for digital image collections. He has published academic works on usability and digital images and as a member of the JISC Images Working Group he was a lead author on the JISC publication *Digital Images in Education: Realizing the Vision*. Earlier in his career he was Technical Manager with English Heritage, developing innovative, image-led interfaces for complex data. He holds a doctorate in Computing Information Systems Engineering, working with Virtual Reality, at the Royal Military College of Science.

Jemima Rellie has worked at the interface of new media and culture for over ten years during which time she has gained extensive experience in cross-platform commissioning and new media developments in both commercial and not-for-profit sectors. She is currently Assistant Director at the Getty Conservation Institute where she is responsible for information and dissemination, both online and offline, including the web, books, a newsletter, an information centre and press. In 2001, she was hired as Tate's first Head of Digital Programmes, with responsibility for public-facing digital content, including a bespoke online programme crucial to establishing Tate Online as a destination in its own right.

Daniela Sirbu is an Associate Professor in the Department of New Media, part of the Faculty of Fine Arts at the University of Lethbridge, Canada. Her academic research is interdisciplinary at the confluence between new media, architecture and fine art. She is currently involved in the WestGrid Collaboration and Visualization Research Program for Western Canadian universities, which is mainly funded by Canada Foundation for Innovation, and she is a principal investigator for two WestGrid projects: I-HEARD (Immersive Hybrid Environments for Architectural Research and Design) and MARVIS (Motion Analysis and Representation in Virtual Interactive Spaces).

Doireann Wallace is a PhD candidate at the Dublin Institute of Technology, Ireland, where she is ABBEST scholar (the ABBEST programme supports exceptional students) in the School of Media. Her research interests are centred on the photographic image in the electronic archive. She had her first solo exhibition, a whole new architecture of reality, at The Lab in Dublin city in 2007. She also lectures part-time in photography and visual culture in the Continuing Education department of the National College of Art and Design, Dublin.

Series Preface

Revisualizing Visual Culture is the sixth volume of *Digital Research in the Arts and Humanities.*

Each of the titles in this series comprises a critical examination of the application of advanced ICT methods in the arts and humanities. That is, the application of formal computationally based methods, in discrete but often interlinked areas of arts and humanities research. Usually developed from Expert Seminars, one of the key activities supported by the Methods Network, these volumes focus on the impact of new technologies in academic research and address issues of fundamental importance to researchers employing advanced methods.

Although generally concerned with particular discipline areas, tools or methods, each title in the series is intended to be broadly accessible to the arts and humanities community as a whole. Individual volumes not only stand alone as guides but collectively form a suite of textbooks reflecting the 'state of the art' in the application of advanced ICT methods within and across arts and humanities disciplines. Each is an important statement of current research at the time of publication, an authoritative voice in the field of digital arts and humanities scholarship.

These publications are the legacy of the AHRC ICT Methods Network and will serve to promote and support the ongoing and increasing recognition of the impact on and vital significance to research of advanced arts and humanities computing methods. The volumes will provide clear evidence of the value of such methods, illustrate methodologies of use and highlight current communities of practice.

Marilyn Deegan, Lorna Hughes, Harold Short
Series Editors
AHRC ICT Methods Network
Centre for Computing in the Humanities
King's College London
2010

About the AHRC ICT Methods Network

The aims of the AHRC ICT Methods Network were to promote, support and develop the use of advanced ICT methods in arts and humanities research and to support the cross-disciplinary network of practitioners from institutions around the UK. It was a multi-disciplinary partnership providing a national forum for the exchange and dissemination of expertise in the use of ICT for arts and humanities research. The Methods Network was funded under the AHRC ICT Programme from 2005 to 2008.

The Methods Network Administrative Centre was based at the Centre for Computing in the Humanities (CCH), King's College London. It coordinated and supported all Methods Network activities and publications, as well as developing outreach to, and collaboration with, other centres of excellence in the UK. The Methods Network was co-directed by Harold Short, Director of CCH, and Marilyn Deegan, Director of Research Development, at CCH, in partnership with Associate Directors: Mark Greengrass, University of Sheffield; Sandra Kemp, Royal College of Art; Andrew Wathey, Royal Holloway, University of London; Sheila Anderson, Arts and Humanities Data Service (AHDS) (2006–2008); and Tony McEnery, University of Lancaster (2005–2006).

The project website (<http://www.methodsnetwork.ac.uk>) provides access to all Methods Network materials and outputs. In the final year of the project a community site, 'Digital Arts and Humanities' (<http://www.arts-humanities. net>) was initiated as a means to sustain community building and outreach in the field of digital arts and humanities scholarship beyond the Methods Network's funding period.

Preface

The study and analysis of the visual arts has been as much affected by the revolutionary emergence of digital technology in recent decades as has any other aspect of cultural life in our society. The effect has been all the more profound because so many of its implications were unforeseen – or unforeseen by all but a few lone voices largely regarded as eccentric. Perhaps this is the case with all revolutions. Once underway, they open up new territory and the unpredictable occurs.

The wide-ranging impact of the new technology on visual culture has been greeted in almost equal measure with wild enthusiasm and horrified reaction. To some extent this is symptomatic of the 'science–art' divide that has characterized Western culture in recent centuries. For 'arts' people the march of science is habitually seen as invasion of barbaric materialism into a world of refinement and sensibility. Yet reaction is usually followed by tacit acceptance once an innovation is found just too good to pass up. Cars, telephones, radios, television all went through this cycle. It might seem that the current technological innovation is of a similar kind. Certainly the impact of digital technology has become so widespread that only the most determinedly ivory tower 'arts' scholar or creator can these days avoid contact with it in almost every walk of life. With the huge gains there always come some losses, but in the end these are usually accepted with an acquiescent shrug.

It is clear then that the world has changed profoundly with the digital. We are very much in the process of this change and sense that there is much more to come, but that does not mean that we should not stop at times to think about what is happening, what we are doing, what is advantageous and what is problematical. This collection of essays provides one of these moments. It is edited by two experts with a profound and longstanding experience of the application of the new technology to the teaching, research and archiving of visual culture. They have brought together a truly broad and comprehensive collection of specialists from both the scientific and art worlds. The original essays contributed come from all sections of the study of visual culture. There are historians, archivists, cultural theorists, curators, technological experts and scientists. An important aspect of this book is that it not only charts the developments that have taken place but also indicates what current developments promise most for the future. For this is an area that is rich in potential and constantly changing. This book provides not only an illuminating map of the current terrain, but also an exciting indication of what may come if the right support and understanding are forthcoming. In this it is polemical as well as analytical. In doing this the authors are also carrying on a tradition established by CHArt – the computers and history of art group that was established more than twenty years ago (and is still going strong) to provide a debating area for such works and to bring together all the different communities. Many of the essays in this collection, indeed, are developments from papers delivered at CHArt conferences.

Perhaps one of the impressions that comes over most strongly from this rich field of development is the way in which the digital appears to have further empowered the visual in our society. The great strength of the digital is its manipulability. It is transferable and transformable. As such it might be seen to be the descendent of film, the archetypal moveable image of the twentieth century. But it does more than film, which moves along a predetermined track. It can change course at any moment and seemingly in any way. There is an argument that film was the defining visual medium of the twentieth century. By the same token it would seem that the digital is set to be (if it is not already) the defining visual medium of the twenty-first century. For the visual this might seem a great gain. This is certainly true in the sense that the visual has become increasingly the medium of communication and expression where once words dominated. Yet in a curious way, this can also be seen as something of a threat to those areas of the visual that have, arguably, traditionally been the visual's main strength. For what has happened with the coming of digitization is that the visual has become increasingly narrativized. There will be those amongst linguistic theorists who will argue that the visual always was a form of discourse. This may be true, in the sense that it was always a form of articulated communication. But it is not true in the sense that the visual is just another form of textual language. While sharing some features with the textual, the visual also has unique features. It is these that have given it its particular strengths. Two of the most fundamental of these are potentially at risk, I think, in the enhanced process of narrativization that the digital introduces to the visual. The first is totality, the ability to present a complete impression on first impact. Naturally this totality does not exhaust what the image has to offer. But it does make its address unique and gives it a particular all-important presence. Such totality exists only in those art forms – be they two- or three-dimensional – that have a single visual manifestation – such as a painting, say, or a ceramic. The second feature is stillness. The traditional visual art form – whether two- or three-dimensional – is static. This might seem to be a weakness, but in fact it is its leading strength – a point that John Berger made forcefully in *Ways of Seeing*. It is that stillness that gives it its contemplative richness, that makes us stop and think and look in the way that the moving image – so much nearer to our daily experience of the transient – does not. Of course the digital does not have to destroy these, but it is capable of overlaying them with its seemingly endless array of changes and multiplicity. This is an issue that we need, I think, to keep in mind.

However, whatever enthusiasms or misgivings we may have about the present situation, the important point is to engage with it, explore it and examine it with critical discrimination. The current book does all these things, and is particularly to be welcomed as a significant intervention at an important moment.

William Vaughan

Acknowledgements

The editors would like to thank Charlie Gere and Mike Pringle, whose contribution and support were invaluable during the initial shaping of this volume.

*We dedicate this volume to the friends and supporters of CHArt
(the Computers and the History of Art group), now in its twenty-fifth year,
and to all researchers and practitioners engaged at the interface
of technology and visual arts research.*

Chapter 1

Introduction: Making Knowledge Visual

Chris Bailey

In the two decades since the origins of computing for arts and humanities the capacity for technology to provide the tools desired by scholars might be thought to have grown sufficiently to provide everything to answer the scholar's prayers. As Will Vaughan comments in his Preface to this volume, the foundation of CHArt[1] – the computers and history of art group – in 1985 and its continuation to date represent a kind of index of development of the field. At around the same time other groups of scholars began to explore the potential of new technologies for history, for languages and linguistics, and the humanities in general. The initial meetings of CHArt were often concerned with the use of computers to analyse visual images, a theme that remains with us, but rather less with the increasing use of ICT for scholarly communication. Looking back at that time – roughly the late 1980s – I recall how this capacity to transfer images and text from distant collections seemed at least as important. This was especially true I suspect for researchers whose object of study was not close by, or who needed access to diverse contextual materials. At the time I was interested in the vast caches of trade literature held by major national collections in the UK and US, and how they might inform the history of design, and perhaps provide a quantitative complement to the mainly formalist accounts then available. Many librarians and information managers, archivists and museum curators shared this interest in making records available in their full richness. Out of this sprang a kind of utopian dream – that freedom of information would lead to a greater equality of access. Michael Ester described the early approach of the Getty Art History Information Program. 'Therefore, about six years ago we began creating a context where we could explore what it is that people in the arts do with images – how they use them in their work, and how we should be shaping technology to address the interests of these professionals.'[2]

If I then look back at how, working in a Midlands polytechnic, I set about getting at this brave new world of information, I see ribbons of file listings on dot matrix printed paper, and instructions to use Anonymous ftp to transfer each image,

---

1 CHArt, the Computers and the History of Art Group, was founded in 1985 and publishes annual conference abstracts to 1997 and conference proceedings from 1999, http://www.chart.ac.uk/, accessed April 2009.

2 M. Ester, *Image Use in Art – Historical Practice* (1993), http://arl.cni.org/symp3/ester.html, accessed April 1999.

painfully slowly, to my desktop PC. No wonder that some colleagues doubted if the slide, or photographic, library would ever be replaced. But access to databases was accompanied by the spread of email from the commercial to the education world, and the convergence of applications in the windows-based interface has unified the previously separate aspects of scholarly practice.

If technical developments have proceeded in a kind of lockstep, with mass-market technological solutions being accompanied by initiatives to create and offer specialized resources, the period has also been punctuated by scholarly reflections on methodology and the ways in which research has itself been shaped by technology. Support for these research communities has often focused on paradigms originally developed within the field of information management, modelled on the process of searching and access, extended in the digital era from verbal to visual resources. Support for scholarly activity which is driven in part by efficiency requirements can sometimes seek to serve a wider community at the expense of depth of support for any one discipline. Sometimes ambitious attempts to circumvent the limitations of text-based searching by retrieving results according to shape, colour or texture ran into a mismatch with what disciplines actually required to advance. As Holt and Hartwick reported of the early development of the QBIC (Query by Image Content) project hosted at University of California, Davis,

> Many of the Art Department faculty are exploring aspects of critical theory in their teaching and research. As a result, an additional aspect of the Art Department's involvement in using this software was to see if the attributes computed by QBIC could pick up areas as subtle as race, class and gender in a given database.[3]

In published descriptions of the methods of researchers in the visual arts there may be found paradigms that offer more comprehensive projections of the future state of the visual arts disciplines. Early studies of digital technology and visual disciplines described the special characteristics of, for instance, art history, as 'an art, with a sizable component of craftsmanship'[4] and seemed generally to applaud the impact of technology without fully examining the implications for the future direction of the discipline. While emphasizing the degree of judgement in doing visual research the effect of access to large-scale image libraries or comprehensive metadata was assumed mainly to have a helpful influence on the work rate. But had the work itself changed? A full decade later the inadequacy of terms used to describe approaches to art historical research was still being lamented by scholars.

---

3   B. Holt and L. Hartwick, '"Quick, Who Painted Fish?"': Searching a Picture Database with the QBIC project at UC Davis', *Information Services and Use*, 14 (1994): 79–90.

4   E. Bakewell, W.O. Beeman and C.M. Reese, *Object Image Inquiry: The Art Historian at Work*; Report on a Collaborative Study by the Getty Art History Information Program (AHIP) and the Institute for Research in Information and Scholarship (IRIS), Brown University (Santa Monica, CA.: AHIP, 1988), p. 72.

As Marilyn Lavin, an early champion of imaging technology to reconstruct works of art, put it:

> What I am looking for is an expression for a mass of material that is intellectually focused on a particular issue, that is constructed and used privately by a scholar in considering a specific problem, and that becomes a permanent retrievable record of a sequence of personal ideas and sources.[5]

Qualitative evidence, drawn from studies of researchers' own accounts of their methods and intentions can be set beside the intentions of research councils and others who have set out to enhance the support for research. Is it still true that digital technology remains limited to providing 'greater availability and access to visual material', and the 'manipulation (and) enhancement of digital images'?[6]

Evidence of a deeper transformation, akin to Lavin's 'conceptual reorientation' reveals that researchers have understood this potential, exploited these techniques, and developed resources, the very existence of which would have seemed unlikely in the pre-digital era, but which can be seen to affect the creation and legitimization of knowledge in the visual field.

The shape of innovation

A number of the chapters in this volume have their origins in presentations and subsequent discussion at an Expert Seminar hosted by Mike Pringle, then Director of AHDS Visual Arts, held on 27 April 2006 at Chelsea School of Art, London, and entitled 'From Pigments to Pixels'. As Lorna Hughes noted in her introduction to the one-day event, the purpose of the series was 'to describe and examine the impact of ICT on research in the field'. This seminar revealed that the impact goes way beyond the introduction of some new tools and methods. Rather, these technologies are radically changing the production of visual culture, its presentation and representation, and its analysis and evaluation. For instance, one of the papers not presented in the current volume, by Tom Morgan, made the point that,

> The discipline image providers have in mind is no longer art history, in which a demand is fulfilled through the supply of an image, but the attachment of multiple meanings to an image by its users, and then sharing these with others. The millions of hits on major museum web sites are being used in ways that echo the strategy of Wikipedia, a structured multi-author work now often considered as reliable as conventional encyclopedias, or the less structured 'cloud tagging'

---

5   M.A. Lavin, 'Making Computers Work for the History of Art', *Art Bulletin*, 79/2 (1997): 198.

6   M.E. Graham and C. Bailey, 'Digital Images and Art Historians', *Art Libraries Journal*, 31/3 (2006): 23.

found on web sites like Flickr. The act of 'tagging' is a form of active listening, which creates meaning for emerging communities of image users.[7]

The discussion which concluded this session questioned whether there is consensus on which approaches would meet the needs of the majority of visual arts researchers, how reliable Wiki-based and folksonomic development of resources would prove to be, and how sustainable very large and very complex databases would be in the light of the economic considerations brought to bear by research councils. The visual arts, in common with much of the humanities, tend to mix up their research approaches depending on context. Some visual artists will almost perversely use outdated software or hardware if they find them effective or interesting, and this makes it much harder to determine when the 'tipping point' might come when most, if not all, researchers in the visual arts might regard some resources and tools as standard.

Just two years later, a final Expert Seminar was convened both to summarize the series and the achievements of the Methods Network as it faced closure after three years, and to confront just this issue: how does an arts and humanities 'e-infrastructure' set about demonstrating its worth? The group that met on 1 April 2008 at the Wellcome Institute, London, took careful account of the inevitable inefficiency of dismantling one structure to create another, but it also recognized how much the policy landscape around pedagogy and research had changed since the early days of arts and humanities computing. As David de Roure, Head of Grid and Pervasive Computing, University of Southampton, commented,

> Generally speaking, Web 2.0 is about ease of participation. One of the key lessons is that you can build software very easily and quickly which has an impact upon the e-infrastructure in a short period of time since people can access it easily and begin using it as soon as it is available ... and this allows new ways of thinking and new questions.[8]

Bruce Brown, Pro-Vice-Chancellor, Research, University of Brighton and RAE Main Panel Chair 2008, also urged that arts and humanities researchers look forward to the convergence of the needs of institutions and users in a context that was now more appropriately seen as an aspect of the creative industries rather than an isolated academic pursuit. He characterized the distance travelled by referring to a recent paper to the JISC Board in which:

---

7   C. Bailey, 'Rapporteur's Report', AHRC ICT Methods Network Expert Seminar on Visual Arts: From Pigments to Pixels (2006), http://www.methodsnetwork.ac.uk/redist/pdf/es5rapreport.pdf, accessed April 2009: 1.

8   AHDS, 'Note of Expert Seminar: Strategic Approaches to Developing the e-infrastructure for Arts and Humanities Research, 1 April 2008, Wellcome Institute, London', unpublished (2008), p. 20.

Ian Dolphin and Paul Walker have observed that whereas early stages of the DNER and Information Environment were characterized by sequential verbs such as: create, publish, manage, curate, locate, request, access and use, current changes in the broader e-environment now demand reconsideration of this model … and need to be extended to include 'shared infrastructure services' that are widened beyond the perceived ownership of what is 'often regarded as a "library" preserve'.[9]

We might also note the cautiously positive endorsement of the increased confidence with which visual arts researchers are employing digital technologies from the Research Assessment Exercise panel Overview Report. They noted about the submissions for the 2008 round that:

The sub-panels' … scrutiny demonstrated that the scholarly infrastructures supporting non-traditional forms of research had both advanced since RAE2001 and were maturing – the majority of submitted outputs included sound evidence of the scholarly apparatus underpinning the research. … There is clear evidence that a greater understanding of methodology is emerging; that evolving networks of resources and references are building the intellectual infrastructure for such research; and, that new ways of harnessing digital resources to conserve, access and disseminate non-traditional scholarly materials are advancing.[10]

Themes

Finding

The chapters in this volume are grouped into three sections, though the concerns of the authors cross these artificial boundaries to deal with related subject matter and technical approaches. A consistent theme of the debate has been the core of 're-search' – the use of technology to improve the search for information. Mike Pringle uses the findings of a research project hosted by AHDS Visual Arts that aimed to discover whether the analytical techniques common in science-based disciplines might have uses in the interpretive and creative arts and humanities. While he sees the potential for quite radical transfer across disciplines, Kirk Martinez and Leif Isaksen argue that using 'domain level ontologies' will provide the best assistance for researchers who want to take advantage of powerful new techniques such as semantic web searches. Stuart Jeffrey sets out to show that successful searching can only become less likely as relevant material on the internet becomes more heterogeneous. Taking archaeology as his example, he argues that interventions

---

9   Ibid., p. 11.

10   HEFCE, Zipped pdf file, Unit 63 Art and Design, RAE 2008 Subject Overview Report (2009), http://www.rae.ac.uk/pubs/2009/ov/, accessed May 2009: 2.

are needed now to ensure that discovery and description issues, especially for complex time-based media, are given the same status now accorded to archiving standards and preservation. In the final chapter in this section Daniela Sirbu is also concerned with how we advance our understanding through improved modelling of data, although in this case the technique is virtual reality applied to historic monuments. As she argues, the three main features of this technique – immersion, interactivity and imaginative inference – work to help us solve complex problems in many fields, sometimes by going beyond what can be directly sensed.

Making

Complementing these practical explorations of resource discovery, the next three chapters are about the shift in professional relationships, and at a deeper level, in the disciplines themselves, caused by engagement through digital forms of the archive.

Doireann Wallace describes how commercial keywording practice may be serving to match images more closely to uses, but that the construction of those uses is itself constrained by the habits and disciplines applied to them. In Sue Breakell's view, the aim of collections to achieve 'full disclosure' is in practice giving way to more complex collaborations as the disclosed content becomes the shared property of archivist and user. Closing this section, James MacDevitt argues more radically that we should abolish the distinction altogether as the user/ archivist both creates and uses the Networked Digital Archive.

Understanding

Always running alongside the creative use of technology has been the interpretation of these forms either within the creative tradition or, sometimes, as antithetical to it, or as a marginal cultural practice. Making historical sense of these transitions in creative practice, and observing absences and discontinuities, Charlotte Frost argues that net art constitutes a category that is currently suppressed in art history. Taking a wider view, Jemima Rellie seeks to map significant innovations in the communication of knowledge and describes how the disruptions to existing channels of communication are part of larger social changes, to the extent that the merging of roles: visitor, curator, scholar, may threaten the distinctiveness of the museum, but seem unlikely to lead to its demise. Decentring of the previously privileged gaze of the specialist is also the subject of the concluding chapter. From the standpoint of cultural theory, Charlie Gere points out that not only is the internet literally decentred, the ramifications of its application can be viewed more optimistically than earlier theorists of the visual supposed, providing scope for making, as well as understanding the realm of visual knowledge. A common feature of many of the chapters in this volume is that intellectual enquiry is situated in specific social practice, and can only be properly understood through reference to the context of policy and social structure. And, of course, so it is with the 'infrastructure' of research, the means by which it is supported and shaped.

Shaping the debate

A complete account of the history of e-infrastructure projects and services in the UK has yet to be written, but it is a virtually universal tenet that the receipt of public funds must be justified by evidence of impact on the 'community', usually conceived as academic staff, teachers and researchers and the information managers with whom they interact. Given this emphasis it is not surprising that these support projects have generally been expressed as partnerships between individual institutions, either at the level of delivery, in which institutions take responsibility for an aspect of the service, or through a governing group with representatives from a number of institutions. As a result of this burgeoning of projects, all aimed at involving an increasing proportion of academic staff in discussion about the application of technology, there has been, for most of the last two decades, a succession of launch events, subject workshops, training events and conferences, with attendant publications and reports.

In general projects are evaluated, often through a process of independent review, but incorporating reflection by the project's staff, its governing body and usually its target community. Some assurance about the effectiveness of resource expenditure is sought, and almost invariably found, in this form of project-by-project evaluation. At the larger scale, however, indicators of the impact of this approach to instigating change in academic practice are harder to identify. To do this the impact of projects would need to be set alongside the whole range of activities that make up academic life, from institutional staff development aimed at supporting changing practice in scholarship or pedagogy, and perhaps most significantly, the role of wider scholarly communications, especially societies, their newsletters, journal and conferences.

In contrast to the needs-based model of funded projects the organs of scholarly communication are driven by the wishes and desires of their participants. This distinction is not surprising. The public sector in general operates on a model in which quantifiable targets can be defined and it is supposedly evident when these are achieved. Scholarly societies on the other hand define their objects in the vaguest terms in order to avoid redundancy at some later point. They rely on voluntary effort, though that is tacitly underwritten for the most part by higher education funding.

There is considerable interaction between projects and societies. In smaller subjects many individuals perform roles in both. This symbiosis may mean that societies' publications and events provide a forum for publication, discussion and development by projects. However, as a rule societies outlive all projects that do not succeed in making themselves indispensable to institutions or become institutions in their own right. To take only one example, a cursory survey of the extensive online archive of CHArt reveals its extensive co-dependence with several generations of ICT projects, such as ADAM, VADS and AHDS Visual Arts (see the CHArt website).

Evidence of value

The decision in 2008 to 'disinvest' in the Arts and Humanities Data Service, in many ways a final evolutionary stage of the various scholarly support services developed since the 1980s, brought into sharp focus the discussion about what the considerable financial investment in digital technology infrastructure has actually secured and posed the question 'has it been worth it?' But how can we know what the impact of these new technologies has really been on the communities of research practice in the visual arts? The use of measurement to assess research quality is hotly debated, no more so than currently, when the transition from the Research Assessment Exercise, the last round of which was in 2008, takes effect and all subjects, including the arts and humanities, must by 2013 expect the new methodologies of the Research Excellence Framework to begin to shape the public funding for research activity in higher education. With it comes a new reliance – for the humanities – on citations and other bibliometric analyses as a measure of research quality.

One approach to understanding the impact of new technology, borrowing this quantitative approach, might be to look at the use of the Technical Appendix, a device whereby researchers describe the technical underpinning of their methodology and indicate whether the data generated might be available in digital form for other research purposes. A Technical Appendix, while not mandatory, was advised for any project involving the handling of large amounts of data. Figures extracted from data published by the Arts and Humanities Data Service, and kindly provided for this essay by David Robey, show some clear trends.

Of the research project proposals supported by the Research Grants programme of the Arts and Humanities Research Council between 1999 and 2006, there is a clear hierarchy of subjects, with some apparently predisposed to including a technical appendix, like modern languages and linguistics (35 per cent), while philosophy, religious studies and law are least likely to include this element (12 per cent). While 23 per cent of proposals in medieval and modern history included a Technical Appendix, only 17 per cent of those submitted to the Visual Arts and Media: practice, history, theory panel did so. When it comes to the AHRC's Resource Enhancement scheme the picture looks different. Proposals to all panels show a much higher proportion with a Technical Appendix. But how should we account for the figure for visual arts and media of 100 per cent? Perhaps this has to do with the strength of interest in shared image databases that has figured in the journal literature, supporting the identification of a 'visual turn' in cultural studies as a whole, and the networking of the many digital library projects affiliated to the Visual Arts Data Service.

While differences between disciplines seem to emerge clearly from the data, supporting the thesis that research in the visual arts tends to be more individualistic and less collaborative than that in other subjects, it is much harder to spot meaningful trends over time. The sample sizes are small at this level, and emerging or increasing enthusiasm for digital technology as a support for research in visual arts cannot be confirmed or disproved by these data.

A scholarly community first shapes its research, but it is in turn shaped by it. The continuum of learning has higher levels of research at one end and at the other the practice of research methods in teaching seems to be taking on quite a new form – one mapped by Lorcan Dempsey as a 'new learning landscape' (see Figure 1.1). In this environment resources are tailored to individual need, communication between scholars takes place in many general as well as specialized forums, and there is greater participation in common tasks by scholars at all levels in the discipline.

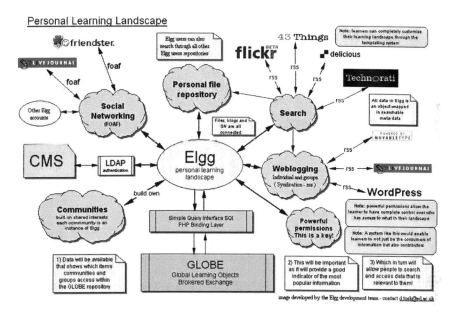

Figure 1.1   Personal Learning Landscape

Source: Image developed by D. Tosh and B. Wurdmuller, for Elgg, the open source social networking service, http://elgg.org/index.php.

Dempsey, blogging in 2005, noted that the University of Rochester was asking itself how its services should change to accommodate working methods that more or less intuitively adopt new technologies:

> In the long run, we envision a system that, first and foremost, supports our faculty members' efforts to 'do their own work' – that is, to organize their resources, do their writing, work with co-authors, and so on. Such a system will include the self-publishing and self-archiving features that the DSpace code already supports, and will rely heavily on preservation, metadata, persistent URLs, and other existing features of DSpace. When we build this system, we will include a

simple mechanism for converting works in progress into self-published or self-archived works, that is, moving documents from an in-progress folder into the IR. We believe that if we support the research process as a whole, and if faculty members find that the product meets their needs and fits their way of work, they will use it, and 'naturally' put more of their work into the IR.[11]

The teaching and research worlds were never more of a continuum than they are now. In many areas of the visual arts – those concerned with making – the discussion of the validation and methodological development of practice-based research has always insisted on the place in the curriculum for exploration of new forms and techniques. In all fields the 'virtual research environment' and the 'virtual learning environment' have come to share many characteristics. The creation of digital repositories by universities that at once capture research content and its metadata, and provide a location for 'learning objects' tend to locate research as a kind of super-independent learning, linked in form and content to many of the tasks set for the undergraduate student.

The intellectual structures of research and its technological forms may be converging just as funding decisions and economic pressures act to frustrate their union. Yet it seems probable that the voluntaristic impulse that has sustained communication for so long will ensure that the futures outlined in this volume come to resemble actuality. If this optimism is warranted it must yet be grounded in a feeling for what research is about, even if its definition has, in Arjun Appadurai's phrase, the 'invisibility of the obvious'[12] and we need the advantage of hindsight to deploy Panofsky's cooler definition of research in the humanistic disciplines as 'a coherent system that makes sense'.[13]

---

11   N.F. Foster and S. Gibbons, 'Understanding Faculty to Improve Content Recruitment for Institutional Repositories', *D-Lib Magazine*, 11/1 (2005), http://www.dlib.org/dlib/january05/foster/01foster.html, accessed June 2009, quoted in Dempsey (2005).

12   A. Appadurai, *Globalization* (Durham, NC: Duke University Press, 2001), p. 10.

13   E. Panofsky, 'The History of Art as a Humanistic Discipline', in *Meaning in the Visual Arts: Papers in and on Art History* (Garden City, NY: Doubleday Anchor Books, 1955), p. 7.

Chapter 2

Do a Thousand Words Paint a Picture?

Mike Pringle

Introduction

In the visual arts, practice, education and research are, not surprisingly, based on, led by and/or executed through a dominantly visual approach. Yet in the digital age, and particularly on the internet, facilities and approaches for sharing or finding visual information are sporadic, inefficient and often highly unsatisfactory. This chapter explores why the image is problematic in the digital age. It describes some of the currently available approaches for exploring visual digital material and discusses how, through combining technological approaches with an increased understanding of user needs, novel methods may be developed for improving the sharing of image-centred information.

Background

From the very moment that Tim Berners-Lee conceived his idea for sending packets of data down a wire, the model for the World Wide Web, as a connector of multiple networks and nodes, was destined to be dominated by the transfer of the written word. Even the name behind the idea, *hypertext*, makes it clear where the emphasis lies. This is highly understandable if we consider the importance of the written word as our core information communication medium. However, regarding the history of internet technologies, it can feel as if this, perhaps inevitable, emphasis on primarily text-based information has dominated research and development ever since, sometimes to the detriment of alternative modes of communication. Indeed, if we consider Berners-Lee's next generation model, the Semantic Web, we see a continuation, even in the name itself, of an explicit word-led agenda. Nonetheless, the capability for embedding other objects – such as images – into a webpage has been an integral part of internet capabilities since the earliest instantiations of Hypertext Mark-up Language (HTML). It was the limits of the early underlying technologies that dictated the word-led approach: narrow bandwidth, slow modems, low screen resolution and lack of processing power made the use of images problematic (compared to their text-based counterparts) for early adopters of the web. This, of course, had serious implications for those professions and areas of study where the image is paramount.

In his discussion of art practice as research, Graeme Sullivan observes that the uncertain world of the digital age offers us new ways to communicate:

Digital technology serves as a site for inquiry where information is clearly no longer a form within which knowledge is found, nor a unit of analysis that lends itself to neat manipulation or interpretation. Yet this uncertain realm of investigative opportunity is just the kind of place where artists, scientists, researchers, cultural theorists, and community activists are speaking to each other in a fresh language of images and ideas.[1]

For the visual arts community, dominated as it is by the practice of art, much of the fresh language comes in the form of digital images, whilst many of the topics discussed relate in some way to digital images and, inevitably, the internet: the key enabling mode of communication of this new language and the discussions it stimulates. However, because of the dominance of text-based approaches in internet research the capabilities of the technology, and the tools developed for it, do not necessarily meet the needs or expectations of many areas of the visual arts community. For example, compare the needs and desires of many members of the visual arts research community – who may wish to explore, exploit or expound via internet technologies from a purely visual perspective – with the more text-dominated approaches of many humanities or science subjects.

What this tends to mean is that much of the integration of visual art resources or methods (on or for the internet) is through use of the word to describe the visual, and on the development of standards, techniques and technologies for manipulating text rather than images. Consequently, the distribution and accessing of visual information is a complex and often unsatisfactory activity – the fresh language that Sullivan promotes is perhaps not yet fully coherent. As ever greater numbers of images join the information superhighway, the reliance of the visual arts community on electronic, rather than analogue, images will inevitably increase. This chapter explores how internet technologies enable, or fail to enable, arts researchers and practitioners to fully exploit, share and explore images in digital form.

A simple problem

Let us take one simple problem: how can images best be shared; how can artists, lecturers, students, librarians or researchers disseminate or discover images in the digital age now that the 35mm slide has declined[2] in usage? Jenny Godfrey[3] defined the problem in terms of:

---

1   G. Sullivan, *Art Practice as Research: Inquiry in the Visual Arts*, Thousand Oaks (CA: Sage Publications, Inc., 2005), pp. xxii, 265.

2   'Kodak Confirms Plans To Stop Making Slide Projectors': <http://www.kodak.com/US/en/corp/pressReleases/pr20030926-01.shtml> (accessed June 2008).

3   J. Godfrey, 'A Digital Future for Slide Libraries?', *Art Libraries Journal*, 29/1 (2004): 10–22.

- There is a serious lack of appropriate images (e.g. subject-specific) in the digital domain
- Legal, IPR and copyright restrictions stifle the ability to create/use digital images
- There is no usable, helpful structure for finding and obtaining images
- There is no structure for facilitating or managing 'loans' of digital images
- Formats, and pixel quality, are not necessarily appropriate for use
- It is difficult to share/pool digital image resources
- There is a lack of use of common standards (or of standards at all)
- Appropriate safeguards and provenance are not available
- There is a lack of resource and support for the use of digital images

However, these issues are all simply symptoms; beneath all of them lies a more fundamental cause. The very nature of digital images is at the root of their own problem: through their make-up of simple pixels or point data they tend to lack useful data for machines to interrogate or interact with. The reason that technology struggles to come to terms with images is because they are, and always have been, complex palimpsests of visual ingredients: information, knowledge, thoughts and abstract concepts, all wrapped in an ever-shifting gossamer web of emotional actions and responses. Text, by comparison, is a simplistic shorthand for communicating the basics of what we see and feel.

A complex problem

In 1911, American newspaper editor Arthur Brisbane gave an instructional talk to the *Syracuse Advertising Men's Club*. His advice included the phrase: 'Use a picture. It's worth a thousand words.'[4] It is unlikely that Brisbane was the first to use this line, but the context of a newspaper editor talking about advertising presents a simple and clear exemplar of the concept behind the phrase. The secondary, and often ignored, concept behind the phrase is the notion that the picture may present a different thousand words to each and every viewer. This is illustrated in Figure 2.1, where two images, both of Paris, are presented.

The left-hand photograph in Figure 2.1 gives a stereotypical view of Paris; it focuses on an iconic representation of the city using the Eiffel Tower as the central motif in a setting 'parisien'. It does not show us a large area of the physicality of Paris, but perhaps it can be said to epitomize some of the characteristics of the city that we all associate with it. In contrast, the right-hand photograph in Figure 2.1 is simply the city of Paris – a panorama of buildings and streets stretching out to the horizon, viewed, in this case, from the Eiffel Tower. This really is Paris, but does it tell us anything about the actual place? Without a label telling us that the photograph is of Paris, it could be any city anywhere in the world. Perhaps more

---

4   http://www.phrases.org.uk/meanings/a-picture-is-worth-a-thousand-words.html, accessed June 2008.

Figure 2.1   Paris

Source: Photographs by the author.

significant than the different ways in which Paris can be presented in photographs is the relationship between the images and a label of this kind. Can the word 'Paris' be said to describe either picture in a meaningful way? To answer this question we need to consider what is *meaningful* in a picture.

Figure 2.2 gives more visual representations of Paris: diagrams of the city's districts, one with accompanying text and one without. Here, the meaning of the labelled version is clear: the image elucidates valuable information about where the districts are in relation to each other, their relative sizes and how they relate to a geographical feature (the River Seine). However, the same diagram without labels loses this value. It becomes a collection of apparently arbitrary lines which, unless you happen to find it aesthetically pleasing, is meaningless.

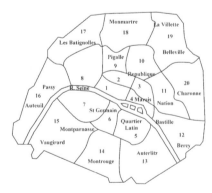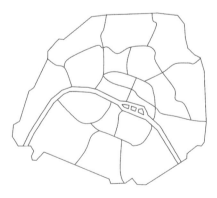

Figure 2.2   Map of Paris districts

To create an image with simple meaning (in terms of informational value), a level of visual abstraction is employed that, in essence, is symbiotic with the text that accompanies it. The words themselves, without the diagram, do not tell us much about Paris, and the same goes for the image.

Taking this idea one step further, we can abstract more from the pictures of Paris in Figure 2.1. The city is represented again in Figure 2.3, as a square on a map of France. In this context, the square is a legitimate abstraction of Paris, simply intended to show the city's whereabouts in France. In any other context, without the map or any labels, what we are left with is just the square. If a user searched on the internet/intranet/image library using the term 'Paris', perhaps looking for a picture that depicted either the 'feel' of the city or the city itself, he/she would be extremely disappointed if all that was returned was a picture of a square.

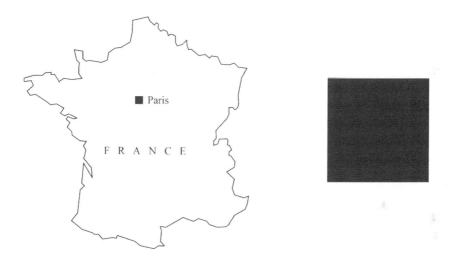

Figure 2.3   Map showing Paris's physical location in France, and a square

The problem of sharing digital images in hyperspace is, essentially, a problem of levels of abstraction. If the meaning of an image centres around its context, i.e. its function is primarily about the elucidation of associated, usually textual, information, then the ease with which the image can be shared/accessed is increased. Unfortunately, the world of art does not abide simply by such illustrative uses of the image. Alan Dix describes language as 'the ultimate formalization tying patterns of electrical and chemical activation'.[5] The key to this statement is *formalization*: language is a formal construct; an abstraction that, while powerful

---

5   A. Dix, *Called xxxxx while Waiting for a Title*, Position paper, HCI, the Arts and Humanities, Kings Manor, York, July 2003, http://www.comp.lancs.ac.uk/~dixa/papers/ xxxxx-2003/, accessed June 2008.

in its own context, is inadequate for describing the meaning of an image where it is the image itself that is key, not the associated information. Dix also notes that 'many artists are still playful: the child caught in the wonder of the world, twirling grass around its fingers to see the patterns it makes.' Where the artistic output of such twirling is a picture, no thousand words can ever fully convey the wonder.

From picture to words

There are, of course, any number of levels of abstraction over information or meaning. However in a hyperspace context some have established themselves more than others, particularly in terms of helping creators/users to share information or meaning through the use of digital images. This section gives a brief, and limited, viewpoint of just a few of the commonly used layers of abstraction, in reference to their relationship to internet technologies and usefulness in the sharing of digital images.

Pictures without words

The technological developments most closely aligned to the visual content of an image, as opposed to any linguistic interpretation, are probably in the realm of what is commonly known as Content-Based Image Retrieval (CBIR). This is the principle of using machine-led technologies to identify and exploit useful information within the digital image itself; for example, shapes, colours or tonal values. With vector graphics, a computer can interrogate the points that represent exact locations in 2D or 3D space and make assumptions about the shapes and patterns that those points create. For bitmap graphics – images made up of pixels – the technology interrogates the stored information about the image's colour patterns. In both cases the technology makes use of developments in areas such as pattern recognition, signal processing and statistical analysis and is therefore not reliant on the addition of textual information. CBIR, as a process, can be summed up thus:

> Line segments, longer linear lines, retained lines, coterminations, 'L' junctions, 'U' junctions, parallel lines, parallel groups, 'significant' parallel groups and polygons. Perceptual grouping rules of similarity, continuity, parallelism and closure are used to extract these features. The presence of these distinguishing features in an image follows the 'principle of nonaccidentalness' and, therefore, are more likely to be generated by manmade objects.[6]

---

6   Q. Iqbal and J.K. Aggarwal, *Combining Structure, Color and Texture for Image Retrieval: A Performance Evaluation*, 16th International Conference on Pattern Recognition (ICPR), Quebec City, QC, Canada, 11–15 August 2002, vol. 2, pp. 438–43.

CBIR offers, at the search interface, a number of ways to interact with images in a large database. Users may have the facility to:

1. Query by example. The user supplies or selects an image and the software finds images similar to it based on criteria such as colour, shape or contrast.
2. Query by sketch. The user draws a rough sketch of the image they are looking for, perhaps with colour, and the software finds images with similar make-up.
3. Colour make-up. The user specifies proportions of colours desired (e.g. '80% red, 20% blue').[7]

Within any of these methods, there is also the potential for refining search results by defining those images that are closer to the desired end result and searching again. Tate has created a simple tool based on this principle – Carousel[8] – this process can also be augmented by the use of text-based information to determine its results.

Clearly, if CBIR could achieve its aims, i.e. determine the content of an image from its digital make-up, such facilities would be invaluable. However, the distance between a computer's understanding of pixels and a human's capacity for interpreting an image is vast. Such limitations suggest that most CBIR technologies are in their infancy and, at present, restricted to very specific functionality. For example, one area where much CBIR research has taken place is in the field of identifying naked bodies to provide automated filters to block pornographic images.[9] Because of the common factors of naked flesh, and a defined need (e.g. to protect children from objectionable images), such research has moved forward considerably, but it is still limited for a number of fundamental reasons, as James Ze Wang et al. note:

> non-uniform image background; textual noise such as phone numbers, URLs, etc; content may range from grey-scale to 24-bit color; may be of very low quality (sharpness); views are taken from a variety of camera positions; may be an indexing image containing many small icons; may contain more than one person; persons in the picture may have different skin colors; may contain both people and animals; may contain only some parts of a person; persons in the picture may be partially dressed.[10]

---

7   Content-based image retrieval: http://en.wikipedia.org/wiki/CBIR, accessed June 2008.

8   http://www.tate.org.uk/collection/carousel/index.htm, accessed July 2008.

9   D.A. Forsyth et al., 'Finding Pictures of Objects in Large Collections of Images', in Object Representation in Computer Vision II, *Lecture Notes in Computer Science*, vol. 1144 (1996), pp. 335–60.

10   J. Ze Wang, J. Li, G. Wiederhold and O. Firschein, 'Classifying Objectionable Websites Based on Image Content', in Interactive Distributed Multimedia Systems and Telecommunication Services, *Lecture Notes in Computer Science*, vol. 1483 (Berlin/ Heidelberg: Springer, 1998), p. 113.

On top of such practical difficulties in identifying naked flesh, there are also the subjective complications of deciding whether an image is actually objectionable or not: if CBIR could successfully identify naked bodies, it would, presumably, also block medical images, innocent holiday snaps and, in art terms, paintings of nudes.

In broader terms, the complications of identifying useful patterns in images present huge challenges for software developers. Ultimately, it may be that systems evolve that allow users to type in simple textual queries such as 'find me pictures that contain a rose'. However, because a rose can be depicted in so many ways, from so many different perspectives, and in so many contexts, such a system is still some way off.

Pictures as words

Abstracting away from the idea of image simply as image, one common use of pictures, both on- and offline, is as metaphors to represent single, sometimes complex concepts instead of, or in association with words. Visual metaphors (or similes) are essentially an extension or development of the principles of symbolism, whereby an archetypal image (or set of images) enables the user to make simple decisions about associated, or underlying, information. They can be informative, i.e. explaining a concept, but are more often illustrative, i.e. providing a commonly understood image to denote the associated concept: for example, using an image of a castle to represent defensive monuments.

Visual symbols have clearly been around a long time. Pictograms – images that look like the thing they represent – are commonplace in ancient 'texts' such as hieroglyphics, as are ideograms – images that have been developed to represent a concept, such as the ankh symbol for life.

In the information age, with the complexity and sheer mass of material, processes and tools that the computer gives us access to, images are a fundamental part of the 'language' of computing. Icons, logos, symbols, diagrams and visual representations are always present on our screens.

Whilst the use of such images is patently useful, it is not universal and again the point can be made about different interpretations of images. For example, in Figure 2.4, four pictograms are given: on the left, a man and a star; on the right, also a man and a star, but this time from an Australian aboriginal perspective[11] (the man is depicted as a kneeling figure from a bird's eye viewpoint). In their own context, and to an audience that has learnt the meaning, these symbols are obvious and clear. But, conversely, out of context or to people who are untrained in their meaning, the symbols are much harder to interpret.

However, in terms of sharing images in a computer environment, apart from the symbols commonly used for navigating collections, it is in the use of thumbnails that the idea of using an image to depict a concept is most commonly found.

---

11   Oceanic art: http://www.oceanicart.com.au/, accessed July 2008.

Figure 2.4   Western man and star; Australian man and star

Most of the time, the thumbnail is simply a reduced version (an abstraction) of the 'original' picture it is associated with; it is a shorthand way of representing the picture that may allow a user to make a better-informed judgement about it than, for example, its title. Such representation is useful insofar as a user is able to scan multiple images on a computer screen rather than looking at each one individually. However, how much information can such a thumbnail seriously impart? Where the user is looking for an 'obvious' image, in a collection of limited size, this approach is excellent, but where there are many images and the user is not sure exactly what they are after, the usefulness wanes. Also, where a thumbnail is used as a 'meta-description', i.e. to depict a collection or a particular school, genre or individual, a single picture may not be sufficient to capture the essence of the subject. What this means is that, in most cases, the use of thumbnails provides a handy filter at the final stage of selection in a large collection of images, but to reach that point the user will, almost certainly, have had to rely on textual search input and corresponding textual information within the database. The homepage of Tate uses icons to represent sections of the website, but they also have textual explanations. In fact the 'pictorial' icon for Young Tate is actually composed entirely of words.

Pictures of words

Visualization of data, particularly in the form of tables, organigrams or hyperbolic trees (see Figure 2.5), makes use of images to display text. Here, the abstraction over the concept is far removed from being a 'picture' of the subject. Rather, it is a collection of words (or numbers) that are arranged in a visual way. Through the representation of relationships, and factors such as relevance (perhaps depicted by size of text), diagrams of this nature assist the user in understanding or browsing information.

In the example given in Figure 2.5 we start to see where the limitations of words lie in relation to enabling us to explore abstract concepts such as those that can be encapsulated in images. The tree on the left is a simplistic picture of Paris, just slightly more abstracted with regard to the concept 'Paris' than the map of districts given in Figure 2.2. The principle of hyperbolic trees is that they are

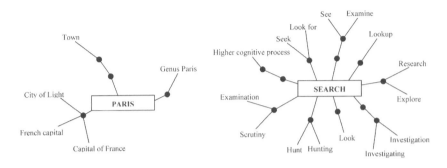

Figure 2.5   Hyperbolic trees – 'Paris' and 'Search'

interactive, allowing the user to explore 'nodes' relating to the core concept. In the hypothetical example above, selecting *town* on the Paris image would lead to a new group of words relating to *town*, including *townspeople*, *township* and *municipality*. Selecting *municipality* gives us *urban area*, *administrative district*, *assemblage* and *gathering*. From *gathering* we move to *gather* and then to *search*. A straightforward chain of logical connections. But consider how far removed the concept of 'search' is from the concept of 'Paris', and consider how, from the list of words relating to *search*, a user might navigate to the picture of Paris.

Shneiderman et al. suggest that visualization methods such as these 'enable users to gain meaningful high-level information from an overview as well as to ascertain the details of each node and link'.[12] This is undoubtedly true in many cases; for example, hyperbolic trees are becoming increasingly commonplace as business tools.[13] The purpose of using the example here is simply to demonstrate how difficult it is to work 'backwards' from a word to a picture, which, at present, is the most common procedure for finding images on the internet.

Words representing pictures

As mentioned in the introduction to this chapter, research into primarily text-based approaches for exploring information in cyberspace has been dominant over other mediums for many, understandable, reasons.

Using words to 'represent' pictures is, in essence, a matter of describing the content of, and providing associated information about, the picture itself. Dunning suggests that perhaps it is this information that is actually the important element of an image; the verbalization of the inherent knowledge.[14] While this makes no

---

12   B. Shneiderman and A. Aris, 'Network Visualization by Semantic Substrates', *IEEE Transactions on Visualization and Computer Graphics*, 12/5 (2006), pp. 733–744.

13   Hyperbolic trees: http://www.thebrain.com/, accessed July 2008.

14   A. Dunning and M. Pringle, *Ban All Digital Cameras?*, http://ahds.ac.uk/news/ban-digital-cameras.htm, accessed June 2008.

sense in terms of the value of the picture, it does give some indication of the sort of logic that can develop to support the word-led development of technology. As is the case with any knowledge source, digital or otherwise, appropriate indexing or cataloguing of images is important. This is particularly relevant for images since, by virtue of their visual nature and the current limitations of technology, they come without any significant 'searchable' information. Without the addition of metadata, we are left with a world full of images that are unsearchable, unidentifiable and, in many ways, unusable.

But even if we put aside the clear limitations of describing an image using any given set of metadata standards, there are other problems. There are clearly issues where terms will mean different things to different people; for example, in the Cedars project, it was noted that:

> the relative novelty of digital preservation as an issue for libraries, and the fact that expertise in this area resides in other sectors (e.g. electronic records management) means that defining what we mean by specific terms is sometimes contentious. Where librarians, archivists, records managers and computing technologists assemble, the term 'archive' can (and does) mean very different things.[15]

As the digital preservation project at the British Library discovered, the need for metadata to meet technological requirements can lead to the overuse of jargon.[16] Not only is this unhelpful for end-users, it also adds a requirement for descriptions of the terms to be added – metadata for the metadata. Also, the simple fact that things change needs to be considered. If the terminology that people are using alters over time then the usefulness of the image, with its terminology based on a fixed point, will diminish. Lehman's Laws (relating to software evolution) state 'in accord with universal experience, that a system must be continually adapted else it becomes progressively less satisfactory'.[17] This is as true of the metadata and other descriptive terminology employed as it is of the images, formats or the system itself. What all this amounts to is a need for a vast amount of textual information to be added to every image: text that can describe every aspect of the image to every possible user, text that provides all background information about the image, and text that will change as perceptions in the outside world change.

To overcome some of these issues, many systems of metadata have evolved; for example, the subject-specific classification system, Iconclass. Iconclass provides a 'hierarchically ordered collection of definitions of objects, persons, events and abstract ideas that can be the subject of an image. Art historians, researchers and

---

15 *CEDARS: Long-term Access and Usability of Digital Resources: The Digital Preservation Conundrum* http://www.ariadne.ac.uk/issue18/cedars/, accessed April 2009.

16 H. Shenton, 'From Talking to Doing: Digital Preservation at the British Library', *The New Review of Academic Librarianship* 6 (2000): 163–177.

17 http://www.doc.ic.ac.uk/~mml/feast2/papers/pdf/556.pdf, accessed April 2009.

curators use it to describe, classify and examine the subject of images represented in various media such as paintings, drawings and photographs.'[18]

Much research is being conducted to try to deal with some of the limits of text-based descriptions. Indeed, as mentioned earlier in this chapter, Berners-Lee's next-generation model for the internet revolves around the Semantic Web: a continuation of an explicit word-led agenda. The basic principle of the Semantic Web and its associated developments, is to reveal ways of creating content that allows machines to interrogate it in increasingly clever ways. Using tools such as the Resource Description Framework (RDF), Web Ontology Language (OWL) and eXtensible Markup Language (XML), creators can 'add meaning to the content, thereby facilitating automated information gathering and research by computers'.[19]

However, as White et al. observe

> search engines, bibliographic databases and digital libraries provide adequate support for users whose information needs are well-defined. However, they do not work well in situations where users lack the knowledge or contextual awareness to formulate queries or navigate complex information spaces. For example, what if you want to find something from a domain where you have a general interest but not specific knowledge? How would you find classical music you might enjoy if you do not know what Beethoven or Berlioz sounds like?[20]

In all cases, word-led systems will never completely meet the possible range of perspectives of users of images. They also have a fundamental Achilles heel: to work in any way they require someone to add the information to the image.

The eye of the beholder

The previous sections have focused on differing technological approaches to the use of images within internet technologies and, in some cases, have alluded to the uses of such images themselves. The common thread across all these discussions is simple: the user. This section, making much reference to a JISC-funded study concerning the preservation of digital images,[21] explores the issues of understanding users.

18   Iconclass: http://www.iconclass.nl/index.html, accessed April 2009.

19   http://en.wikipedia.org/wiki/Semantic_Web, accessed April 2009.

20   R.W. White, B. Kules and B. Bederson, *Exploratory Search Interfaces: Categorization, Clustering and Beyond,* Report on the XSI 2005 Workshop at the Human-Computer Interaction Laboratory, University of Maryland, 2005, Communications of the ACM, Volume 49, Number 4 (2006), pp. 36–39.

21   AHDS Digital Images Archiving Study: http://ahds.ac.uk/about/projects/archiving-studies/digital-images-archiving-study.pdf, accessed April 2009.

Most of the 'problems' with sharing images in cyberspace relate to the fact that the meaning or information value of an image is dependent on the perception of the user, more than the intentions of the provider:

> While the observer is only the onlooker, this 'looking' is a kind of movement. It embodies 'active observation'. From a certain moment when the observer becomes immersed in the action, his 'passive onlooking' is replaced by 'active observation'. The observer discovers that he – and not the artist – is the one creating the situation.[22]

The essence of successfully sharing images may reside not so much in exploring technologies but in developing our understanding of the observers – the people who want digital images. Crucially, in Information Communication Technology (ICT), it is the *people* aspects that are the most important, i.e. the informing and the communicating. The technology is simply the conduit.[23] What is the purpose of placing an image on the internet, or in any other virtual reservoir, if it is not to meet the needs, expectations, entertainment or interests of some known, or unknown, person or persons?

The following quotations from an AHDS Visual Arts survey illustrate this:

> People seem to work from the point of view of the digi-expert, web designer, archive owner. The user should be considered first.

> Access (that's the point, isn't it?).

Also, regarding the link between access and textual information:

> Access: what's the point of *the image* existing if it cannot be accessed? Metadata: there is no point in *the image* existing if it cannot be found.

In 2000 Neil Beagrie identified a need to establish strategies and services for long-term *access* of digital resources in UK HE/FE communities,[24] but inevitably such strategies and services are, in many ways, limited by today's technologies, which, as we have seen, are inadequate for providing access to images without the use of text. Consequently, much of the focus is on text-based approaches to image access. However, it is now widely understood that the development of digital systems, like that of non-digital systems, should be led by an understanding of the needs of the

---

22   M. Fleischmann and W. Strauss, 'Images of the Body in the House of Illusion', first published in C. Sommerer and L. Mignonneau (eds), *Art and Science* (Berlin, 1998), pp. 133–147.

23   M. Pringle, 'The People Versus Technology', *Art Libraries Journal*, 31/3 (2006): 16–20.

24   N. Beagrie, 'The JISC Digital Preservation Focus and the Digital Preservation Coalition', *New Review of Academic Librarianship*, 6 (2000): 257–67.

people who will use it. The JISC-funded Digital Repositories Review states that 'it is vital that repositories meet the needs of users; there is a need to explore user requirements and prioritize them in the development of repositories; the process needs to engage the user community in a real way'.[25] On a bigger scale, the House of Commons Education and Skills Committee report, following the low uptake of the £50m UK e-University, noted that it 'failed largely because it took a supply-driven rather than demand-led approach'.[26]

Who are we talking about?

In every web-based development it is now commonplace for 'usability' to be a component. What is less clear is any evidence that genuine users are in any way involved in the process of developing a system 'for them'. Instead, it is often the developers of the system, or the images, who make decisions *on behalf* of users. For this to be of any value, there must obviously be a clear understanding of just who the users are. If images are to be shared in cyberspace, we must first define what we mean by 'users' of those images and, subsequently, identify just who the actual people involved might be.

Broadly speaking, users of digital images can be divided into two categories: those who create digital images or are involved in their creation through commissioning, managing or perhaps financing the creation; and those who make use of those images as part of their work through, for example, manipulation of the image, study of the subject matter or interest in the digital object itself. Although any system or digital image resource should be developed in light of its end-user (its *raison d'être*), imperatives from 'behind the scenes' can often be more influential: for example, the requirements of legal entities, branding experts or funding bodies or, as mentioned above, the beliefs of the developer/creator. It is therefore necessary to explore the needs of both sets of users, and to establish the impact that each will have on the other's needs or requirements. Both groups are 'stakeholders' in the strategies, processes and systems needed for sharing digital images.

Perhaps, for ease of reference, the behind-the-scenes participants should be referred to as 'start-users': the individuals or organizations who contribute to the creation, development, deployment or expansion of the image resource. However, it is important to recognize that there will always be overlap between the two groups and of course some users will wear different hats at different times.

Figure 2.6, as well as illustrating two simplistic groups of users of digital images, also illustrates just how varied the participants in those two groups can be. Referring back to our 'simple' problem – how can artists, lecturers, students, librarians or researchers disseminate or discover images in the digital age? – let us take a look at just what 'users' means in terms of images in an arts education community.

25   S. Anderson and R. Heery, *Digital Repositories Review* (2005), para. 4.1, p. 15.

26   House of Commons Education and Skills Committee, *UK e-University: Third Report* (2004–2005), summary, p. 3.

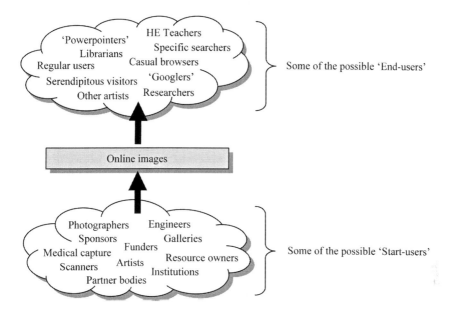

Figure 2.6   Examples of stakeholders

It could mean: users of online, education-led services (e.g. the Visual Arts Data Service, the National Gallery, the Courtauld Institute of Art); users of internal institution provision (e.g. intranets, Virtual Learning Environments); users of images in different areas of education (e.g. lifelong learning, higher education, post-doctoral research); users with different roles (e.g. researchers, support staff, librarians); users with different learning needs (e.g. dyslexia, physical impairment); or users with different subject needs (e.g. creative arts and sport, engineering, social sciences).[27] We should also consider some other types of user. Users of born-digital images vs users of digitized images; different criteria may be important to users depending on whether the image is a digitized surrogate of an analogue object, or an object originally created in a computer environment. Users of different generations may consider different things to be important, in terms of what online images provide. As well as different age groups, we should consider differences between the needs of 'digital natives' – those who have grown up in the digital environment, and 'digital immigrants' – those for whom the digital environment has been a relatively recent introduction.[28] It is likely that in some (many?) cases, the users of differing image types or formats will have differing approaches to their use.

The breadth of possible user scenarios that the above list could produce is, at the least, daunting and, at best, impractical, particularly given that for every item on the list there will be an equally complex list of further possible scenarios. For example, a category comprising creative arts and sport clearly represents an extremely wide range of different people with a correspondingly wide range of circumstances for using digital images. Furthermore, it is true to say that user needs could be defined in a wider way: for example, the particular needs that an institution or a Virtual Learning Environment might have. Most importantly, this list only touches on some of the possible people who might use images; it does not even scratch the surface of *how* people might use images.

Conclusions

This chapter has explored some of the ways that images are used in the digital era and, in particular, how, to be of value, those images are for the most part dependent on text. In fact this is, of course, also true in the non-digital world when we consider images as information, or are dealing with information that is primarily concerned with images.

Imaging technology has a considerable way to go before it can match our natural, intuitive methods for navigating through or to images but, in the meantime, there are ways in which we can improve the navigation of visual material in the digital arena. Even given the limitations of text-based approaches 'behind the scenes', the development of interfaces that are more visual in nature offers vast potential. For example, at present, most image search tools on the web return a page of thumbnails that are invariably sorted according to unknown textual references, and the user navigates the images according to that invisible order. But why can a user not search, or refine a search, according to a whole raft of different text-based orders: for example, by subject, or date? An example of how this might work as a way to explore images is given in Figure 2.7; it was suggested by an art student in an anonymous usability session.

The reason this approach is not yet the norm relates to simple technological limitations – computer developments with text have outstripped those with images for the same reason. To enable users to make decisions in real time would involve considerable bandwidth and formidable processing power. Nonetheless, if more research was conducted into the use of such mechanisms, solutions would soon evolve. Of course this approach could also exploit the benefits of CBIR through provision of crude drawing tools, colour/shade/contrast choices, or even the capacity to upload a picture as the basis of a similarity search. Such research is already starting to take place, with projects such as SCULPTEUR at the University of Southampton, which exploits ontological approaches to information but also acknowledges that 'it is valuable to provide graphical visualization tools for a

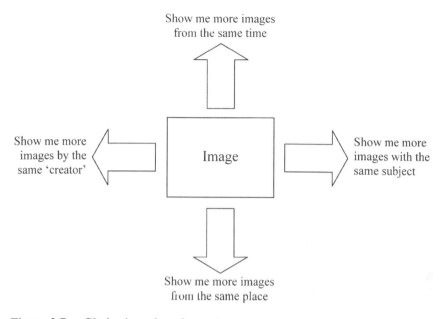

Figure 2.7   Choice in order of search returns

user whose background is different from a given domain as a way of supporting better understanding'.[29] Most importantly, the SCULPTEUR developers recognize that research into the problem domain – 'the landscape of the visual arts' – is key to development of the interface between visual arts people and visual arts information.

In fact, domain knowledge is so crucial, that in some cases – for example, the Apollo space missions – the creation of software is left to the domain experts themselves rather than being trusted to dedicated computer experts.[30] Of course, domain experts for NASA were scientists and possibly, by their nature, comfortable with computer development. In the visual arts, although there are many who engage with computers as part of their practice or research, there are few who will make the shift from artist to CBIR code writer. Furthermore, such an idea can lead to considerable duplication of effort and re-invention of the wheel.

29   S. Kim, P. Lewis and K. Martinez, *SCULPTEUR D7.1 Semantic Network of Concepts and their Relationships* – Public Version, IAM, ECS, University of Southampton, 2004 at http://www.sculpteurweb.org/html/events/D7.1_Public.zip, accessed 27 May 2009.

30   http://jayanthr.wordpress.com/2008/06/18/software-bottleneck-and-its-resolution/, accessed April 2009.

The answer then, is not to focus on arts people becoming computer experts, nor computer experts becoming artists, but to focus on understanding how people interact with images. Essentially, what we have at present is a bottleneck. On one side we have a rich array of visual information presented in myriad ways, on the other a vast array of different users and reasons for interacting with images. The bottleneck is at the interface between these two complex entities; quite literally, the human–computer interface. It is here that we are truly able to make progress, but we need a shift in approach: if we are to fully exploit the use of digital images on the web, we need to shift some of our effort from developmental methodologies to more exploration of the 'problem domain'.

In real terms this probably means less time spent on developing new 'prototyping' or 'waterfall' systems and more time trying to understand how people use images. It probably also means less quantitative data and more qualitative data; less machine readable tables and more thoughtful opinion. It is about increasing focus on what Brooks calls the 'essences' of the problem, rather than focusing on what he calls the 'accidents' arising from computer development.[31]

31   F.P. Brooks, 'No Silver Bullet – Essence and Accident in Software Engineering', *Proceedings of the IFIP Tenth World Computing Conference*, 1986, pp. 1069–1076.

Chapter 3

The Semantic Web Approach to Increasing Access to Cultural Heritage

Kirk Martinez and Leif Isaksen

Introduction: The successes and failures of today's web

The Web today provides a massive amount of information for researchers. A major contributing factor to its success is the simplicity of *publishing* almost any type of data. *Discovery*, however, is much more inefficient, generally using a term-based paradigm that requires entering keywords into a search engine and browsing through results, refining the terms to improve the accuracy of the returns. The ranking algorithms used frequently show the most significant sites in terms of links but at the expense of obscuring the 'long tail' which may also contain valuable information. We are also hidden from the 'deep web' of resources either invisible to search engines or blocked through access controls. The reason why systems cannot automatically crawl the web and index data of a particular type is that web pages are generally not machine-readable, i.e. the elements of information on a typical web page are not marked up with the conceptual nature of their content, so a Natural Language Processing approach is the only feasible way of automatically parsing and comparing the text.

The most common approach towards supporting the marking-up process is the use of metadata. Whilst this may be as simple as a single keyword tag, it opens the door to interoperability in two ways, either by providing standardized fields with content of a known nature, or by drawing on thesauri, wordlists and other Knowledge Organization Systems so as to provide 'universal' values (or both). Dublin Core is perhaps the best-known case of the former approach, and many in the arts community will be familiar with the Getty Thesauri as an example of the latter. Using documents marked up in this way, search engines can (and do) use live access interfaces such as the Open Archives Initiative's OAI-PMH[1] to directly query collections. There are, however, limits to the utility of common metadata standards. The most immediate is the natural tension between the generic nature of a schema and the complexity of the instances which are to be described by it. Either extensions are made, which makes the standard more complex; fields are reinterpreted, which conflates meaning; or information is excluded and thus remains undiscoverable.

---

[1] Open Archives Initiative Protocol for Metadata Harvesting, http://www.openarchives.org/pmh/, accessed July 2008.

In this chapter we will discuss one of the key initiatives intended to ameliorate these problems, known as the Semantic Web. In the first section we provide some background to the reasons for its development and the state of play today. In the second section, we look at how it has been received in the cultural heritage domain, arguing that it has suffered from a confusion arising from its (false) association with Web 2.0 phenomena. The third section is an introduction to the key technologies behind it and is intended to clarify both what the Semantic Web is and what it is not. Section four presents several case studies of successful Semantic Web applications in cultural heritage which we hope will inspire further efforts in this area. In the final section we reflect on current and future challenges in this space.

The Semantic Web

The idea of a 'web of data', in contrast to a 'web of documents', goes back almost to the earliest days of the World Wide Web. The ability to aggregate information across multiple repositories without the danger of conceptual conflation would hugely improve our ability to make meaningful queries that are not determined by arbitrary data structures and boundaries. Although a vast repository of human-readable content is available online, the well-known challenges associated with Natural Language Processing and implicit semantics render it largely useless for machine inference. By being explicit about the semantic content of data 'fragments', however, the potential is opened up for automated (or semi-automated) integration and cross-querying, thereby increasing the information retrieval power of the internet by orders of magnitude.

The Semantic Web Roadmap[2] was published by the World Wide Web Consortium (W3C) in 1998 as an attempt to help guide research in this area, and over the last decade the technologies which formalize these semantics, in particular Uniform Resource Identifiers (URIs), Resource Description Framework (RDF) along with its SPARQL[3] query language, and the Web Ontology Language (OWL)[4] have become well established. High-level services, like the SIMILE project,[5] which enable data suppliers or third parties to disseminate, manipulate or 'mash-up' information using these techniques, are increasingly available. The

2   Semantic Web roadmap http://www.w3.org/DesignIssues/Semantic.html, accessed July 2008.

3   SPARQL Protocol and RDF Query Language.

4   Web Naming and Addressing Overview http://www.w3.org/Addressing/, accessed June 2008; Resource Description Framework (RDF)/W3C Semantic Web Activity http://www.w3.org/RDF/, accessed June 2008; SPARQL Query Language for RDF http://www.w3.org/TR/rdf-sparql-query/, accessed June 2008; OWL Web Ontology Language Overview http://www.w3.org/TR/owl-features/, accessed June 2008.

5   SIMILE Project http://simile.mit.edu/, accessed June 2008.

phrase 'Semantic Web' in turn has now come to mean both a body of semantically-interlinked data hosted across the internet, and the set of formal and conceptual technologies used to create and embody that data.

This is an important distinction because many early successes, most notably in e-Science and medicine,[6] have related to projects that integrate data held between institutions for research purposes, rather than for dissemination to the general public. It is in large part this lack of publicly accessible semantic data that has restricted further viral growth and it remains true that, as of summer 2008, there are still only islands of information available and they apply to limited domains. This is of paramount concern, for although the community of interested users has grown and there are an increasing number of local success stories in applying such technology, this has not yet been sufficient to provoke uptake on a global scale. Whether this will require a so-called 'killer app' or merely a critical mass of users is unclear, but it is at least certain that utility will grow with increased adoption. Developments such as the Linked Data Initiative[7] which seek to maximize connectivity across Semantic Web applications, will play a key role in this process. Moreover, considerable work still needs to be done at domain level – in the words of three protagonists of the Semantic Web vision, 'the ontologies that will furnish the semantics for the Semantic Web must be developed, managed, and endorsed by practice communities'.[8]

The Semantic Web in cultural heritage

The cultural heritage sector has taken note of the potential power of the Semantic Web and the museums and archives community in particular have been quick to explore it. This has been in the form of both theoretical discussions and practical implementation. The former has generally been through workshops and symposia which, whilst making important contributions, have often swung between hubris and pessimism. The DigiCULT project[9] brought together a panel of thirteen European experts in 2003 to discuss Semantic Web development in cultural heritage but the plethora of nascent (and competing) technologies at that time, along with an apparent requirement for the agent-based applications mentioned

---

6   Katy Wolstencroft et al., 'A Little Semantic Web Goes a Long Way in Biology', in *The Semantic Web – ISWC 2005: 4th International Semantic Web Conference, ISWC 2005, Galway, Ireland, November 6–10, 2005. Proceedings* (Berlin, 2005).

7   Linked Data http://linkeddata.org/, accessed June 2008.

8   Nigel Shadbolt et al., 'The Semantic Web Revisited', *IEEE Intelligent Systems*, 21/3 (2006): 99.

9   DigiCULT, *DigiCULT Issue 3: Towards a Semantic Web for Heritage Resources* (2003).

Table 3.1   The Semantic Web and Web 2.0

Semantic Web	Web 2.0
Emphasizes Web semantics.	Emphasizes Web participation.
Prescriptive. A specific research agenda, defined and directed by the W3C.	Descriptive. A set of observations about emergent web cultures, initiated by Tim O'Reilly.
Focus on content and datastructures.	Focus on user interaction and interfaces.
The separation of meaning from instances of that meaning (eg specific words).	Re/usability, crowdsourcing, tagging, multimedia.
Improves computational engagement with data.	Improves human engagement with data.
Clearly defined technology stack (principally URIs, RDF(S), OWL).	Loosely defined technology group (RSS, web APIs, AJAX inter alia).

in a seminal 2001 *Scientific American* article,[10] resulted in the Semantic Web being described as a 'Shangri-La' surrounded by a 'veil of mystery'. Nonetheless, a number of participants concluded that 'they would put their money on the Semantic Web' whilst other contributors maintained that 'the heritage sector is likely to be left behind'.[11] Five years later, the Semantic Web Think Tank project, a series of workshops for the museum sector, funded by the AHRC, concluded in 2008 that 'There is no coherent answer to the question "How do I do the Semantic Web?" and almost no information with which to make an informed decision about technologies, platforms, models and methodologies.' This appeared to create a gap between the vision and the reality of the Semantic Web 'which critically undermines the ability of the sector to move forward in a clear and constructive way.'[12]

We believe that this pessimism is largely due to a misunderstanding of the Semantic Web project or, at best, discussion of a (lower case) 'semantic web' that is so broad as to inevitably be incoherent and hence unpractical. Both the final and online reports of the SWTT meetings[13] frequently mix discussion of Semantic Web technologies with a variety of concepts and applications – including tagging, folksonomies, topic maps, social networks, Flickr, Google Base and Yahoo Pipes

---

10   Tim Berners-Lee et al., 'The Semantic Web', *Scientific American*, May 2001, http://www.sciam.com/article.cfm?id=the-semantic-web, accessed April 2009.

11   DigiCULT, *DigiCULT Issue 3*: 6–7, 10, 14.

12   Ross Parry et al., 'Semantic Dissonance: Do We Need (And Do We Understand) The Semantic Web?', in *Museums and the Web 2008* (Montreal, Canada, 2008).

13   UK Museums and the Semantic Web, http://culturalsemanticweb.wordpress.com/, accessed July 2008.

– which are not related to the Semantic Web project as outlined by the W3C. Whilst there is no question that these emerging tools are potentially of great value to the museum community, we feel that it is important to keep them under the separate banner of 'Web 2.0'.[14] The differences between these two web paradigms are summarized in Table 3.1, which we hope will make clear that any evaluation of the Semantic Web is best done on its own terms.

It is important to emphasize that these are not competing visions of the web. Indeed, Web 2.0 is not really a vision at all, merely a description of contemporary trends in cyberspace. Nevertheless, they both provide important conceptual and technical toolkits that we can bring to bear on the problems of information dissemination, and fortunately there is no conflict between them. Further discussion of Web 2.0 is, however, beyond the scope of this chapter in which we shall go into greater detail about the technologies that constitute the Semantic Web, indicating along the way why they are relevant to both researchers and curators of cultural heritage.

How it works

In order to demonstrate how the Semantic Web works, let us imagine a typical situation encountered when we try to combine information from separate databases. Perhaps we are interested in the works of Pieter Breugel the Elder and are able to obtain the metadata associated with paintings in two separate collection databases, as shown in Tables 3.2 and 3.3.

Table 3.2   Extract from Collection A

Artwork	Painter
The Tower of Babel	Pieter Breughel

Table 3.3   Extract from Collection B

Object	Artist
The Wedding Dance	Breughel the Elder

Those familiar with the Breughel dynasty will be aware that such a problem is by no means as simple as it initially appears. Does the first entry refer to *The Tower of Babel* by Pieter Breughel the Younger or *The Tower of Babel* by Pieter Breugel

---

14   What Is Web 2.0, http://www.oreillynet.com/pub/a/oreilly/tim/news/2005/09/30/what-is-web-20.html, accessed July 2008.

the Elder? (the missing 'h' in the 'Breughel' name is no help – he only dropped it from his signature later in life). Could *The Wedding Dance* be by Jan Breughel the Elder? There is no means of telling which artist (and thus which artworks) are referred to by the records here. Better metadata that might enable an expert to make an educated guess is of little or no help to an automated cross-querying process for a number of reasons.

Identity

A relational database cannot guarantee the global uniqueness of any identifier. Even if the identifier refers to a Knowledge Organization System (such as the Getty Thesaurus), the association between the ID and its term list is only implicit within the relational structure and hence undiscoverable by an automated agent.

Category

There is no cross-identification between types of data. In our example, the columns 'Artwork' and 'Object', and 'Painter' and 'Artist', hold the same categories of information that we are interested in but, again, this not transparent to an automated process. Dublin Core has helped here to a limited degree by providing a generally accepted set of basic metadata categories (such as 'creator') but they are of necessity extremely broad with well-documented consequences.[15]

Conceptual association

The great advantage of establishing what concepts our data refers to is that we can then map associations between them. Thus it interests us not only that Breugel is the creator of the *The Tower of Babel*, but also a person with familial ties, and hence potentially part of an artist's dynasty.

Fortunately, the technical means by which to formalize such semantics, Uniform Resource Identifiers (URIs), Resource Description Framework (RDF) and Ontologies, are now established.

Uniform Resource Identifiers

URIs, most commonly encountered as the HTTP web addresses displayed in an internet browser, provide a solution to the problem of identity and form the fundamental building blocks of the Semantic Web. As globally unique (and generally resolvable) identifiers, they can be associated with any given concept, either entity or property. So,

---

15 Martin Doerr et al., 'The Dream of a Global Knowledge Network – A New Approach', *Journal on Computing and Cultural Heritage*, 1/1 (2008): 1.

> http://www.collection_a.com/painters/pieter_breugel

might refer to an artist,

> http://www.collection_a.com/artworks/the_tower_of_babel

could refer to a painting, and

> http://www.collection_a.com/concepts/created_by

may identify a relationship between them. Of course, the possibility is still there for other organizations to use different URIs to refer to the same real-world entities (whether concrete or abstract). This 'problem of co-reference', whilst challenging, is not insurmountable, as we shall see. Of much greater importance is the ability it gives resource providers to use the same URI when they want to refer to the same entity. And because any concept can be referred to by means of a URI, there are no limits to what is potentially cross-searchable across institutions.

Ontologies

Ontologies in computer science are 'an explicit specification of a conceptualization'.[16] They define not only the concepts associated with a branch of knowledge but the relationships between them. Essentially an ontology is a schema which may define any or all of the following:

- a list of possible classes whose scope has been defined;
- a list of entities which instantiate those classes;
- a list of possible relationships whose scope has been defined;
- a specification of which relationships are associated with which classes.

Depending on the ontology, both classes and relationships may also inherit features from parent classes and relationships, enabling querying to take place at varying levels of granularity. This is best demonstrated with an ontology which might apply to our problem.

In the domain described in the ontology in Figure 3.1, there are several kinds of things in the world – which include paintings and persons – and they have very specific relationships. Persons can be artists who create paintings or other art objects which enables us to ask questions such as 'Who created painting *x*?',

---

16   Thomas R. Gruber, 'Towards Principles for the Design of Ontologies Used for Knowledge Sharing', in Nicola Guarino et al. (eds), *Formal Ontology in Conceptual Analysis and Knowledge Representation*, special issue of the *International Journal of Human and Computer Studies* (Deventer, 1995).

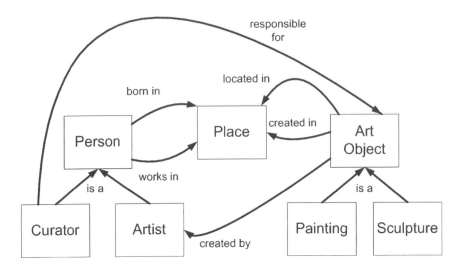

Figure 3.1   Simple example of an ontology showing concepts and relationships

'What paintings did *y* create?' or even simply 'Who created what?' To do so, however, we have to find a way of associating the instances from our databases with the classes and relationships which form our ontology. Fortunately, because we can use URIs to express these general categories in the same way in which we can use them to refer to specific cases, all we need is a language to combine our URIs into meaningful statements.

Resource Description Framework is that language. Its sentences come in the form of *triples* – sets of three URIs (or two URIs and a literal such as a number or character string) and represent a subject-predicate-object statement in the nature of '*x* has relation *y* to *z*'. As the same URIs can be used across multiple statements they collectively form a network, or graph, of information which can be traversed by a query engine. How do we formulate a query about Pieter Breugel the Elder? We simply find the URI that corresponds to him and then request all the statements that refer to it (as either subject or object). These might tell us that he is, for instance, <of type> <painter> or that he <created> <The Tower of Babel>.

It is important to note that RDF is only a conceptual language. It can be expressed in any number of ways, from visual diagrams to the spoken word. Computationally, a number of different notations can be used, including N3, Turtle and RDF/XML. For the purposes of clarity however, we will here simply express them as triplets of URIs listed consecutively. Thus, collection A might hold the following three triples:

(1)
http://www.collection_a.com/artworks/the_tower_of_babel
http://www.our_ontology.com/created_by
http://www.collection_a.com/painters/pieter_breugel

(2)
http://www.collection_a.com/artworks/the_tower_of_babel
http://www.w3.org/1999/02/22-rdf-syntax-ns#type
http://www.our_ontology.com/painting

(3)
http://www.collection_a.com/painters/pieter_breugel
http://www.w3.org/1999/02/22-rdf-syntax-ns#type
http://www.our_ontology.com/painter

What do the predicate (i.e. second) URIs in (2) and (3) mean? They are URIs provided by W3C that give a global definition to the concept that an instance *I* has the 'type' of class *C*. Together these triples tell us that a specific painter (represented by a URI) created a specific painting (represented by another URI). Collection B might alternatively represent its information as follows:

(1')
http://www.collection_b.com/objects/the_wedding_dance
http://www.our_ontology.com/created_by
http://www.collection_b.com/artists/breughel_the_elder

(2')
http://www.collection_b.com/objects/the_wedding_dance
http://www.w3.org/1999/02/22-rdf-syntax-ns#type
http://www.our_ontology.com/painting

(3')
http://www.collection_b.com/artists/breughel_the_elder
http://www.w3.org/1999/02/22-rdf-syntax-ns#type
http://www.our_ontology.com/painter

Of course we're still left with our problem of co-reference: how do we know that our two painter URIs refer to the same thing? The problem is easily resolved with an extra triple (which might be stored at collection A or collection B or somewhere else):

(4)
http://www.collection_a.com/painters/pieter_breugel
http://www.w3.org/2002/07/owl/sameAs
http://www.collection_b.com/artists/breughel_the_elder

Using the power of the higher-level ontology language known as OWL (Web Ontology Language), we can associate (or dissociate) our local concepts with any other concepts held in RDF out there on the web. These may also be associated with a scope note in the form of a string of text so that human readers can be sure what they refer to. We can also store this connective information anywhere we like, perhaps at one or other of the collections, or locally, or even at a completely different repository. The triples above are enough to tell us that the painting *The Wedding Dance,* and the painting *The Tower of Babel*, were created by the same painter, and that might well be enough for our needs, but for truly powerful searching we would want to be able to map our local ontology to a global one.

RDF, RDFS and OWL

Any attempt to record information in RDF will almost certainly require the use of the standard URI vocabularies hosted at W3C. The basic RDF vocabulary, which records URIs for concepts like 'type' and 'property', can be found at: http://www.w3.org/1999/02/22-rdf-syntax-ns (accessed April 2009). RDF provides the essential building blocks for making subject-predicate-object statements. Looking at the URI in your Web browser is likely to present you with a nicely formatted list that describes them, but if you open the page source, you will see that it is in fact also written in RDF (using an XML application called RDF/XML). In other words, RDF is self-describing. RDF Schema (RDFS – see http://www.w3.org/2000/01/rdf-schema, accessed April 2009) provides an important set of further URIs for building simple ontologies and includes concepts such as 'class'.

Whereas RDF and RDFS enable us to build closed ontologies, OWL was designed as a set of concepts that enables us to use them in a distributed, web-centric fashion. Generally speaking, OWL concepts (which include 'sameAs', 'differentFrom' and 'intersectionOf') enable us to define concepts by relating them to others (or groups of others). As a result, the possibility of mapping between and merging ontologies held in otherwise disparate domains is opened up. However, there is a price tag that comes with this. Use of the full OWL ontology is potentially so complex (especially over large numbers of triples) that resolving queries over them, known as *inferencing*, can become intractable. For that reason, two subsets of the OWL ontology (known as 'OWL DL' and 'OWL Lite') are more commonly used in order to create ontologies with more limited expressive power that won't cause your server to grind to a halt.

The CIDOC Conceptual Reference Model

Perhaps the most important Semantic Web development in the cultural heritage sphere is the establishment of a 'core ontology' known as the Conceptual Reference Model (or CRM) created by the Comité International pour la Documentation des

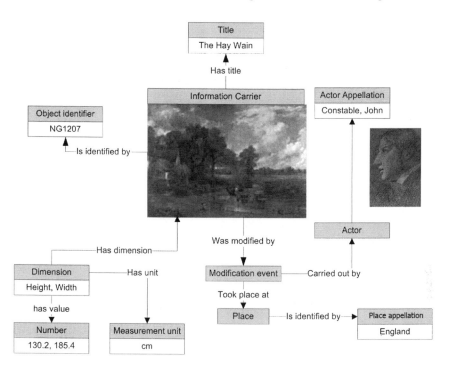

Figure 3.2   Mapping existing Dublin Core metadata to the CIDOC CRM

Musées (CIDOC).[17] The CIDOC CRM is intended to cover the full spectrum of cultural heritage knowledge and has recently been extended to cover the production of literary and musical entities in more depth. Although currently incorporating eighty-four entity types and 141 property types it is remarkably compact and efficient given its extremely broad scope. It also has an inherently epistemological structure based around temporal 'events' in order to deal with the innate uncertainty of information about the past.[18] It received ISO standard status in 2006 (ISO 21127:2006) and is now the dominant domain ontology in cultural heritage. The greatest challenge in mapping legacy datasets to the CIDOC CRM, however, has been the considerable mental leap required of both museum creators and their technical staff to map their datasets to such an abstract conceptualization. Although CIDOC have had a number of successes in mapping legacy data to the

---

17   Nicholas Crofts et al., 'Definition of the CIDOC Conceptual Reference Model. Version 4.2.4' (2008) http://cidoc.ics.forth.gr/docs/cidoc_crm_version_4.2.4_March2008_.pdf.

18   Martin Doerr, 'The CIDOC Conceptual Reference Module: An Ontological Approach to Semantic Interoperability of Metadata', *AI Magazine*, 24/3 (2003).

ontology,[19] and encourage an adaptive approach which restricts and/or extends the ontology, the process generally requires extensive collaboration between curators, IT professionals and CRM experts.[20] The recent release of the AMA tool[21] may help to ease this process, but there are still too few case studies for a formal evaluation of its utility. A recent publication gives an interesting overview of CIDOC's future intentions in this area.[22]

The Semantic Web in cultural heritage today

Further to these central developments, several research projects have been successful at producing end-to-end semantic systems. Many of them have an online presence, which we encourage readers to experiment with.

Case studies

MuseumFinland/CultureSampo[23]

The first major deployment of Semantic Web technologies in the museum sector was the MuseumFinland project's provision of tools and services so that Finnish museums could present their collections online through a common Semantic Web interface. A central ontology was developed for the project and contributing institutions make their data available as XML. This is then mapped to the ontology, although the approach is reflexive and new concepts can be added globally where required. A website allows users to search and browse cultural artefacts in a 'follow-your-nose' fashion via their properties. Coming second in

---

19   Nicholas Crofts, 'Combining Data Sources – Prototype Applications Developed for Geneva's Department of Historical Sites and Monuments based on the CIDOC CRM' (2004); Martin Doerr et al., 'Integration of Complementary Archaeological Sources', in *Proceedings of Computer Applications and Quantitative Methods in Archaeology Conference 2004* (Prato, 2004).

20   Matthew Addis et al., 'New Ways to Search, Navigate and Use Multimedia Museum Collections over the Web', in *Museums and the Web 2005* (Vancouver, 2005).

21   Oyvind Eide et al., 'Encoding Cultural Heritage Information for the Semantic Web. Procedures for Data Integration through CIDOC-CRM Mapping', in David Arnold et al. (eds), *Open Digital Cultural Heritage Systems, EPOCH Final Event Rome, February 2008* (EPOCH, 2008).

22   Martin Doerr et al., 'The Dream of a Global Knowledge Network: A New Approach', *Journal on Computing and Cultural Heritage*, vol. 1, no. 1 (2008).

23   Eero Hyvönen et al., 'MuseumFinland – Finnish Museums on the Semantic Web', *Web Semantics: Science, Services and Agents on the World Wide Web*, 3/2–3 (2005); Eero Hyvönen et al., 'CultureSampo – Finnish Culture on the Semantic Web: The Vision and First Results', in *Information Technology for the Virtual Museum* (Berlin, 2007).

the 2004 Semantic Web Challenge (an award given annually at the International Semantic Web Conference), it also forms part of a wider initiative by the Finnish government to enable public web services semantically. A follow-up project, the CultureSampo portal, extended the MuseumFinland ontology in order to represent events and processes. This enables the embedding of artefacts in narratives, helping to provide greater contextualization.

ARTISTE/SCULPTEUR/eCHASE[24]

Building on the previous ARTISTE project which provided cross-archival search capabilities for galleries using RDF, SCULPTEUR uses an ontology-driven approach to provide adaptive search and visualization mechanisms for 2D and 3D objects. Datatypes include digital images, 3D models, associated metadata, free text documents and numerical tables. Museum databases were mapped to the CIDOC CRM (with several extensions) and an ontology of the system components enabled dynamic interface modification to suit the heterogeneous nature of the data returned. Key amongst these navigation tools was the mSpace browser.[25] The ensuing eCHASE project, funded by the European Commission, was more directly focused on the creation of a toolset and framework by which third parties could both contribute and draw multimedia entities from a semantically integrated network of repositories across Europe, chiefly with the aim of catalysing increased exploitation of otherwise moribund resources.

MultimediaN E-culture/CHIP@STITCH[26]

MultimediaN E-culture is a prototype system that brings together multiple online cultural heritage repositories in the Netherlands. Winner of the 2006 Semantic Web Challenge, it is aimed at public users and non-technical researchers with a generic browser, '/facet', that enables users to explore the databases along any

---

24   Matthew Addis et al., 'New Ways to Search, Navigate and Use Multimedia Museum Collections over the Web'; Matthew Addis et al., 'The eCHASE System for Cross-border Use of European Multimedia Cultural Heritage Content in Education and Publishing', in *AXMEDIS 2006: 2nd International Conference on Automated Production of Cross Media Content for Multi-channel Distribution, Leeds, UK* (2006).

25   mc schraefel et al., 'The Evolving mSpace Platform: Leveraging the Semantic Web on the Trail of the Memex', in *Proceedings of the sixteenth ACM conference on Hypertext and hypermedia. Salzburg, Austria* (ACM, 2005).

26   Jacco van Ossenbruggen et al., 'Searching and Annotating Virtual Heritage Collections with Semantic-Web Techniques', in *Museums and the Web 2007* (2007); Lora Aroyo et al., 'CHIP Demonstrator: Semantics-Driven Recommendations and Museum Tour Generation', in *The Semantic Web. 6th International Semantic Web Conference, 2nd Asian Semantic Web Conference, ISWC 2007 + ASWC 2007, Busan, Korea, November 11–15, 2007. Proceedings* (Berlin, 2008).

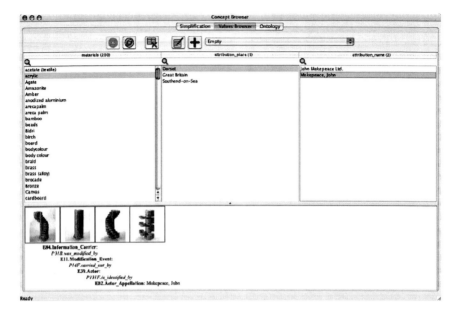

Figure 3.3   The mSpace faceted browser

facet – whether artist, genre, period or otherwise.[27] Ontologies were developed for individual databases as well as the Getty thesauri (Art and Architecture Thesaurus and Union List of Artist Names) and then aligned by hand.[28] The CHIP browser, drawing on ontology mappings from the CATCH STITCH project, as well as MultiMediaN E-culture, combines data from the Rijksmuseum's ARIA database with RDF from the IconClass and Getty thesauri. The results are used to provide an automated Artwork Recommender that creates suggestions based on users 'rating' other examples as well as personalized tours of the museum that can be downloaded to a handheld device.

---

27   Michiel Hildebrand et al., '/facet: A Browser for Heterogeneous Semantic Web Repositories', in *The Semantic Web – ISWC 2006. 5th International Semantic Web Conference, ISWC 2006, Athens, GA, USA, November 5–9, 2006. Proceedings* (Berlin, 2006).

28   Getty Vocabulary Program http://getty.edu/research/conducting_research/vocabularies/, accessed June 2008.

CIDOC CRM-EH/STAR[29]

In 2004 the English Heritage Research and Standards Group undertook a project in conjunction with CIDOC to develop a CRM extension that would adequately describe the wide variety of archaeological datasets which they hold in-house as well as permit integration with excavation data from County Councils. This is an important step forward for archaeologists, as the CRM was developed with a focus on the needs of the museums and archive community. Following this work, the STAR project, run in partnership with the Hypermedia Research Unit, University of Glamorgan, is now developing tools to help third-party organizations map their resources to this ontology. These include SKOS services that are capable of providing archaeological thesauri[30] and a demonstrator of several archaeological databases aggregated into RDF following the CRM-EH ontology.

The Future of the Semantic Web

Whilst all of these projects and others have remained confident that semantic approaches can prove highly beneficial, they also generally underline the current challenges of mapping legacy datasets to ontologies – especially those with a high degree of complexity. This issue is exacerbated by the frequent adoption of centralized approaches to mapping that attempt to convert relational and textual data into RDF using a single generic ontology. We believe this is unhelpful on two counts and that it is better for cultural resource providers to first map data to their own local ontologies, and only then to align them with more generic Domain Ontologies (such as the CIDOC CRM) as a second step. The first reason for this is purely pragmatic. Whilst it may require slightly more labour, the two-step process is conceptually far more tractable. It is quite difficult enough to map between two explicit worldviews, let alone convert between data formats and implicit ontologies at the same time! Second, there is a growing realization of the importance of multivocality in cultural heritage. Although this is most evident in the needs of indigenous groups and areas of contested heritage,[31] it is important to realize that the cultural heritage community is not one, but many 'knowledge societies', each with potentially different conceptualizations of our common material legacy. We do not want to throw the baby out with the bathwater by creating 'one ontology to rule them all'. It is our belief that the next step to be taken by the cultural heritage sector is for separate discipline communities to develop their own ontologies and

---

29   Paul Cripps et al., 'Ontological Modelling of the Work of the Centre for Archaeology' (2004); STAR Project, http://hypermedia.research.glam.ac.uk/kos/STAR/, accessed June 2008.

30   INSCRIPTION, http://www.fish-forum.info/inscript.htm, accessed June 2008.

31   Robin Boast et al., 'Return to Babel: Emergent Diversity, Digital Resources, and Local Knowledge', *The Information Society*, 23/5 (2007), pp. 395–403.

host it as linked data. Once they are able to express the 'deep' nature of the data in their possession, we can begin to align them and, in so doing, create a much more powerful body of information than has previously been available.

Conclusions

Semantic Web tools have developed sufficiently for the next generation of knowledge on the web to evolve. However this will require effort on the part of information providers in order to publish their data. The benefits will be considerable as it will provide the raw material for a new generation of search engines and web tools which allow a deeper exploration of cultural heritage knowledge than is currently available. Interlinking millions of information sources has already shown its worth in the existing web – this new semantic wave has the potential to further improve the usefulness, availability and accuracy of retrieved information.

Acknowledgements

Our thanks to many collaborators including Patrick Sinclair, Forth, C2RMF, Artiste, SCULPTEUR and eCHASE consortia. Also to the European Commission Framework programmes for funding.

Chapter 4

Resource Discovery and Curation of Complex and Interactive Digital Datasets

Stuart Jeffrey

The realm of the visual record, like almost all forms of information, has long since divorced itself solely from the physical. Much material that began life in one format – oil on canvas, text on paper, silver nitrate film – has gone through the ubiquitous and, many would argue, liberating, transformational process of digitization into an intricately coded collection of binary data. In this form it can, in theory at least, be infinitely manipulated, infinitely copied and infinitely accessed. Any constraints on its transmission and accessibility are a function of its legal or social context, and not the technological limits of the digital form. Of course, a digital version of a physical object is, as it is correctly termed, a surrogate; it is not the duplicate of an original, and our modes of interacting with, analysing and enjoying the surrogate are very different from how we experience the original. At the same time as many physical records are making the transition to digital surrogate, even more material is being created initially in digital form.

These objects, both born-digital and digitized, are often gathered together for long-term storage and preservation in the context of archives, libraries and galleries. In practice the gathering process can be notional as the physical storage sites for digital media can be, some say should be,[1] geographically distributed. However, the user may perceive them as being a single location because their access point makes them appear accessible from a single web location, normally a search interface or catalogue. In fact for many users the phrase 'on the internet' almost implies the concept of a single place. This is testament to the power of the internet, particularly the World Wide Web, to present itself as a unified whole with the web browser apparently acting as a window on a single semi-coherent collection of information. Users show little tolerance for the difficulties that exist in making diverse datasets fully discoverable and cross-searchable. This is because conceptually the data appear to be already stored in the same place, i.e. on 'the internet' and in the same format, i.e. 'digital'. The user might then ask: surely it is an easy matter to search quickly and comprehensively for all things digital on the internet? In fact discovering what resources exist on the internet, either for the purposes of research

---

1 Distributed physical storage, at least of copies of material, is considered a prerequisite of safe archival practices on the understanding that catastrophic events, war, fire, earthquake, etc., are less likely to affect two remote geographical locations simultaneously.

or simply to consume and enjoy, is far from straightforward. The whole world of resource search and discovery is bound up with complex commercial, economic and social issues that for the moment allow the most simple search paradigms, such as the Google 'search box', to dominate. In fact, in terms of volume of searches the Google search engine itself dominates the internet, being by far the most used.[2] How this type of search works, essentially a brute-force free-text search, is somewhat naïve when compared to the sophisticated cataloguing and resource discovery mechanisms familiar from the world of libraries and archives. More importantly it does not (and does not claim to) search what is known as the 'deep web'. The deep web (sometimes called the invisible web) is not normally searchable by standard search engines such as Yahoo and Google and is generally thought to constitute the major part of the web, although putting an exact figure on how much is searchable and how much is 'deep' is virtually impossible as the border between the two is fluid and changes constantly with policy and technology changes. Some estimates assess the amount of information available on the web, but not accessible by search engines, and therefore 'deep', as many tens of times larger than the total amount of data on the surface web.[3] An example of deep web material might be data held behind a database interface or held on web servers that exclude access by Web Crawlers and Spiders[4] as a matter of policy. How much access a search engine has to this material can to a certain extent be dictated by the data provider. However, the question that library or archive-based data providers might find themselves asking is why they have built sophisticated catalogue systems, relying on finely tuned categorization schema and delivered by a bespoke database interface, when a standard generic search engine will simply discard all that richness in favour of a simple text search? For organizations with a commitment to providing access to their data to a broad range of audiences, and for organizations whose performance is judged directly on the level of web usage, it is entirely necessary to open up their resources to as much search engine cataloguing as possible. This, after all, is how the majority of users will find their way to the resources in practice. However, it is important that other forms of resource discovery are not discarded. Those forms of discovery that rely on rich categorization – rich metadata – to describe the resource, and sophisticated and reliable search mechanisms, have often arisen from, and remain part of, professional or academic practice, and should continue to be valued as long as they remain useful to those audiences.

---

2   Nielsen NetRatings Search Engine Ratings in July 2006 gave Google 49.2% of all search engine usage with the nearest rival on 23.8%: http://searchenginewatch.com/showPage.html?page=2156451, accessed July 2008.

3   For more detail on the deep web and useful references see Wikipedia: http://en.wikipedia.org/wiki/Deep_Web, accessed July 2008.

4   Web Crawlers and Web Spiders are the terms for the automated software agents employed by search engine companies, such as Google, Yahoo and Microsoft (sometimes known collectively as GYM), to 'crawl' the web and pre-index word occurrence on web pages.

In many arts and humanities disciplines the pros and cons of various forms of categorization and the value of categorization itself remain the subject of debate.[5] It is indeed a truism that categorization schemas are the manifestation of a particular view of the world and therefore necessarily privilege that originating world view over the myriad others that we know to exist. In critical thought, this is one of a number of fundamental notions that must be constantly held in mind: how a 'thing' is intellectually conceived, constructed, and referred to is negotiable and dynamic. The process of categorization necessarily stems this process, locking the 'thing' into a near-rigid intellectual framework. Understanding this means that while a categorization schema or ontology may indeed be a manifestation of a particular world view it need not necessarily be seen as a statement of the intrinsic 'rightness' of that particular way of seeing the world. It can in fact be viewed as a pragmatic solution to allowing the discovery of a specific item of interest from a vast, near-overwhelming volume of potentially relevant data.

The Archaeology Data Service (ADS)[6] holds a large collection of digital resources that are intended to act as source material for both the teaching of archaeology in Higher Education and further research in archaeology within the higher education sector. Many of the resources the ADS holds comprise multiple file forms such as text, still images, spreadsheets and audio-visual material. Increasingly frequently they comprise databases, 3D, VR and Geographic Information System (GIS) files. These file types are designed to have an element of interactivity and, in the case of databases and GIS files, are designed to allow user-defined queries in order to derive full benefit from them. Unlike many types of data they cannot simply be passively consumed.

Archaeology as a discipline has a long tradition of experimenting with novel methods of recording its primary data. Consequently, the curation and delivery methodologies of these data have grown up to reflect this tradition, allowing for the discovery and reuse of such resources as photographic images, text documents, maps, plans and geophysical survey plots. More recently, driven in no small part by the explosion of user-friendly application programmer's interfaces (APIs) to common programmes, newly adopted methodologies are producing outputs that incorporate a degree of interaction with the data that are actually integral to the understanding of the data themselves. Examples of these include complex database front-ends, virtual reality models and GIS data. Also included are more standard formats such as those produced in the audio and video recording of archaeological sites and archaeologists' practice. Many of these new outputs are both ground-breaking and aesthetically pleasing and sit at the cutting edge of what is possible and what can be imagined as a way of presenting data about our past and its inhabitants.

5　For an example of the nature of this debate in archaeology see A. Baines and K. Brophy, 'What's Another Word for Thesaurus? Data Standards and Classifying the Past', in P. Daly and T.L. Evans (eds), *Digital Archaeology: Bridging Method and Theory* (London, 2006), p. 237.

6　The Archaeology Data Service website: http://ads.ahds.ac.uk/, accessed July 2008.

Ever-increasing linkages between the data and the software applications that deliver it, and even the nature of the digital infrastructure by which it is served up, challenge the normal practice of digital curation where deconstruction of the resource to simple open-source formats for preservation has been the norm. The core of digital preservation approaches such as the Open Archival Information System (OAIS) reference model is that data held in preservation formats can be easily reconstructed into a delivery package which represents the best, most current way to deliver a particular type of data. ('best' here usually means the most accessible rather than the most elegant in pure informatics terms). How does such an approach function when the data cannot be logically broken down to preservation formats without rendering it meaningless, and the ways of describing degrees and forms of interactivity in this context have not been specified? This increasing integration of archaeological data with its mode of delivery throws up two major issues for those tasked with curating it for the long term. How do we allow resource discovery within (rather than simply of) time-based media and, perhaps more significantly, how do we describe the significant properties of interactive resources?

This richness in interactivity raises a number of challenges for organizations hosting and delivering such resources. Included amongst these are the following questions. Is additional software needed and available to access the files? Without downloading and experimenting with a large dataset how might the user be informed of the levels of interactivity available and/or required? Does the user require an understanding of the underlying processes and data structures when interacting with the data? If so, how are they to be informed? How can the user target the right data at the right level of detail for their purposes without downloading and examining it? All of the above issues are to some degree relevant for passively consumed data, but the impact and implications for resources that require some kind of interaction are far greater, especially when data volume and application specificity are considered. Potentially very useful resources will remain untapped because the likely user community is not aware of what they are and what they are capable of doing. In the following sections some of the above issues are explored and, although there is no obvious solution to many of them, future directions for facilitating the best possible access to this material are suggested.

The key tool in the resource discovery of a digital dataset, or indeed any dataset, is the concept of metadata, or data describing data. Metadata is used to describe a record or an archived resource in such a way, and using such descriptors, that a researcher can easily discover that it contains information relevant to their researches. Some metadata is extremely straightforward, to the point of being obvious. For example the 'title' of a resource, say the title of a book, is often a useful bit of information. If you are looking for a book on the theory and practice of archaeology, then the title *Archaeology, Theories, Methods and*

Practice[7] would look like an obvious choice and would almost certainly come up in a search for 'archaeological theory'. Similarly, if you know that Colin Renfrew writes on archaeological methods then searching on that author's name will also return the book *Archaeology, Theories, Methods and Practice*. Unfortunately not all titles are as helpful as this and a researcher does not always know the author or year or publication of all works that might be relevant. Here is where a more rigorous approach to resource discovery becomes useful. Dating back to 1873, one of the earliest and most widely adopted approaches that could be described as a metadata schema[8] is the Dewey Decimal Classification[9] system (DDC) used extensively in libraries. This system recognizes that it would be useful to be able to classify documents by their content as well as by their author, date, title and so on. DDC categorizes 'field of knowledge' broad headings and then develops them hierarchically so that at each level of the hierarchy the category is more focused. The following example[10] shows the classification for texts dealing with caring for cats and dogs:

600	Technology
630	Agriculture and related technologies
636	Animal husbandry
636.7	Dogs
636.8	Cats

There are many hundreds of categories and subcategories allowing books in a library to be discovered by topic. In the example above, the number 636.8, when assigned to a book on cat welfare, would allow for its discovery in searches for 'technology', 'agriculture' and 'animal husbandry'.

This form of metadata, which uses a controlled list of words to organize general knowledge can obviously be applied to digital objects also, although frequently a much more liberal approach to describing content is taken. The hierarchical approach of the DDC system is reflected in archaeological classification systems such as the Thesaurus of Monument Types (TMT),[11] which is used to assign a specific term to each of the huge and varied range of records about monuments

---

7   C. Renfrew and P. Bahn, *Archaeology, Theories, Methods and Practice* (London, 1991).

8   A metadata schema is a proscriptive, although possibly extensible, system for creating metadata.

9   A full list of the DDC categorization system is available on the OCLC website: http://www.oclc.org/dewey/resources/summaries/default.htm, accessed July 2008.

10   This example is drawn from the OCLC's own documentation available from the OCLC website referenced above.

11   The TMT was created by English Heritage National Monuments Record, it can be explored online at: http://thesaurus.english-heritage.org.uk/, accessed July 2008.

held in either national monuments records or historic environment records.[12] Because of this the TMT can be used to assign a specific metadata term relating to monument type in all forms of record that relate to that monument.[13] As well as performing a function describing the content of a digital resource, or indicating its associations in the case of the TMT, other metadata elements can deal with technical aspects of the resource and are intended to be of use to the archive rather than being a tool for resource discovery, although they are often used as such. An example of this type of metadata might be drawn from the Dublin Core metadata schema, which was specifically developed for archiving and discovery of a broad range of digital material. The 'core' of the Dublin Core[14] is fifteen properties of a resource that help to describe it. As well as the expected properties, such as 'title', 'creator' and 'publisher', there are also properties that allow for the description of a resource's file formats, data types and even aspects of copyright and intellectual property law relating to it. It should be obvious that the file format of digitally archived data is essential to its discovery as well as to its archiving. A researcher may be looking specifically for text, audio, video or a 3D model; the file format is a key indicator for this. The relationship between file type and resource discovery is an important one and the proliferation of sophisticated and highly specialized delivery mechanisms for media like digital video, but more particularly 3D models, digital panoramas, pseudo-immersive VR models and so on, means that a researcher may wish to narrow a search to the formats he or she can meaningfully access. When the choice is between image formats such as TIFF, JPEG and GIF then this is trivial. When it comes to differing (and proprietary) video 'Codecs' (coding and decoding algorithms)[15] the choice becomes harder. Ultimately when the distinction is between formats used to store and deliver highly interactive datasets, such as the pseudo-immersive VR mentioned above, the choice is often a very simple one, i.e. is there an application available to read this format and does the researcher have access to it?[16]

12   In the UK, National Monuments Records are curated by the appropriate national body for England, Scotland, Wales and Northern Ireland. Historic Environment Records (sometimes called Sites and Monuments Records) are held by local authorities and perform a role specific to local authority responsibility for the planning process. However, they also represent a significant HE research resource.

13   For example, a digitized journal article that refers to a particular site might have a term from the TMT used in its metadata.

14   The Dublin Core Metadata Element Set, Version 1.1 is available from the Dublin Core website: http://dublincore.org/documents/dces/, accessed July 2008.

15   The coding and decoding algorithms used in digital audio and video are often considered as key intellectual property of the companies that developed them and as a result are closely guarded secrets made available to other software developers only at significant cost, if at all.

16   It is major plank of good practice in digital archiving to recognize that software companies and the codecs they own the rights to should not be assumed to be permanently available.

There is another approach to metadata for digital resources, including time-based media such as audio and video. It is most apparent in so-called Web 2.0 contexts where the content of a website might be created by the people who are also using the website. This is commonly known as user-generated content or UGC. Far from their origins as a fringe activity, these types of site now hold very large volumes of data. For some, the explosion of user-generated content, whether it be still images, audio or video or more complex file types, has gone hand-in-hand with an entirely different attitude to resource discovery (and also technical metadata). Sites such as Napster,[17] Flickr[18] and YouTube[19] would seem at first blush to operate as a kind of archive for audio, images and videos. Leaving aside the numerous issues surrounding the legal, social, technical and ethical positions of these services as they are currently structured, what is of interest here is the notion of unstructured user-generated metadata. In Web 2.0 jargon this concept is most frequently referred to as tagging, social tagging or user-generated tags. How exactly tagging is implemented may vary from site to site, but the principle remains the same, the original depositor and then subsequent site visitors can choose and associate words and phrases to describe a resource. The terms that are most frequently given are assumed to be the most useful. Here is a partial list of tags drawn from an image of Stonehenge on Flickr:[20]

> Stonehenge, Wiltshire, UK, BRAVO, ABigFave, Superbmasterpiece, BlueRibbonWinner, ExcellentPhotographer, Awards, amazingamateur, ancient Mesolithic, bronze, stone, circles, sunset, landmark ...

As can be seen from this list, many of the tags act as relevant metadata for one purpose, say archaeological research, while some clearly refer to the subjective quality of the image ('Superbmasterpiece') and others refer to non-archaeological features of the image ('sunset') and finally, others appear to have no general relevance at all ('BRAVO, ABigFave'). Despite the shortcomings of this approach for resource discovery in a research context, it is undeniable that different conceptions of a monument might be elucidated by this type of tagging. While this is most likely a desirable outcome and would be generally welcomed in archaeology it is only ever likely to be complementary to more rigorous systems.

It is very important to remember that these sites, and even search engines such as those controlled by the market leaders, do not actually have as their highest

---

17   Napster is a peer-to-peer file sharing site that was subject to intense legal pressure over alleged copyright infringement relating to content when the company first started. It is owned by Roxio Inc.: http://trial.napster.co.uk/, accessed July 2008.

18   Flickr is a photo-sharing site owned by Yahoo!: http://www.flickr.com/, accessed July 2008.

19   YouTube is a video-clip-sharing site, owned by Google since 2006: http://www.YouTube.com/, accessed July 2008.

20   http://www.flickr.com/photos/nardip/1433903816/, accessed July 2008.

priority facilitating the easy and quick discovery of information or resources that might be relevant to a focused user query. All these services are commercial enterprises, irrespective of how they originally emerged. As such they are now driven primarily by the profit motive. The actual business models by which profit is delivered or is going to be delivered by these sites is still a somewhat unresolved question and new models emerge, are tested, and then are replaced by others on a frequent basis. Currently, the two dominant models are versions of the sale of advertising space on web pages. This is often augmented by tailoring advert presentation based on a user profile, and the sale of information on customer (user) behaviour on the internet. Clearly the first model echoes that of traditional media such as newspapers and commercial television and, in common with these media, the veracity, quality and discoverability of the content are only considered relevant if they have a direct impact on the levels of usage of the medium, i.e. reading a paper, watching television or using the internet. Therefore this type of site may hold vast amounts of material, it might even be tagged with significant amounts of useful pointers to its content, but this is ancillary to the function of the site, which is to sell advertising. The waters are muddied still further by a trend to disguise advertising as content, for example film trailers on YouTube, and the fact that actually making things harder to discover, say by presenting a search result in conjunction with other content that is associated in some way, or even only tangentially relevant, keeps a user on the site, and therefore exposed to advertising, for longer.

In addition to the direct use of audio and visual techniques for archaeological recording and owing to a broad general public interest in archaeology, the discipline has benefited over the years from a substantial volume of broadcast documentaries and reconstructions. Much of this material is of significant interest to the research community and is beginning to be offered to the relevant digital archives, such as the ADS. Metadata provision has been identified as one of the most significant stumbling blocks confronting archivists in the field of time-based media.[21] Historically, time-based media has not required widely usable metadata or metadata suitable for public searching or research purposes (i.e. resource discovery, rather than technical or management metadata) as they were until recently held only by the organizations that created and broadcast them. All general access to these media was dictated entirely by the broadcaster and there was little or no private consumption. Resource discovery was via a published schedule such as the *Radio Times*.[22] Recent trends in play-on-demand (over the internet), such as BBC

---

21   See Section 1.6 in A. Wilson et al., *AHDS Moving Images and Sound Archiving Study* (AHDS, London, 2006): http://ahds.ac.uk/about/projects/archiving-studies/index. htm, accessed July 2008.

22   *Radio Times*, BBC Publications, London: http://www.radiotimes.com/, accessed July 2008. The exception being video/DVDs. Here the description of the content, beyond technical information, BBFC Classification, etc. is intended primarily to sell the product.

iPlayer,[23] and the vast collections of user-generated content on YouTube and similar sites have served simply to highlight the deficiencies in resource description for users looking for specific elements of content. The problem associated with time-based media, the opaqueness of media content,[24] is well known. It is very hard to know what the content of a time-based media resource is without watching it all the way through. The approaches to resource discovery offered by these online services may be just about acceptable for content designed as entertainment, but where the content is relevant to research, more suitable ways of finding it, and what lies within it, are needed.

Organizations that archive and broadcast these media have developed techniques for describing such content. The most widely used is 'logging' whereby individual scenes inside a video (or audio clip) have their timestamp associated with their content. For audio and video, logged metadata is just as important as the classic forms of bibliographic and descriptive metadata detailed earlier. The simplest form of logging data is a transcription of the words heard in a soundtrack. Often this accompanied by the description of 'keyframes' or scenes within the video. A very simple example of this type of logging might look like this:

Table 4.1   An example extract from a frame logging document

In Point	Out Point	Name	Comment/Description
00:00:20	00:00:60	Introduction	Introduction to the film including an overview presented Jack Smith.
00:00:60	00:01:20	Scene One	Helicopter flypast of Stonehenge in winter with voiceover describing elements of the monument.

There are numerous schemas that perform this content description function, but, as already pointed out, there is no universally accepted way of doing this. Another problem with this approach is that, as in the example above, the actual description is not very helpful and in this case does not relate to any knowledge organization system that would facilitate meaningful discovery of, or searching within, the resource. The transcription of audio-only or video soundtracks provides a searchable text and is much more amenable to meaningful searching.[25] Some

23   The BBC iPlayer is a web based 'play on demand' service offering a selection of previously broadcast content: http://www.bbc.co.uk/iplayer/, accessed July 2008.

24   See K. Green, 'More-accurate Video Search', in *Technology Review*, 12 June 2007, http://www.technologyreview.com/read_article.aspx?ch=specialsectionsandsc=sear chandid=18847anda=f, accessed July 2008.

25   A commercial example of this approach is the EveryZing system: http://www. everyzing.com, accessed 7 July 2008.

digital time-based formats, such as MPEG-7, are designed to encapsulate this type of logging. In addition, this type of content description can easily be expressed in an extensible mark-up language (XML)[26] and reused for both resource discovery and intra-resource searching. There is a strong possibility that speech recognition in tandem with natural language processing (NLP)[27] on the resulting text will actually deliver meaningful and highly structured metadata, however this will be contingent on appropriate ontological structures, such as the TMT in archaeology, being available to capture the semantics of the text. Clearly video that does not contain the spoken word or which does not have the appropriate quality of speech (speech that actually gives an indication of the visual content) is never going to succumb to an automated metadata extraction process relying on either speech recognition or NLP.

Earlier in this chapter a number of approaches to resource discovery and technical metadata that we see in digital archives and online libraries were outlined. Some systems, such as DDC, describe content in relation to a specific form of knowledge organization. Other systems, such as decimal classification (DC), describe content in a more open way, but usually still in relation to some form of knowledge organization. Further systems, such as tagging, exert no control over how a resource is described. In addition to the different approaches to formalizing the metadata into schema, the different approaches to creating the metadata – creator-generated, user-generated and automatically generated – have also been touched upon. However, there are other issues around the structure and creation of metadata, which concern the increasing complexity and interactivity of digital objects and their relationship to the techniques of data curation.

As discussed above, the ADS is a data archive, facilitating access to numerous data resources. This means that the mission of the ADS is not just about resource discovery but also about developing procedures and systems that keep these resources safe and accessible for the long term. This is not the place for a discussion on the fragility of digital data and the need for well thought through preservation strategies, as this is dealt with extensively in the literature,[28] but there are aspects of the preservation process that have a direct bearing on time-based media, complex digital objects and hardware-dependent objects. In order to draw

---

26   XML is a widely used general-purpose specification for creating custom mark-up languages; it allows the specification of custom tags, thus allowing an XML document to capture the quite specific features of such things as video logging schemas: http://www.w3.org/XML/, accessed July 2008.

27   An example of the use of NLP to extract keywords automatically from archaeological text to populate a pre-existing ontology and thereby automatically generate resource discovery metadata can be seen in the Archaeotools project: http://ads.ahds.ac.uk/archaeotools, accessed July 2008.

28   For example: F. Condron, J. Richards, D. Robinson and A.Wise, *Strategies for Digital Data* (Archaeology Data Service, York, 1999): http://ads.ahds.ac.uk/project/strategies/, accessed July 2008.

out the relationship between these types of archival object and the nature of the archival systems it is first necessary to understand some of the principles behind digital archiving in general.

The Open Archival Information System (OAIS)[29] reference model has, in the absence of any serious competition, established itself as the *de facto* standard for digital archiving in a number of sectors, such as UK higher education, including the ADS. Already widely used, OAIS, developed by the Consultative Committee for Space Data Systems, in fact became an ISO Standard in 2003. The standard itself is represented by a large and complex document, but in essence it defines a way of thinking about archiving digital material that ensures all the key issues in the process are addressed. OAIS identifies six major functions of the digital archive:

- Negotiate for appropriate deposits
- Obtain sufficient control of resources
- Determine scope of community
- Ensure independent utility of data
- Follow procedures for preservation
- Disseminate to the designated community

The point that is of most concern in the context of this discussion is the fourth one, 'ensure independent utility of the data'. Especially problematic is the word 'independent'. In implementing an OAIS-based system this core function is often tackled by migrating the submitted data to a number of different information 'packages'. These are termed:

- SIP – Submission Information Package
- AIP – Archival Information Package
- DIP – Dissemination Information Package

Each of these packages represents a different manifestation of the submitted data, each with a specific purpose. The SIP is the untransformed package initially submitted by a depositor to the archive. The AIP represents a form of that same data that is designed to assure independent utility of the data. The DIP is a form of the data that is most suitable for dissemination. An example of why these distinctions are necessary might be as follows:

---

29   OAIS became an ISO standard in 2003, ISO 14721:2003. The full OAIS specification is available as a PDF document from: http://public.ccsds.org/publications/archive/650x0b1.pdf, accessed July 2008.

SIP: A Microsoft Word document
Rationale: A very popular word processing format, this is how the document is submitted to the archive by the depositor. The SIP maintains this format unchanged and it is held in deep storage as an 'original'.

AIP: An ASCII[30] text file and associated TIF[31] images
Rationale: MS Word is a proprietary format and there is no guarantee that the software to access it will be freely available and supported in the future. Extracting the text into ASCII and the images into TIFs ensures their accessibility into the future in open formats. However, it renders them unsuitable for delivery in most contexts.

DIP: An Adobe Portable Document Format (PDF) document
Rationale: The archive can't rely on every potential user having access to Microsoft Office and would also like to distribute only an uneditable version of the document. The AIP version would require the user to piece the document together from its separately-archived elements. PDF uses a freely available reader and allows a document to be locked for editing.

It is clear from the above that the key to fulfilling the role of a digital archive is intimately bound up with the ability to move data freely from format to format, both to ensure its preservation in a neutral 'open' format, protecting it from the vagaries of a rapidly changing commercial software environment and to ensure its reusability as a disseminated item. Thus the traditional archival model clearly draws a distinction between the data and the mode of delivery. However, when we examine more complex digital objects this barrier begins to break down. Compromises have ultimately to be made where an unbreakable link exists between the data and either the software that created it or the software that delivers it or even between the data and the hardware by which it is delivered. An example of each of these three cases is given below.

1. The clearest and most common example of an unbreakable link between data and the software that created it is where that software is proprietary and there is no equivalent format, open or otherwise. If the data cannot be migrated to some accessible format it has no useful life when dissociated from its intended software. Unfortunately historical attempts to defend market share meant that commercial software developers on occasion deliberately made it difficult to convert their files to alternative formats.

---

30   ASCII stands for the American Standard Code for Information Interchange and dates back to the days when text was encoded for transmission along telegraph wires.
31   Tagged Interchange Format, or TIF, although not actually an open standard – it is still technically owned by Sun – is generally considered open as it is fully published and described in the literature.

For a number of technical and commercial reasons this is becoming less of a problem, but lack of access to original software remains a significant problem for digital archives dealing with legacy datasets.

2. An example of a situation where the relationship between data and the software that created it is crucial is Agent Based Modelling or ABM.[32] This approach involves the running and re-running of computer simulations containing models of both environments and agents within the environment. These simulations might be run for many cycles and then reset with new variables relating to environmental factors or agent behaviour and then rerun. It is the honing of these elements of the simulation that represent the research process just as much as the outcomes of the model. Indeed, the simulation is constructed from the interaction of the model elements, which might be expressed as 'data' and the algorithms embedded within the simulation software. In short, the raw data is only meaningful when used with one particular piece of software. The ADS has, as a matter of policy, not accepted software for archiving. This is because archiving software, with the associated issues of versioning, porting and commercial exploitation is felt to be outside the remit of the ADS. If ABM modelling material is to be archived then the ADS or a similar organization would have to accept that this is a more complex task than simply archiving a series of digital outputs.

3. Links have always existed between data, software and hardware. Even the simplest file type needs to be translated via an application into a readable form for display on a computer screen. In most situations for archiving purposes this does not present a significant issue. If the data can be made independent of the software it is normally automatically independent of the hardware. However where the means of display or interaction with the data go beyond simple pictures and sound via a screen and speakers this relationship can become problematic. In the world of head-mounted displays for fully immersive VR models or hemispherical displays or even haptic devices relaying tactile information about a model, the data may be so closely linked to the form of its ultimate dissemination that there is no other meaningful form in which it can be archived. The question then arises, is it worthwhile archiving it at all if its associated hardware is not likely to be accessible over the long lifetime of the archive?

The three scenarios above should be considered in combination with the resource discovery and intra-resource discovery problems discussed earlier in this chapter.

---

32   Agent Based Modelling is not new in archaeology, but is undergoing a renaissance owing to, amongst other things, the increased availability of high end computing. A current example of this type of project is the AHRC-EPSRC-JISC e-Science funded MWGrid: Medieval Warfare on the Grid project at the University of Birmingham. http://www. cs.bham.ac.uk/research/projects/mwgrid/, accessed July 2008.

There is one final, vital complication in creating meaningful metadata that should be noted. Novel and sophisticated modes of presentation such as Quick Time Virtual Reality (QTVR),[33] panoramas or object movies and Virtual Reality Modeling Language (VRML) models allow rich and varied modes of interaction with the data being presented (the panorama, the object or the VRML model). The levels of interactivity offered, and often how that interactivity is exploited, are not standard. For example, the frame-passing function of QTVR might be utilized to change lighting angles or lighting conditions on an object rather than the more usual approach of using each frame to change the angle of view[34] (see Plate 4.1). In these cases the functionality offered can be key to understanding the data, yet there is no standard way of describing this functionality. Metadata, as discussed above, might describe the object of the data, but it will not yet allow us to describe how we can interact with the data in a formal and universally understood fashion. A user might even understand the general levels of interactivity offered by QTVR, so the metadata element that indicates an object is of this file type should indicate to some extent how the data can be interacted with. However there is no metadata element or formal terminology that allows the archivist to say 'this particular file changes angle of lighting rather than angle of view', but this difference in functionality results in a significantly different resource. Although the above example might seem trivial, the problem it represents, the blurring of the division between data and delivery method and the inability to describe functionality for resource discovery purposes, raises some potentially serious problems for the digital archivist that will only increase with the complexity of the objects being deposited for archive.

Where then does this overview suggest we currently stand with regard to both finding and searching within complex digital media? Finding one's favourite web resource or digital object is not always as straightforward as we might like it to be. It would be good to think that this situation will resolve itself somewhat in the future by various means. For the majority of internet content right now, which is predominantly text and images (although often presented in sophisticated ways), this may well be the case.

The ADS is actively engaged in research and development activities designed to enhance researchers' abilities to discover relevant resources that we either hold ourselves or provide access to by aggregating resource discovery metadata. Where metadata schemas have been adhered to and where they are underpinned

---

33   QTVR is a proprietary from of pseudo-immersive virtual reality owned by Apple: http://www.apple.com/quicktime/technologies/qtvr/, accessed July 2008.

34   Examples of this type of unexpected use of interactivity can be seen in this night/ day object movie of a standing stone from Machrie moor on Arran (see Plate 4.1) and the variable angle lighting of a medieval inscribed stone, both downloadable from the ADS, S. Jeffrey, *Three Dimensional Modelling of Scottish Early Medieval Sculpted Stones* (unpublished PhD Thesis, University of Glasgow, 2003): http://ads.ahds.ac.uk/catalogue/library/theses/jeffrey_2004/, accessed July 2008.

by rigorous (and rigorously managed) thesauri and word lists, this offers the possibility for faceted classification. Faceted classification is a very simple concept, but extremely powerful. Faceted classification browsing systems offer the most likely challenger to the broad-brush search approaches offered by 'type and hope' search boxes.[35] In essence a faceted classification browser allows a user to navigate a hierarchical knowledge organization structure, or tree, by clicking on the most relevant facets. For searching purposes in archaeology the facets that are most useful are: where, what and when. An archaeological example of a hierarchy of facets might look like this:

When – Medieval
　　　　Early Medieval

Where – United Kingdom
　　　　England
　　　　　　Yorkshire
　　　　　　　　York

What – Military and Defensive
　　　　Defended buildings
　　　　　　Castles

Each of the three facets can be selected by mouse clicks and, providing that the classification against the facts has been thorough, the user should have full confidence in the completeness and relevance of the returned results (in the case above, early medieval castles in York). This level of confidence is impossible if only using a text search box. The ADS created a proof of concept faceted classification browser interface with UK HE funding in 2004. Following workshops held by the AHRC ICT Methods Network in 2006, the ADS and the computer science department at the University of Sheffield gained funding from the e-Science Research Grants Scheme (funded by AHRC, EPSRC and JISC) for a project to bring to service a faceted classification browser based on archaeological monument inventory data. This system will be fully functional by early 2009.[36]

It is looking very likely that the internet of the future will be host to vast amounts of rich forms of data such as audio, video, 3D models, geographical data and databases, as well as forms and formats that we cannot yet imagine. As research material presented in these formats becomes standard in the arts and humanities, discovery mechanisms that have evolved to cope with text and images will struggle to maintain their usefulness for researchers' day-to-day use. The

---

35 A number of demonstrations of faceted classification approaches can be seen at Facetmap: http://facetmap.com/browse, accessed July 2008.

36 http://ads.ahds.ac.uk/project/archaeotools/, accessed July 2008.

current archival structures, and resource and object description schemas are simply not designed to cope with the explosion of time-based media, complex digital objects or software dependent digital objects. One thing is clear, however: just as the challenges of metadata creation for time-based media are beginning to be addressed,[37] new challenges requiring the ability to describe the levels and forms of interactivity offered by even more complex digital objects arise. The difficulties of archiving complex forms of data may require a more flexible approach to the notion of independent utility. Certainly, in the case of objects like the outputs from ABM and collections of data inextricably or very strongly linked with particular hardware suites, re-use cases for the data should be very clearly made before the data is considered for archiving in the usual way.

It may be argued that current resource discovery and archival approaches have plenty of time to adapt to changes in the nature of the resources they deal with. In fact, to date, all the 3D material archived with and disseminated by the ADS was created specifically as part of projects looking into the usage of 3D recording and modelling in archaeological practice or was created at such an early stage that no standard metadata schema for this form of material could be expected to have arisen. Despite this, the history of rapid media development, format development and even assorted broad paradigm shifts since the opening of the internet to the public and commerce suggests that now is the time to tackle the problems of dealing with resource discovery and curation of complex digital objects. Just as a core theme in digital archiving best practice is that archival strategies for data should be thought about at the very outset of a project, perhaps format and application developers in interactive media should be thinking more about discovery and description issues from the outset of the design process.

---

37   For example, recent work by the Technical Advisory Service for Images (TASI) includes reviews of moving image technologies and search engines for moving images and audio: http://www.tasi.ac.uk/, accessed July 2008.

Chapter 5

Digital Exploration of Past Design Concepts in Architecture

Daniela Sirbu

Introduction

Various forms of visualization have long been used as design, research and communication tools in architecture. The emergence of digital 3D visualization in the course of the last two decades has now enabled dynamic ways of investigating architecture. This marks a significant departure in architectural visualization; a move from static representations towards the dynamic experience of architecture in the virtual realm. This may open new avenues of research in architectural history, some of which are studied in this chapter.

One of the most dramatic shifts brought about by visualization tools is the promise of experiencing architecture through digital reconstructions. However, this also raises the question that is the focus of this chapter: is the experience of digital 3D representations of architecture a valid way of enhancing our understanding of real architecture?

To answer this question we need to understand the true nature of 3D visualizations as digital entities. This may clarify the type of changes that architecture undergoes in the process of translation from one medium to another and how interactions with digital environments may inform our understanding of real architecture. Much of the present analysis relates to a number of research projects based on 3D reconstructions of built and *unbuilt* architecture.[1] While some of the projects discussed are based on photorealistic 3D visualizations of architecture, other projects examine the design process of the architect by translating architectural drawings into navigable 3D environments reminiscent of the graphic style of the architect.

There are numerous uses of 3D visualization tools in architecture; however, the goals of this chapter span a more specialized area of study. We review how the investigation of architecture mediated by 3D computer visualizations provides valuable tools in the study of historical architecture that is not available for direct exploration. We include in this category lost, ruined and unbuilt architecture.

---

1 Architectural projects that have never been constructed are referred to as unbuilt architecture in this chapter.

Experiencing architecture in the real world

Our understanding of architecture that is unavailable for physical exploration can be enhanced through the development of digitally navigable 3D reconstructions. It is important to see how the exploration of such digital reconstructions can be mapped to experiencing architecture in real life. For this purpose, we briefly analyse the process of experiencing real architecture; the nature of 3D computer reconstructions of architecture; and the manner in which the two forms merge in the digital exploration of past architecture. Following this we analyse how experiencing architecture works in the digital medium, through a number of 3D visualization-based research examples.

To understand architecture, we must experience the way in which spaces flow into a functional and aesthetic structure when we move inside the building. This experience is mediated by scale and the proportional relationships between architectural elements and their relation to human size; by the kind of mobility we naturally acquire in the building; by the contrasting effects between solids and hollows; by the selection of colours; by the interplay of light on forms; by the tactile dimension embedded in textural effects; and by the acoustic quality of the space. Furthermore, when experiencing a building in the real world, we can observe purposively or feel intuitively how the building has been designed with a certain function in mind. Architectural design is attuned to the general expectations of people at a certain moment in time, and we perceive the specific rhythm of life characteristic of the building's era.[2]

There is also a personal aspect to experiencing architecture that has to do with dwelling in its spaces and forming memories associated with those spaces. Once formed, these memories subjectively influence how architecture is perceived. This process is defined in architectural theory as place-making, and in-depth analyses related to the psychological, philosophical and social aspects of place-making have been developed.[3]

We are interested in the concept of place and the distinction made in architectural theory between its two fundamental components: space and character. Space is defined by the physical components of architecture, and space acquires character through the projection of our memories onto the spaces we have lived in.[4] How our memories operate in relation to architecture, as a social group and at an individual level, broadly spans what experiencing architecture means in real life.

To clarify how experiencing architecture is mapped into experiencing digital architecture, we investigate the nature of space in digital reconstructions of

---

2   See Steen Eiler Rasmussen, *Experiencing Architecture* (Cambridge, MA, 1982) and Jeff Malpas, *Place and Experience: A Philosophical Topography* (Cambridge, 2007).

3   See Malpas, *Place and Experience*; Christian Norberg-Schulz, *Genius Loci. Towards a Phenomenology of Architecture* (New York, 1984), and David Canter, *The Psychology of Place* (London, 1977).

4   See Norberg-Schultz, *Genius Loci*, pp. 11–23.

architecture and the modalities through which digital space acquires character through memories formed in interactions with the virtual environments.

Experiencing digital architecture

The digital medium is active and dynamic. Consequently, we consider the ways in which the nature of the digital medium influences content and its delivery.[5] We analyse these in relation to 3D computer visualizations of architecture in order to understand how virtual architecture acquires, from the digital medium, the particular properties that define it as an entity distinct from real architecture.

The two functions of 3D visualizations: Cultural content and interface

The type of navigation we can experience in an artificial environment has its own logic which is different from the way we navigate and interact with architecture in the natural world. When using digital media we expect to have certain features available such as interactivity, non-linearity of the textual discourse, and discontinuous navigation of space.

For example, in the 3D interactive reconstruction of Teatro Olimpico,[6] what we see first is a representation of the theatre. We can move in this space, coming closer or stepping away from different parts of the theatre. If we click on interactive elements within the theatre, for example one of the statues, we may also access information about whom the statue represents, how the history of the theatre links to that person, and so on. The additional information may be provided through text, static images, sound or short movies. The digital representation of buildings, through computer models, becomes the 3D interface. It is based on the familiar form of architecture as a metaphor around which information is structured. It makes the user's orientation and the access to information intuitive within a medium whose workings are based on the abstract logic of computer algorithms and programming.[7] Approached from this perspective, investigating architecture through 3D reconstructions of buildings is a special case of human–computer

---

5 See Marshall McLuhan, *Understanding Media: The Extensions of Man* (London, 2001).

6 The reconstruction of Teatro Olimpico, together with other 3D computer reconstructions of Renaissance buildings designed by Italian architect Andrea Palladio (1508–80) is available online through *IL PORTALE Internet Culturale* at: http://www.internetculturale.it/genera.jsp?id=1032, accessed June 2008. The reconstructions have been developed as part of the project *La Biblioteca Digitale Italiana e il Network Turistico Culturale (BDI&NTC)*. The project is co-funded by the Italian *Ministero per i Beni e le Attività Culturali* and the *Comitato dei Ministri per la Società dell'Informazione (CMSI)*.

7 See Lev Manovich, *The Language of New Media* (Cambridge, MA, 2001), pp. 69–93 for further theoretical developments on cultural interfaces and new media theory.

interaction (HCI) where the information is structured around representations of architecture. The interface, as a 3D representation of the building, is part of the informational content available within this environment. We emphasize the double role of the 3D visualization as interface and cultural content. In this context, the 3D representations of architectural forms define the configuration of an information space. Some authors recognize this spatialization of information as a typical phenomenon within 3D navigable environments.[8]

The actions we take within digital architectural environments draw interconnections between the database associated with the environment and the navigation.[9] The metaphor of architecture embeds meaning in the distribution of cultural data throughout the digital space. The navigational actions in such environments are inspired and informed by our everyday interactions with real architecture. These actions link data in meaningful sequences. The metaphor of real-life architecture underlies the logic of the digital architecture in both structuring and linking cultural data in meaningful sequences.

There is an intimate and intuitive intermeshing between the external forms of digital architecture, the informational content, and the logic of the conceptual model of interaction[10] based on the metaphor of real-life architecture. However, we often feel awkward interacting in such environments. This is most often because the developers of such 3D computer reconstructions of architecture parallel the way we experience architecture in real life, for example by walking from one place to another, and neglect to apply and systematically adapt the HCI design principles[11] to the goals of 3D visualizations of architecture.

Most frequently, the development of ineffective interaction models for 3D reconstructions of architecture stems from insufficient integration between the real-life architecture metaphor and the specifics of digital environments. Our familiarity with the digital medium has increased enough during the last two decades to compete with other forms of interaction within the natural environment. A fluent and effective navigation of 3D computer visualizations should merge these forms appropriately.

In addition, depending on the nature of the digital simulation and the type of interaction enabled within the artificial world, different computer reconstructions of architecture emulate older and better-established media through a cultural mechanism defined as remediation.[12] We often meet remediations of photography and film, for example, which are very conspicuous in a medium that is still in

---

8   Ibid., p. 78.

9   Ibid., p. 212–83.

10   See Ben Shneiderman and Catherine Plaisant, *Designing the User Interface: Strategies for Effective Human–Computer Interaction* (Boston, 2005) for more details on interaction styles.

11   Ibid.

12   See David Jay Bolder and Richard Grusin, *Remediation: Understanding New Media* (Cambridge, MA, 1999).

the process of developing a specific form of expression. This medium will have matured enough when the exploration of digital architecture allows the focus of the experience to be placed on the architectural form rather than the operations that draw attention to the digital medium.

Finally, the concept of place acquires new meaning in relation to digital, interactive environments emulating architecture. The digital space is structured around representations of architecture, but acquires new meaning as an information space. Dwelling in such spaces is related to human–computer interactions mediated by interfaces structured around the more familiar metaphor of architecture in real life. An adaptation of the concepts of space and place is necessary to reflect the specific nature of the digital space and digital place-making.[13]

Several case studies are given below. These illustrate various aspects of constructing and experiencing 3D visualizations of architecture that are not available for direct exploration.

Digital reconstructions of Louis Kahn's unbuilt work

A series of photorealistic images created by Kent Larson[14] of MIT Media Lab shows key aspects of Louis Kahn's unrealized projects.[15]

Analysis of Kahn's design concept

Larson's interpretation of Kahn's design concept is based on an analysis of archival material[16] and of the built work of the architect. These show an important change in Kahn's work in the 1950s after his one-year residency at the American Academy in Rome. During this time, Kahn's new interpretation of architectural space emerged, drawing on the Roman conception of architecture as ritualistic space. In his research, Larson discovered that Kahn and Frank E. Brown, whose residencies at the American Academy in Rome overlapped at the beginning of the 1950s, had similar ideas about the shaping and articulation of Roman architectural

---

13   For a more extended analysis of the concept of digital place-making with application to the internet see Yehuda Kalay and John Marx, 'The Role of Place in Cyberspace', in Hal Thwaites and Lon Addison (eds), *Seventh International Conference on Virtual Systems and Multimedia (VSMM'01)* (Berkeley, 2001), pp. 770–79.

14   See a list of Kahn's unbuilt projects and sample images from Larson's reconstructions at http://architecture.mit.edu/~kll/kahn.html, accessed June 2008. See Kent Larson, *Louis I. Kahn. Unbuilt Masterworks* (New York, 2000).

15   See Larson, *Louis I. Kahn.*

16   The archival material indicated in Larson, *Louis I Khan. Unbuilt Masterworks* includes design documentation, correspondence, original drawings and written notes by the architect, lectures, and other unpublished materials relevant to Kahn's work. Other primary sources, such as interviews with the architect's collaborators and family, were also used.

spaces in the spirit of the ritual.[17] The sacral spirit and actions, which disappear as the ritualistic performance unfolds, are captured and permanently contained in the architectural space.

Emerging from these Roman studies was Kahn's idea that architecture must be informed by and in turn support the ritualistic activities of human institutions. He makes a clear distinction between *form* and *design* as two concepts encapsulating two distinct aspects in his approach to architecture. *Design* refers to solving problems in a given location with available means, while *form* responds to the ritualistic actions of the human institution to be served. Thus *form* responds to a principle ingrained in human nature and is not dependent on particular aspects of an instance in time and location. The architectural space must contain this permanent principle, which has to do with ritual and is rooted in the human nature of its actions. In this sense, Kahn's architecture from the 1950s onwards reflects the archaic spirit of Roman architecture. This spirit is embedded in the space of a modern architecture based on simplified geometric purity and on subtle interplays of light on architectural forms. Larson's goal is to reveal this immaterial archaic quality in Kahn's space, capturing the essence of his architectural concept:

> The computer-graphics images [...] attempt to capture something of Kahn's genius: the ability to incorporate the spirit of the archaic and the deep understanding of fundamentals into a timeless, styleless architectural vision. [...] These new studies focus on what the archival material does not reveal – the complex play of form, light, and materials fundamental to all Kahn's later built work.[18]

Through carefully selected viewpoints and lighting, Larson emphasizes the abstract geometric nature of the forms, capturing Kahn's intention to embed in the architectural space the ritualistic essence of the human activities served. Larson explains that images rendered from 3D computer reconstructions of Kahn's unbuilt work are studies of the architect's use of light.[19]

The series of photorealistic renderings of Kahn's unrealized projects naturally completes the idea formed about the architect based on his built work and allows a more in-depth understanding of how Kahn's concept evolved in time. We are given a better overall view of Kahn's architectural vision in the context of the second half of the twentieth century. The series of digital images visually communicate Larson's academic discourse on Kahn's work and bring into this discourse the component of 'experiencing' Kahn's unbuilt architecture in a way that is made possible only through research using 3D visualization tools.

---

17   See Larson, *Louis I. Kahn. Unbuilt Masterworks* and Frank Edward Brown, *Roman Architecture* (New York, 1961).

18   See Larson, *Louis I. Kahn*, p. 12.

19   Ibid.

Kent Larson's academic discourse

The careful design of shots taken with the virtual camera represents the way Larson conveys, in a structured and accurate manner, his interpretation of Kahn's architectural concept. The quality of this academic discourse depends on two aspects: the quality of the information sources that document the 3D reconstructions and the degree to which current technology allows the matching of research ideas through visualizations.

Larson used primary design documents, interviews with Kahn's collaborators, and on-site documentation of Kahn's built work. This research shows that in Kahn's design process there is usually an information gap between the architect's design sketches and final design documents, which are developed by draftsmen based on Kahn's verbal explanations. The architect's elevation drawings are usually missing so it is necessary to attempt to deduce the building's appearance from sketches and final technical drawings.

The design process often incorporates inaccuracies and sometimes information is missing, matters which are usually resolved during later design stages. However, for unrealized projects, the missing information has to be inferred by the researcher from the available sources. There is always a degree of uncertainty that comes with these decisions. In terms of the clarity of the academic discourse, it would have been important to specify which parts of the reconstructions are based on accurate information and which parts are Larson's interpretations based on existing information sources. The photorealistic representations show the architectural forms as we would presumably have seen them built in reality. This allows the architect's intentions to be read and serves appropriately the defined goals of the research.

Furthermore, photorealistic representation was used because Kahn's design process lacked the elevation drawing as a direct expression of his concept in a more elaborated visual form. Existing buildings have been used as source material, grounding ideas about how the unbuilt projects might have looked if constructed. The use of technical drawing specifications and built architecture directed Larson towards his photorealistic reconstruction of the unbuilt projects.

Larson's idea was that reconstructions provide what archival material cannot convey: that is, how space acquires character through the interplay of light on the architectural form. The reconstructions allow a viewer to experience the unbuilt projects through virtual representations, leading to what we refer to in this chapter as the digital exploration of unbuilt architecture.

The digital exploration might have been enriched with interactive or even immersive navigation of the virtual architecture. However, technical limitations imposed by real-time 3D authoring programs at that time were severe enough on both mesh density, number of dynamic lights in the environment, and texture map resolution, scale and aspect ratio. These limitations would have reduced the image quality drastically while a real-time 3D-navigation engine would not have significantly improved the illusion of experiencing architecture through movement within the digital environment.

A Virtual Reality (VR) simulation would have imposed even more drastic limitations on visual quality in favour of a feeling of immersion. The feeling of immersion in the simulated space is important for understanding architecture. For this reason, Larson designed an off-line interactive installation emulating the CAVE VR system,[20] the main difference being that the illusion of space is created with projections of static rather than moving images. The projected static images of high photorealistic quality create the illusion of immersion within the virtual world with a fixed viewpoint. Although a dynamic exploration of the digital space is not possible, a feeling of immersion is created while Kahn's concept is conveyed with clarity through high-quality images.[21]

Digital reconstruction of Teatro Olimpico

At the beginning of 1580, Andrea Palladio (1508–80) advanced two designs for Teatro Olimpico.[22] One of these was realized in the still existing Teatro Olimpico in Vicenza in Italy, which was constructed mainly by Palladio's successors[23] after his death on 19 August 1580. The other design was never used. Each design is preserved side by side on the same sheet of paper.

Some aspects of Palladio's original designs are not fully clarified by the architect. For example, solutions for the ceiling of the theatre, for the space behind the central arch, and the four lateral openings of the *proscenium* have caused numerous controversies among scholars. Various written and graphical historical sources suggest different design solutions for the missing information in the original designs. Several repairs and the replacement of the ceiling provide further reasons for debate, as it is uncertain whether the present ceiling reflects Palladio's original intentions or those of his successors. Different and sometimes opposing hypotheses about static versus dynamic and open versus closed space conceptions are supported by the different design solutions for the ceiling, *proscenium*, and the ellipse form of the *cavea*. The 3D computer reconstruction of Teatro Olimpico developed by the VR Lab, University of Lethbridge, provides a platform for testing various ideas about Palladio's concept of space in the design of the theatre.[24] A 3D

20   See a definition of virtual reality (VR) in William R. Sherman and Alan B. Craig, *Understanding Virtual Reality: Interface, Application, and Design* (Boston, 2003), p. 13. See a description of a CAVE VR system in Carolina Cruz-Neira et al., 'The Cave – Audio Visual Experience Automatic Virtual Environment', *Commun. ACM*, 35/6 (1992): 64–72.

21   See a detailed description of the installation and exhibition at: http://architecture. mit.edu/~kll/www_compton/exhibit.html, accessed May 2008.

22   See RIBA: Palladio XIII/5, 1580 London.

23   Among Palladio's successors, Vicenzo Scamozzi (1548–1616) designed the 3D illusionistic perspective behind the *proscenium* and supervised most of the construction work after Palladio's death.

24   See Daniela Sirbu, 'Virtual Exploration of Teatro Olimpico', in Xavier Perrot (ed.), *Digital Culture and Heritage. Proceedings of ICHIM05* (Paris, 2005), pp. 23–6, http://www.archimuse.com/publishing/ichim05/Daniela_Sirbu.pdf, accessed June 2008.

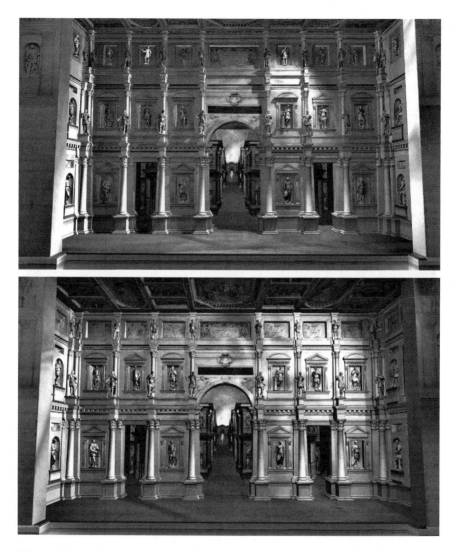

**Figure 5.1   Computer reconstruction of the built and unbuilt designs of
Teatro Olimpico. Architect: Andrea Palladio (1508–80)**

Source: Computer reconstruction by Daniela Sirbu, University of Lethbridge, and Val
Sirbu, University of Alberta.

visualization of the existing Teatro Olimpico was developed. It shows the building
as preserved in Vicenza, bearing the wear and tear of time (see Plates 5.1–5.3). The
reconstruction of the existing theatre has three main purposes. First, the quality
and validity of the photorealistic reconstruction may be assessed by comparison

Figure 5.2   Computer reconstruction of the existing Teatro Olimpico. Architect: Andrea Palladio (1508–80)

Source: 3D-Illusionistic perspective designed by Vicenzo Scamozzi. Computer reconstruction by Val Sirbu, University of Alberta, and Daniela Sirbu, University of Lethbridge.

Figure 5.3 Unification of the *proscenium* and *auditorium* spaces into a unitary pictorial space in the computer reconstruction of Teatro Olimpico. Architect: Andrea Palladio (1508–80)

Source: 3D Computer reconstruction by Daniela Sirbu, University of Lethbridge, and Val Sirbu, University of Alberta.

**Figure 5.4   Comparative views of the painted ceiling in the computer
             reconstructions of the built and unbuilt designs of Teatro
             Olimpico. Architect: Andrea Palladio (1508–80)**

Source: 3D Computer reconstruction by Daniela Sirbu, University of Lethbridge, and Val
Sirbu, University of Alberta.

with the real theatre and with photographs of it. Second, this comparison provides
grounds for the assessment of the photorealistic reconstruction of the unbuilt
design version (see Plate 5.4). Third, various hypotheses about Palladio's space
design concept can be investigated in new experiential ways for both the built and
unbuilt design versions (see Figure 5.1).

Figure 5.5   Space extension through the 3D illusionistic perspective in the computer reconstructions of the unbuilt and built designs for Teatro Olimpico. Architect: Andrea Palladio (1508–80)

Source: 3D Computer reconstruction by Val Sirbu, University of Alberta, and Daniela Sirbu, University of Lethbridge.

The hypothesis of Teatro Olimpico as a precursor of the contemporary concept of immersive virtual space could be studied in experiential ways following several directions: analysis of the dynamics of multiple layers of immersive 'space in space' (see Figure 5.2); illusionary unification of the *proscenium* and *cavea* spaces into one pictorial space (see Figure 5.3); and the extension of the theatre space through the painted ceiling (see Figure 5.4) and through Vicenzo Scamozzi's 3D illusionist perspective with the seven streets of Thebes (see Figure 5.5).

The project provides a series of photorealistic static images from selected locations illustrating the ideas of illusionary space extension within the digital theatre. Other selected shots take various positions within the digital space, attempting to grasp how the *cavea* and the stage are separated or unified in one common space. This kind of testing extends theoretical speculations with an experiential approach to the interpretations of space configuration within the theatre. Visual studies of digital Palladian reconstructions show how the space configuration may shape the physical expression of the dramatic performance and how the illusionary space extension operates, breaking space delimitation towards an open horizon (see Figure 5.5).

While the analysis of illusionary space extension within the theatre is rather speculative, the analysis of the functions of space in both design versions could be concretely relevant for a better understanding of Palladio's design concept. The unbuilt design version changes proportional relationships between components of the *proscenium*. The change is propagated throughout the entire theatre owing to the fact that the proportional relationships between *proscenium* parts determine the proportional relationships between *auditorium* components. The 3D reconstruction of the unbuilt project allows some grasp of how the new rhythm of forms within the theatre might have worked if the unbuilt version had been constructed (see Plate 5.1, Plate 5.4 and Figure 5.6).

So far, the main forms of digital exploration of the theatre are based on static images and cinematic navigations. Current technology allows a photorealistic quality in such reconstructions, conveying how the unbuilt design might have looked if constructed. A photorealistic approach is necessary because the analysed space conceptions integrate real and illusionary spaces through a fusion of details. This places firm requirements on detail rendering and, as a result, on the photorealistic quality of the digital simulation.

The requirements for photorealism raise a number of technical difficulties. Usually, detailed and realistic modelling of architecture leads to complex computer models. With current technology it is still difficult to operate with such models in a real-time interactive navigation of the digital environment. However, the purpose of the project is to allow the experience of digital architecture through cinematic and interactive navigation of the virtual space. Although a compromise has been attempted between photorealistic quality and low polygonal modelling, the final polygon count is not low enough to allow smooth real-time navigation in the virtual environment. Cinematic explorations of the digital architecture were used instead, but the computer model of the theatre is economical enough to be transferred into a real-time interactive 3D simulation platform. The program used for the 3D modelling of the theatre is Autodesk's 3DS Max, versions 7 through 2008. For the development of the real-time interactive 3D exploration, the software used is Virtools Dev 3.0 and

Figure 5.6   Multiple views from the computer reconstruction of the unbuilt design for Teatro Olimpico. Architect: Andrea Palladio (1508–80)

Source: 3D Computer reconstruction by Val Sirbu, University of Alberta, and Daniela Sirbu, University of Lethbridge.

Virtools VR Pack from Behavior Company.[25] The visualization is based on the passive stereoscopic projection system Barco Gemini VR.

Digital reconstruction of *Pont destine à réunir la France à l'Italie*

Pont destine à réunir la France à l'Italie is the final project presented by Henri Labrouste (1801–75) at the end of his *grand prix de Rome* residency in Italy, in 1830. This project was designed by Labrouste with the knowledge that it would never be built and it is a symbolic expression, in particular the elevation drawing, of a new idea about architecture that goes against the academic establishment of the epoch. While the main aspect of the new approach is related to the need for a flexible architecture responding to available location, materials, and technology, it has reverberations within a complex fabric of interrelated philosophical, artistic, social and symbolic meaning in the academic environment of the *École des Beaux-Arts* institution of the time.

A short film based on the 3D computer reconstruction of the unbuilt project (see Figure 5.7) explores the symbolic meaning and the poetics of architecture, approaching the bridge from the outside and performing the rite of passage.[26] The overall movement in the cinematic navigation follows the main lines of force defined in the visual composition of the elevation drawing.

Figure 5.7   **Computer reconstruction of the final design of the unbuilt project *Pont destine à réunir la France à l'Italie*. Architect: Henri Labrouste (1801–75)**

Source: 3D Computer reconstruction by Daniela Sirbu, University of Lethbridge.

---

25   Virtools was acquired in 2005 by Dassault Systèmes and is currently developed as part the Dassault Systèmes' 3DVIA brand. For additional information see http://www.virtools.com/company/index.asp, accessed June 2008.

26   See Daniela Sirbu, 'Digital Exploration of Unbuilt Architecture: A Non-Photorealistic Approach', in Kevin R. Klinger (ed.), *Connecting: Crossroads of Digital Discourse, ACADIA 2003 Conference Proceedings* (Indianapolis, 2003), pp. 234–45.

The reconstruction is based on information provided directly in the drawings and indirectly through research and documentation related to the evolution of Labrouste's design. The design of the bridge is part of a longer process closely interwoven with Labrouste's studies of ancient ruins during his five-year residency in Italy. This study period led to major changes in Labrouste's concept of architecture. The digital exploration of the bridge visually investigates parallel ideas the architect might have developed in the course of the design process.

Figure 5.8   Various views from the 3D computer reconstruction of design sketches for the unbuilt project *Pont destine à réunir la France à l'Italie*. Architect: Henri Labrouste (1801–75)

Source: 3D Computer reconstruction by Daniela Sirbu, University of Lethbridge.

The various sketches and the final design drawings are the direct output and the most accurate reflections of the architect's creative process. For this reason, the 3D computer reconstruction of the project maintains the graphical style of the architect, a goal that is achieved through both modelling and texturing. The resulting virtual environment is reminiscent of the architect's graphic style. The exploration of the digital space provides visualizations of design sketches (see Figure 5.8) and final design drawings (see Figure 5.7) showing the bridge from viewpoints not available in the original project documents. In the digital exploration of the bridge, ideas are linked in a filmic manner that visually conveys alternative possibilities in the creative thought process of the architect.

The digital reconstruction has two main components: a digital reconstruction of the final design[27] and digital reconstructions of various design sketches. All these are navigated cinematically, with the reconstruction of the final design exploring the bridge along the directional lines of force suggested in the elevation drawing. Reconstructions of design sketches provide short cinematic sequences that explore dynamically the 3D reconstruction of the sketches through various camera movements within the virtual space. In this case, the project goals dictated a non-photorealistic approach to the 3D computer reconstruction of the bridge.

It is important to observe that, depending on the information available to the researcher and the established goals of the 3D visualization-based projects; both photorealistic and non-photorealistic reconstructions may serve the purpose of exploring the architect's design concept. However, only computer technology allows the dynamic forms of photorealistic reconstructions that bring to life Louis Kahn's unbuilt projects or the non-photorealistic reconstruction of Labrouste's unbuilt bridge project. It also allows the dynamic exploration of navigable 3D virtual worlds reminiscent of original design sketches.

Physical expressions in historical dramaturgy through 3D reconstructions

Richard Beacham's 3D computer reconstructions of ancient theatre architecture and, in particular, temporary stage sets, emerged from previous research on physical aspects of the Roman theatre. This preoccupation was inspired by depictions of ancient stage sets in Pompeii and Herculaneum frescoes. The main research objective was to enhance the understanding of ancient Roman theatre by experientially investigating its physical form of expression. For this purpose, full-scale real-life replicas of the first temporary Roman stages and their scenic apparatus have been constructed. The enactment of an ancient play in this context places the viewer within the physical surroundings of an ancient Roman theatre and explores Roman dramaturgy in live interaction with an audience. This may improve in new, experiential ways our understanding of Roman theatre as a

---

27   See additional sample renderings at http://www.chart.ac.uk/chart2003/papers/sirbu.html, accessed June 2008.

cultural form. It also raises new questions about how the society of the time is reflected in theatre and how theatre, in turn, may have actively impacted Roman society at large.[28]

Throughout the 1980s, the research project was based on real-life reconstructions of ancient stage sets. During the 1990s, the development of 3D computer models of lost ancient, medieval, and Renaissance theatres and stage sets have complemented this approach.[29] Textual and other resources that informed the reconstructions have never been of such a nature as to document with photographic quality any of these structures. The computer models of the Roman temporary wooden stage sets were largely based on their descriptions through ancient wall paintings, but other sources have been used when available. Such reconstructions allow navigation in real-time of the digital space, assuming various viewpoints in the audience and on the stage. They allow the staging possibilities of various epoch plays to be explored, and an understanding of how physical surroundings and various ambient factors such as lighting and acoustics might have shaped the live interaction of actors on stage and with the audience. They allow the overall expressive qualities of the dramaturgic live performance in ancient Roman society to be conjectured. The digital reconstruction of various temporary ancient wood stage sets developed within the framework of projects like Skenographia[30] are primarily meant to provide an intuitive understanding of how physical performance might have been shaped by the temporary stage sets and the details are not of major importance. An effective approach in relation to the purpose of the research requires accuracy in proportional relationships among architectural components to allow a good grasp of the spatial configuration of the temporary theatres. However, spending computing resources on photorealistic details, which are approximately inferred from secondary sources, is not effective. Instead, a schematic non-photorealistic approach is adopted. This approach provides enough relevant data for understanding the definition of the performance spaces of various temporary theatres.

In contrast, Beacham's[31] reconstruction of the Theatre of Pompey benefited from rich archaeological data, making it possible to achieve a photorealistic computer reconstruction.[32] A separate 3D navigable model was built and adapted to the limitations of real-time 3D web interactive applications to allow quick

---

28   See Richard Beacham, *The Roman Theatre and Its Audience* (London, 1991) and Richard Beacham, 'Reconstructing Ancient Theatre with the Aid of Computer Simulation', *Crossing the Stages: The Production, Performance, and Reception of Ancient Theater, Syllecta Classica*, 10 (1999): 189–208.

29   Here we refer to a number of different projects based on 3D computer reconstructions of theatre architecture. See http://www.kvl.cch.kcl.ac.uk/index.html, accessed June 2008.

30   See Skenographia project at http://www.skenographia.cch.kcl.ac.uk, accessed 10 June 2008.

31   See Richard Beacham and Hugh Denard, 'The Pompey Project: Digital Research and Virtual Reconstruction of Rome's First Theatre', *Computers and the Humanities*, 37/1 (2003): 129–39.

32   See http://www.pompey.cch.kcl.ac.uk/Burge.htm, accessed June 2008.

rendering for fast interactive response in the digital exploration of the theatre architecture (see Plate 5.5).[33] The two 3D reconstructions complement each other in creating a more complete description and better understanding of the Theatre of Pompey, of its importance in the power structure and social fabric of the epoch, and in understanding how the configuration of the theatre architecture might have shaped live performances.

Immersive 3D reconstructions of architecture

Immersive reconstructions of architecture based on CAVE VR systems or large size semicircular surrounding screens with rear projection are some of the applications that come closest to the experience of architecture by means of digital simulations. In a VR world, the space seems to go beyond the limits of peripheral vision and closes around the participant. In such environments, the tactile quality of textured surfaces could be experienced through feedback mechanisms based on haptic equipment, which a participant wears or manipulates in some form. Atmospheric effects alter the colour and shape of objects, conveying their distance from the user. Artificial soundscapes are designed to indicate the location of sound-generating events in relation to the user. Some VR systems may also address the olfactory sensory channel, but this is still rare in current systems.[34]

To maintain the illusion of immersion, animations must be generated in real time at a rate of at least sixty frames per second. This is the minimum rate required to ensure continuity in the simulated environment through projected imagery. Furthermore, the VR system must handle in real time a large amount of additional non-graphic information. Three-dimensional position trackers continuously read the location of the user in the environment,[35] navigation and manipulation interfaces[36] work in conjunction with gesture interfaces[37] to update the input data to the system, and the action of forces such as gravity, friction and pressure are emulated through physics simulations.

In VR systems, the manipulation in real time of such large amounts of visual and non-visual information is essential for inducing a feeling of immersion. However, the high demands on processing power usually translate into typical simplified representations of architecture and a limited range of motion within the virtual environment. While we still have to wait for the technology to mature to overcome

---

33   See the interactive real-time navigation of the Theatre of Pompey at http://www. pompey.cch.kcl.ac.uk/Blazeby.htm, accessed June 2008.

34   See Grigore Burdea and Philippe Coiffet, *Virtual Reality Technology*, 2nd edn (Hoboken, 2003), pp. 3, for more details on how VR systems address the sense of smell as an input sensory channel for the participant.

35   Ibid., p. 17.

36   Ibid., p. 41.

37   Ibid., p. 46.

these limitations, VR systems remain useful owing to the fact that we understand through mental processing more than is seen and sensed. This imaginative, cognitive dimension works in an integrated manner with the interactivity and immersive dimensions to create the specific nature of the VR environments. There are various applications based on VR technology that illustrate how the three integrated features of immersion, interactivity and imaginative inference work to solve complex real-life problems in areas such as high-precision surgery; rehabilitation medicine; training based on virtual anatomy; military, manufacturing and robotics information visualization; and so forth. This ability to gather more information than is directly sensed in the VR environment makes the digital experiencing of architecture a useful form of exploration of past architecture with possible insights that might not be available through any other digital forms.

Currently, experiencing architecture in VR environments cannot expand significantly beyond short visits to the artificial space. This is because the simulation of human interactions with the real world is limited owing to the amount of information that can be handled by computer technology at a given time. It is also because many aspects of human interaction with the natural world are not well understood, and consequently cannot be simulated. In addition, our understanding of the human sensorimotor response is limited and, as a result, the effects of immersion and interaction with VR systems may produce hazardous health and safety effects. An average of about 70 per cent of users of VR systems experience cybersickness manifested through oculomotor problems, along with disorientation and nausea.[38] Neural conflict may easily be induced through the lack of information coordination between different sensory channels. This is a normal occurrence owing to the current limitations of VR technology.[39] Consequently, we cannot speak about defining digital place in VR environments, as prolonged immersion in such systems is not possible.

Even if 'dwelling' in VR environments were possible and the simulation of architecture more realistic than technology currently allows, interactions with digital architecture are still mediated by characteristics that are common to all digital environments, but which are very different from real life. For example, owing to such specific features, the user may be discontinuously transferred from one location to another in the digital environment. This breaks the flow of spaces that characterizes experiencing architecture in real life. Such unrealistic interactions may be avoided through programming, but most users have enough experience with computer environments to know that these types of interactions are possible and it is generally expected that such interactions are available. This illustrates that

---

38   See Kay M. Stanney (ed.), *Handbook of Virtual Environments: Design, Implementation, and Applications* (Mahwah, NJ, 2002) and Burdea and Coiffet, *Virtual Reality Technology*.

39   Deborah Harm, 'Motion Sickness Neurophysiology, Physiological Correlates and Treatment', in Stanney (ed.), *Handbook of Virtual Environments: Design, Implementation, and Applications*, pp. 637–61.

effective user experiences in digital environments require interactions that make the medium conspicuous. As the digital medium matures, we expect it to become less intrusive, allowing content to come to the forefront of the user experience.

Conclusion

We conclude by emphasizing that digital explorations of architecture are still mainly informative, allowing us to navigate the virtual environment as observers, while being aware that the experience is mediated by an artificial medium. The key element is the ability to mentally infer much more information than the digital experience provides. Although emulating real architecture through explorations of computer reconstructions is fragmentary in terms of mapping human interactions with the built environment, 3D computer visualizations of architecture are singular in providing the means to explore architecture that is not physically available. Interactions with digital reconstructions open the possibility to test hypotheses about lost, ruined or unbuilt architecture and thus expand our understanding of architectural thinking of the past.

Experiencing architecture digitally, through VR systems, or through other forms discussed in this chapter, should be understood in relation to its specific digital nature. A good understanding of the double function of 3D visualizations as interfaces and cultural content provides the grounds for effective design of 3D computer reconstructions as interactive environments.

Theoretical investigations of the function and aesthetics of digital architecture require the definition of adequate concepts to operate with. Following the direction opened by Kalay and Marx in their analysis of the role of place in cyberspace, concepts of space and place may be borrowed from established theories of architecture and adapted to capture the essence of how computer reconstructions of architecture function. A brief explanation of how such concepts operate is introduced in the present chapter, but these could be further analysed. The important aspect is that we deal with an emerging domain that still needs definition both in the area of theoretical enquiry and in its operation as a supporting methodological tool for research in other areas. While the theoretical framework is still in the process of being defined, we should be aware of its dynamic evolution in relation to computer technology.

Chapter 6

Words as Keys to the Image Bank

Doireann Wallace

In the archive, images have always been subject to verbal classification: labelled, stored and indexed for retrieval, which has then entailed negotiating the spatial geography of the archive with reference to the indexing system as a kind of map. In the networked digital archive, this is replaced by search engines that summon images stored as code in distant databases for display on computer screens; and from the point of view of computing, and the technicalities of locating and retrieving data, the bit-stream image is not qualitatively distinct from its metadata labels: the 'meta-medium of the digital computer' levels all differences.[1] Inevitably, this produces new forms of archival organization, and new archival relationships between image and text – including, most radically, the possibility that images may be searched for and retrieved 'on their own terms', as media archaeologist Wolfgang Ernst puts it.

For Ernst, the possibilities of CBIR (content-based image retrieval) techniques, which enable image retrieval on the basis of pixel distribution, promise to overcome the containment of the image by verbal labels, giving rise to an 'anarchive of sensory data', in which direct correspondence between image and image bursts apart the order of the word: 'I am talking about a truly multi-media archive, which stores images on an image-based method and sound in its own medium (no longer subject to verbal, i.e. semantical indexing).' Ernst, for whom the computer is the exemplary Foucauldian archaeologist, shunning interpretation for the purely descriptive identification of regularities, views textual labelling as representative of a 'conservative desire' to reduce this anarchive 'to classificatory order once again'.[2]

Faced with the need to develop practicable 'real-world' solutions to finding images in sprawling digital databases, the aspirations of CBIR researchers are somewhat more conventionally archival. Having experienced relative success in the first decade or so of research into image-matching by 'low-level' content – purely visual features such as colour, texture and shape – the principal challenge facing further development has been identified as the reduction of the 'semantic

---

1   Lev Manovich, *The Language of New Media* (Cambridge, MA and London, 2001).

2   Wolfgang Ernst, 'Dis/continuities: Does the Archive Become Metaphorical in Multi-Media Space?', in Wendy Hui Kyong Chun and Thomas Keenan (eds), *New Media, Old Media: A History and Theory Reader* (New York, 2006), pp. 105–23.

gap' between low-level content and higher-level concepts.[3] Image searches need to be able to return *meaningful* matches to have widespread application beyond specialist domains.

As it stands, textual metadata remains a necessary intermediary in most image search techniques. Informal, user-generated verbal tags label personal images in photo-sharing platforms such as Flickr, while keyword classification is currently the dominant mode of classifying and retrieving images in online stock image agencies, which constitute a multi-billion dollar global trade in the reproduction rights to 'visual content' of all kinds, ranging from advertising photographs and illustrations to fashion, celebrity, photojournalist, archival and art historical images.[4] Although user-generated 'folksonomies' have begun to generate some interest, keywording, despite its ubiquity, has attracted little critical attention to date.[5] In his influential study of the visual content industry, Paul Frosh dismisses it as a failed experiment – cumbersome, expensive, and ultimately incapable of taking over the interpretive role of the human picture researcher.[6]

Keywording is not typically regarded as a technical innovation in any way. It is, however, an emergent classificatory practice that is significantly different from traditional forms of archival indexing, allowing images to be multiply classified and searched for by any number of terms, with each label functioning as a hyperlink to a further catalogue of images. As such it has become an important archival technology in the image bank, and merits close analysis. Focusing on keywording practice in the stock image industry, this chapter aims to address this gap.

---

3   For a comprehensive survey of the current state of CBIR research, see Ritendra Datta et al., 'Image Retrieval: Ideas, Influences, and Trends of the New Age', *ACM Computing Surveys*, 40/2, Article 5 (April 2008); a wider multimedia perspective is provided in Michael S. Lew et al., 'Content-Based Multimedia Information Retrieval: State of the Art and Challenges', *ACM Transactions on Multimedia Computing, Communications, and Applications* (February 2006); for a survey of the early years of research, see Arnold W.M. Smeulders et al., 'Content-based Image Retrieval at the End of the Early Years', *IEEE Transactions on Pattern Analysis and Machine Intelligence* 22/12 (December 2000): 1349–80.

4   Some of the better known of these agencies include Getty Images, http://www.gettyimages.com, Istockphoto, http://www.istockphoto.com, now owned by Getty, and Bill Gates' Corbis, http://pro.corbis.com, all accessed April 2009.

5   See, for instance, Daniel Rubinstein and Katrina Sluis, 'A Life More Photographic: Mapping the Networked Image', *Photographies*, 1/1 (2008): 9–28, for an outline sketch of the archival dynamics of Flickr. For a rather reductive discussion of classification in image banks that doesn't account for the implications of digital technology, see David Machin, 'Building the World's Visual Language: The Increasing Global Importance of Image Banks in Corporate Media', *Visual Communication*, 3/3 (2004): 316–36.

6   Paul Frosh, *The Image Factory* (New York, 2003).

Programming the archive

To begin with, it is impossible to understand keywording without grasping the significance of the archival shift in which it is implicated. Long associated with a paradigm of centralized storage and bureaucratic control, it is easy to imagine that archival order has been severely shaken by the distributed networks of digital databases and the incessant transfer of data. It seems, as Mike Featherstone comments, that 'the shifts in the digital archive between flows and classification take us to the heart of the questions about the constitution, formation and storage of knowledge in the current age'.[7] This is true, but not because the archive has become liquid. What is structurally novel about electronic substrate is the fact that the archive and its techniques have in effect been denaturalized by digitization, which opens up the possibility of a critical access to the archive as a form of production, or at the very least renders these techniques opaque.[8] Tradition no longer suffices to determine the order of the archive. Its processes must be broken up – discretized – and logically analysed, for the purpose of designing computer programs that will replicate its functions. Alan Turing famously hypothesized that the computer could imitate any machine, or any process, whose functionality could be reduced to a series of logical operations; and this is precisely what every archival technique – from institution, classification and storage to retrieval and access – is now subject to.[9]

Crucially, programmatic descriptions of archival functions as 'model systems', as Peter Bøgh Andersen describes them, are also stored – fixed in the form of software – that is to say, techniques that were formerly the purview of archivists and picture researchers are now themselves subject to archivization.[10] One result of the growth of the desktop computer industry and the internet is that the majority of computer users find themselves engaged in archival practices of sorting, filing, annotating, searching for and retrieving information on a daily basis, whether for work or leisure, and many software packages on the market, as well as internet photo-sharing sites and the like, are directed towards aiding in, or to some extent automating, this task. Far from transforming the archive into a space of flows, the digital thus extends its reach. Far from crumbling, archival order is *restructured* in

7   Mike Featherstone, 'The Archive', *Theory, Culture and Society*, 23/2–3 (2007): 591–6.

8   For a similar perspective on the digital photograph, see Bernard Stiegler, 'The Discrete Image', in Jacques Derrida and Bernard Stiegler, *Echographies of Television* (Cambridge and Malden, MA, 2002).

9   Alan Turing, 'Computing Machinery and Intelligence', in Noah Wardrip-Fruin and Nick Montfort (eds), *The New Media Reader* (Cambridge, MA and London, 2004), pp. 50–64.

10   The program, as Andersen observes, is basically an analytical model of a set of techniques, or 'referent system' that describes the instructions for performing these processes in a language the computer can understand and act on. See Peter Bøgh Andersen, *A Theory of Computer Semiotics* (Cambridge, 1999).

the economy of the digital archive.[11] Within this domain, keywording, and keyword-based search engines, are central to the restructuring of archival classification and retrieval – the erstwhile roles of picture researchers and archivists. What, then, is the order of keywords?

Classification and archival order

In his discussion of classification in *Everything is Miscellaneous*, David Weinberger draws attention to the material logic behind the famous taxonomic ordering system created by Linnaeus in the eighteenth century to classify the natural world. Linnaeus used a single index card to organize the position of each individual species in his 'kingdoms', with the result that each could therefore occupy only a single place in his taxonomic tree.[12] Taxonomic ordering systems are invariably paradigmatic in this way, as evidenced by the necessity, in the traditional archive, of classifying images as this *or* that *or* the other, to place them into one box *or* another – a single location. For Weinberger, this 'second order of order' is exemplified by the traditional image archive, in which physical locations are indexed by a single, or very limited, number of classificatory labels.[13] Both keywording and CBIR represent what Weinberger calls the 'third order of order' – the possibility that the label may be theoretically unlimited, even to the point of coinciding with the image data itself. In the place-bound photographic archive, ordering systems are usually 'either taxonomic or diachronic', Allan Sekula tells us, and 'in most archives both methods are used, but at different, often alternating, levels of organization. Taxonomic orders might be based on sponsorship, authorship, genre, technique, iconography, subject matter, and so on, depending on the range of the archive'.[14] The point is that all of these are oriented around putting information *in its place*. Indeed, the traditional understanding of a classification system is as 'a set of boxes (metaphorical or literal) into which things can be put', and of categories as (ideally, at least) mutually exclusive, 'clearly demarcated bins, into which any object addressed by the system will neatly and uniquely fit'.[15]

---

11   I use the term 'restructuration' in the sense Derrida gives it in 'The Book to Come'. See Jacques Derrida, *Paper Machine* (Stanford, 2005). On the related notion of the archive as economic intersection of place (or media) and law, see Derrida, *Archive Fever* (Chicago, 1996).

12   David Weinberger, *Everything is Miscellaneous* (New York, 2007).

13   Weinberger contrasts the Bettmann archive of historical photographs, now housed by Corbis in an underground preservation facility, with the online operations of corbis.com, as representative of the second and third orders respectively.

14   Allan Sekula, 'Reading an Archive: Photography Between Labour and Capital', in Jessica Evans and Stuart Hall (eds), *Visual Culture: The Reader* (London, 1999), p. 185.

15   Geoffrey C. Bowker and Susan Leigh Star, *Sorting Things Out: Classification and its Consequences* (Cambridge, MA, 1999), p. 10.

The same logic and the same limitations apply to the printed stock photography catalogue as to the materially bound archive. Each image must occupy a single place in the catalogue, and must therefore be categorized by a single term: 'People' *or* 'Business' *or* 'Summer Holidays' *or* 'Forces of Nature', for instance.[16] Following Sekula, Frosh argues that the ordering system of stock photographs in the printed catalogues he analyses is taxonomic (rather than diachronic) for the practical reason that it is oriented towards the potential consumers of the image, who are more concerned with the content of the image than the date of its production or acquisition by the stock agency.[17] What he overlooks, however, is that the material limitations of the book form actually necessitate this order, and he ignores the fact that this is not strictly applicable in the digital archive. It would be difficult to imagine a workable alternative to taxonomic categorization in the printed catalogue. Similarly, classification by multiple keyword is necessitated by the use of search engines as points of access to vast databases of images, increasing the chance of finding the right image quickly, and facilitating more refined searches. The automated search engine, through which users are obliged to conduct their own image searches, restructures the role of the archivist and the picture researcher, and this technological base is crucial to understanding the order of keywording. But how exactly does this affect verbal classification as an archival technique? If the image is always to some extent contained and constrained by its label in the taxonomic order of the traditional archive in which, by virtue of its indexical function, the word specifies what the image is supposedly 'of', and not just where it is located, how has this changed in the electronic archive?

Within the printed catalogue, the photograph is always showcased as an example of a single generic category that is broad enough to contain a diversity of images. Images furnish illustrative examples of such consumer-oriented categories as 'Connected Business', 'Contemporary Lifestyles', 'Emotional Intelligence', and so on, but – despite their various possible applications – each one occurs only once, in a single category. Image content is loosely anchored by the category label that designates 'what' the image illustrates. On the websites of stock image agencies, as is evident at a glance, each image is labelled by a sizeable cluster of keywords that includes terms pertaining to image content, theme, possible concepts that could be brought to bear on it, and often any notable formal qualities, or style. By way of example, an image of a young man and woman on a couch with a laptop that could have served as an example of 'Contemporary Lifestyles' in a printed catalogue is tagged with the following keywords on the website of royalty-free visual content agency *Veer*:

---

16   My examples of categories are taken from two late 1990s printed stock catalogues advertising image CDs: *Resource Kit* Volumes 1 and 2, published by Irish stock photography agency Stockbyte. Stockbyte was purchased by Getty Images in 2006.

17   Frosh, *The Image Factory*, p. 100.

20s, 30s, Arms around shoulders, Black hair, Boyfriends, Buying, Contentment, Couches, Convenience, Credit and bank cards, Curly hair, Customers, Day, e-Commerce, Efficiency, Girlfriends, Happy, Holding, Husbands, Indoors, Jeans, Laptop computers, Lifestyles, Looking at camera, Metallic, Online shopping, Portraits, Shaved heads, Side by side, Sitting, Smiling, Three-quarter length, Two people, Viewed from above, Windows, Wives.[18]

Here, the relationship of classificatory labels to the image is very far from a model of containment. No single word or phrase attempts to determine what the image is of, and in fact even the terminology used to describe the work of classifying images in digital archives – annotating, tagging, keywording – all frame the word as a point of access, or supplement, to the image, rather than a container. Professional photographer and author Michal Heron advises image annotators to 'think of every word that would bring up your image, both in the specifics as well as the conceptual use', but insists that keywords 'don't describe the photograph so much as they create triggers that might fit a particular image and jog the memory – yours and that of the software'.[19] Essentially, the keywords by which archived digital images are classified do not *indicate* the location of the hidden image, but need to *stand in* for it, so that a correspondence between search term and keyword will allow the image to be retrieved by a search engine. We might say that the keyword cluster aspires to be *synonymous* with the image.

Word and image

Stock images have primarily an illustrative function. Their use lies in their ability to stand in for things in the world metonymically, and often through their contextual deployment to effect a metaphoric transfer of the attributes or associations of these things. In and of themselves, these images are latent examples of concepts, subject matter, moods or themes, which are typically reflected in classificatory labels or keywords. An image seeker using a search engine expects to be presented with examples – visual instantiations – of whatever it is they have in mind by the query term and, in order to maintain the illusion of transparency and correspondence that is the mark of an effective interface or program, keywords need to supplement the illustrative capacity of the image. Rather than 'containing' the image in the manner of a taxonomic category, then, keywords stand in for images through a non-hierarchical verbal system of synonyms that aims to be equivalent to the image in its signifying role. Although many stock image websites continue to deploy hierarchical taxonomic categories similar to the examples from printed catalogues cited above, these are far too general to use in isolation for the purpose of searching

---

18   http://www.veer.com>, accessed July 2008. Image code: SBP0316047.

19   Michal Heron, *Digital Stock Photography: How to Shoot and Sell* (New York, 2007), p. 162.

multi-million-image digital databases, and are useful only in conjunction with other keywords and categories in refining a search. Such categories no longer function as containers, but as filters. Instead of broad subject headings that contain images, individual keywords or their combinations, as well as generic category terms, are 'plugged into' the search engine, establishing its parameters. They constitute mobile elements in logical assemblages – 'couple' *and* 'laptop' *and* 'horizontal' – patched together to form filters through which the search engine sieves and matches metadata, generating a provisional and malleable catalogue of corresponding images.

In many search engines, this system – what I will term a system of correspondence – is direct. Search terms are only matched with actually present keyword metadata. Where thesauri are used to search for synonyms or to match entries with broader or narrower categories, as is the case with larger agencies such as Corbis and Getty Images, a secondary system of synonymy is included as a sub-function of the system of correspondence. This technical system has its necessary correlate at the level of image classification by keyword, where the cataloguer establishes a system of synonyms that attempts to verbally replicate the illustrative potential of the image – its specific capacity to refer to and stand in for things in the world. This word-to-image equivalence anticipates the expectations and the conceptual and interpretive frameworks of the image (re)searcher, so that their search terms will match the keywords, but it must also be as concise as possible in order to achieve the right signal-to-noise ratio, and to return suitable images. These two interconnected systems might be illustrated as follows:

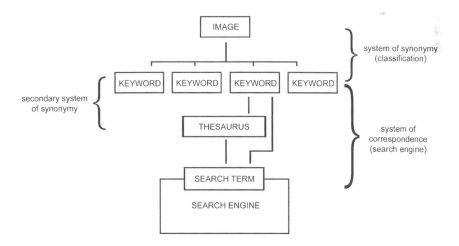

Figure 6.1   Keyword image search system

The system of synonymy attempts to model how viewers and users of images see the referential function and illustrative potential of the image, while the system of correspondence models the techniques of archival retrieval, formerly the province of archivists and picture researchers. Both model interpretive processes in the attempt to match entered search terms with appropriate images from the archive.

Modelling interpretive systems is no easy task, and keywording practices can be seen to vary across stock agencies. Getty Images and Corbis work with controlled, editor-defined vocabularies, using software designed to aid exhaustive classification and identify synonyms and categories, in an effort to systematize image classification to some extent, although this is often more aspirational than actual. Weinberger describes the process by which Corbis assigns keywords to images:

> A team of nine full-time catalogers categorize each image Corbis acquires, anticipating how users are going to search. When a new image comes into the collection, one of the cataloguers uses special software to browse the 61,000 'preferred terms' in the Corbis thesaurus for those that best describe the content of the image, typically attaching 10 to 30 terms to each one. The system incorporates about 33,000 synonyms ... as well as more than 500,000 permutations of names of people, movies, artworks, places, and more.[20]

Despite efforts to systematize, search terms can vary between visually similar images even within the Corbis and Getty collections, and a comparison between agencies shows even less terminological correspondence, indicating the ultimate difficulty of systematizing how images are viewed and interpreted. For Frosh, it is these difficulties, as well as the high labour costs involved in keywording, that make it ultimately impractical.[21] Such problems notwithstanding, keywording remains the dominant classificatory technology in use in image banks. With the proliferation of low-cost 'micro-stock' agencies, which allow their submitters to upload images to the archive at any time, the costs of keywording are offset by also outsourcing keywording to image submitters. The problem, then, for professional cataloguers and individual submitters alike, remains how to keyword in order to maximize correspondence between what the client is seeking and which images are retrieved.

Achieving this balance is difficult. Getty Images tend to be parsimonious with their search terms, limiting each image to three concepts, while content submitters on self-annotating sites such as Shutterstock[22] sometimes saturate an image with barely relevant terms in the hope of increasing its visibility. The problem with this is that an image may be seen frequently, but not always in a context in which

---

20 Weinberger, *Everything is Miscellaneous*, p. 20.

21 Frosh puts the cost of cataloguing a single image at around $10. Frosh, *The Image Factory*, p. 179.

22 http://www.shutterstock.com, accessed July 2008.

it matches user expectations. A novel solution is being pioneered by UK agency Alamy[23] – currently the largest stock photo provider on the Web – with the recently introduced 'Alamy Rank', a system designed to create an incentive for submitters to keyword effectively and concisely in the absence of direct editorial control. Submitters are assigned a rank according to the ratio of views to purchases of their images (calculated algorithmically), so that those whose systems of synonyms consistently match searcher expectations will rise to the top of the system, with their images represented closer to the top of search results. This requires an ongoing attempt, on the part of the submitter/cataloguer, to anticipate how images are interpreted and used, and to model these processes through the creation of systems of synonyms that match keywords with images.[24]

Extending the taxonomic

Taxonomies break up elements into distinct hierarchical classes and categories. Indeed, for this very reason they remain invaluable for ordering the masses of information available on the internet. It seems quite clear, however, that image keywords are not subject to this logic of differentiation and hierarchical organization, but run parallel to the image, modelling and supplementing its illustrative potential. I have already argued that archival order is extended rather than exploded in the electronic archive, due to the archivization of techniques in the program, and this claim must now be examined in relation to classification. In eluding the model of categorical containment traditionally associated with linguistic taxonomies, how does keywording as a classificatory practice explode or extend the realm of the taxonomic?

Paul Ricoeur describes taxonomies as the 'inventories and combinations' yielded by a closed language system and governed by semiotics as a mode of analysis.[25] Semiotics itself, according to Emile Benveniste, is fundamentally oriented around 'the identification of units, the description of characteristic features, and the discovery of increasingly fine criteria of their distinctiveness'.[26] In this, taxonomies and the semiotic are directly opposed to the domains of

---

23   http://www.alamy.com, accessed July 2008.

24   Efforts to systematize how we understand images are ongoing but still limited. Burford, Briggs and Eakins attempt to construct a taxonomy of the image from the point of view of user functionality, drawing on art historical and cognitive theories of perception, but when applied this results in no more systematic a keywording practice than any reasonable effort seen on self-annotating stock image sites. See Bryan Burford, Pamela Briggs and John P. Eakins, 'A Taxonomy of the Image: On the Classification of Content for Image Retrieval', *Visual Communication* 2/2 (2003): 123–61.

25   Paul Ricoeur, 'Structure, Word, Event', in *The Conflict of Interpretation* (London, 2004), p. 77.

26   Emile Benveniste, 'The Semiology of Language', in Robert E. Innis (ed.), *Semiotics: An Introductory Anthology* (Bloomington, 1985), p. 242.

semantics (meaning) and pragmatics (context) that are held to lie outside the closed paradigmatic system of language, in the realm of speech or discourse. Keyword clusters, aiming to be synonymous with the image, do not occupy the realm of the semiotic, and the constitution of meaning by internal differences between signifiers, but that of the semantic, meaning and reference. 'Semiotic systems,' Benveniste argues, 'are not "synonymous"; we are not able to say "the same thing" with spoken words that we can with music, as they are systems with different bases.'[27] The same holds for words and images. Semiotics is intralinguistic, 'in principle cut off and independent of all reference', whereas semantics operates at the level of the utterance, of discourse, of extralinguistic reference.[28] It is only in the domain of semantics, then, that referential correspondences can be established between words and images, as they are in keywording.

This does not mean that keywording is an open-ended interpretive process of free combination outside systematization. How images are seen as referring to the world may not be easily systematized, but the process is now subject to logical analysis and inscription in the development of proprietary, controlled vocabularies – both within individual agencies and on the open market – as well as personal keywording systems. Again, Alamy proves a particularly interesting example, requesting submitters to keyword their images according to three distinct levels of priority: 'essential' (very limited in number and 'very high priority'), 'main' ('high priority' and moderately limited), and 'comprehensive' ('medium priority' and allowing inclusion of relevant but non-essential terms). In tandem with 'Alamy Rank', how a submitter makes use of this keyword hierarchy can have a significant impact on their level of success and exposure. What is striking about the system is that 'essential' and 'main' keywords are hidden from viewers of the image on the open website in order to protect the 'intellectual property' of the submitter.

At present, ideas cannot be legally copyrighted, but only particular materializations or actualizations of an idea. Like an idea, an interpretive system is not legally protected as property unless it is formalized as a piece of software. Besides systems such as Alamy's, which formalizes interpretive systems as property, several software packages offering controlled vocabularies for keyword annotation are currently available. Heron regards David Reik's package[29] – which combines a taxonomic hierarchy of categories, listing subcategories for broader ones, with a thesaurus for synonyms – as one of the best currently available, although more recently Image Keyworder have increased their profile by upgrading their Windows-based software to include a customized 'Alamy Mode', developed specifically for that agency's subscribers.[30] Both include lists of conceptual terms

---

27   Ibid., p. 235.

28   Benveniste, 'The Semiology of Language', p. 242.

29   http://controlledvocabulary.com, accessed July 2008.

30   http://www.imagekeyworder.com, accessed July 2008. The software includes a thesaurus with over 40,000 terms, and automatically adds synonyms, alternate forms and plurals. Recently, a further upgrade was announced which allows users to propose terms

and stylistic descriptors, and offer advice regarding the exhaustive but efficient keywording of images, but it remains the task of the individual annotator to choose the appropriate terms to stand in for the image in the first place.

Regardless of whether it is even possible to systematize interpretive processes exhaustively, the order of keywording is based on aspirations to do just this – to build verbal systems of synonymy that functionally model the referential qualities of the image in depicting, and providing a vehicle for conceptualizing, the world. Controlled vocabularies attempt to formalize this semantic domain, which is not entirely 'free', but subject to cultural and generic laws of discursive closure. Interpretive processes must be presumed to be 'iterable', in Derridean terms, even to approach the task of supplementing the illustrative potential of an image with keywords.[31] For the purposes of computer programming, all processes must be viewed as iterable structures with determinable regularities that can be logically described and functionally modelled. In the context of classification, I will call the ordering of referential and contextual meaning in keywording practices a *taxo-semantic order*. If taxonomy (taxis + nomos) is the law of order or classification – the rules governing a particular (proper) order of things – and is inextricable from a material archival paradigm in which interpretation and narrativization are always exterior to the archive, the taxo-semantic order marks a significant restructuration of interpretation and meaning, which are themselves archived in the digital image archive, both through classificatory practices and through the computer program.[32]

The taxo-semantic order operates at the level of the program as well as of image classification, and sees the extension of the semiotic, or taxonomic, not merely in the sense of a paradigmatic inventory, but as an inscription and ordering (and thus an *archivization*) of combination, association, context, process – everything typically regarded as outside the language system, here seen as iterable regularities of praxis. The system of synonymy by which the referential aspect of the stock image is functionally modelled does not treat the image as a semantically *available* paradigmatic unit within a larger categorical container, but as a relatively full, semantically *determined*, unit of discourse, which already actualizes and

---

to boost the controlled vocabulary. http://www.stockphototalk.com/the_stock_photo_ industry_/2008/06/image-keyworder.html#more, accessed July 2008. The use of taxonomic categorization for the identification of appropriate terms in such software, it should be noted, is an intralinguistic relationship of word to word, and should not be mistakenly projected onto the relationship between keywords and images.

31   Derrida criticizes J.L. Austin's pragmatics for presuming that context is external to communication, when in fact it too is an iterable condition of communicative efficacy. Derrida, 'Signature Event Context', in *Margins of Philosophy* (Chicago, 1982), pp. 307–30.

32   In linguistics, semantics is traditionally the domain of meaning and reference, while context falls under pragmatics. However, the interface between the two is notoriously fuzzy. I use the term 'semantics' in the expanded, 'encyclopaedic' sense that modern linguists give it, acknowledging that context is a crucial determinant of so-called semantic meaning.

circumscribes a specific set of referential and illustrative possibilities.[33] While the system of synonymy supplements the image itself, the system of correspondence, centred on the search engine, is at the root of this restructuration. As the system for which images are classified, it is a functional model of the process of seeking and retrieving an image from the archive.

Classificatory technologies

How does keywording as an archival technology measure up against the more striking technical innovations of content-based methods? At present, applications of CBIR in stock image banks are limited to supplementary colour search features on a small number of stock photo websites,[34] and xcavator.net,[35] a stock image portal that retrieves images matching an uploaded JPEG or URL from three micro-stock agencies. The fact that agencies such as Getty Images and Corbis, struggling to maintain a high-end, high-priced rights-managed image market, have so far chosen not to incorporate such an option, points to the implication of such low-level CBIR techniques in the economic division between expensive rights-managed images, which are marketed on the basis of a rhetoric of aesthetic and communicative 'power', and cheap royalty free images, sold as malleable graphic substance. A growing trend towards the latter may indeed see the increased use of CBIR in the industry, but given that stock images continue to have a primarily illustrative function, the identification of conceptual content will remain crucial to finding appropriate images in large databases. The acknowledgement of this imperative in image banks generally is leading CBIR researchers to explore multimodal solutions, combining content-based and text-based search paradigms, in an effort to overcome the individual limitations of both.

While words remain central to this endeavour, is it foreseeable that CBIR could ever succeed in supplanting or fully automating keywording practices? Perhaps the best way to assess this possibility is to compare keywording with current efforts to overcome the limitations of manual image annotation (its high cost, time-consuming nature, and potential unreliability), through the automatic indexing of images based on the extraction of low-level visual features. In Jia Li and James Z. Wang's ALIPR (Automatic Linguistic Indexing of Pictures in Real-time) program,[36] a 'trained dictionary of semantic concepts' is constructed,

---

33   The notion of 'semantic availability' is central to Sekula's classic definition of the condition of the decontextualized photograph within the archive in 'Reading an Archive'.

34   For instance http://www.shutterstock.com and http://www.photos.com, accessed July 2008.

35   http://www.xcavator.net, accessed July 2008.

36   See Jia Li and James Z. Wang, 'Automatic Linguistic Indexing of Pictures by a Statistical Modelling Approach', *IEEE Transactions on Pattern Analysis and Machine Intelligence*, 25/9 (2003): 1075–88; Li and Wang, 'Real-Time Computerized Annotation of

consisting of a lexicon of correlations between concept models – representing statistical regularities based on various visual features extracted from general-purpose photographic images in a 'training set' – and verbal concepts.[37] When an image is uploaded as a search query, its 'image signature' is obtained and compared to the concept models in the dictionary. It is then labelled, based on its closest similarity to the concept models. Concepts, broadly speaking, are semantic entities that represent a certain body of knowledge about something which may be precise, or loosely defined and encyclopaedic, incorporating a diversity of experiential, referential and contextual connections.[38] In this sense, all keywords and classificatory labels are concepts, even when they are referred to as 'subject' or 'style' terms. If successful, a program like ALIPR could eventually 'hide' the verbal concepts within its underlying architecture, apparently achieving its goal of direct semantic matching of images – but how successful can it be?

Rather than basing such a judgement on current levels of success, it would be more prudent to consider the limitations of the system itself, and the reasons for these. The problem of the semantic gap between word and image is essentially one of the relationship of concepts (which are semantic) to sensory experience (such as visual perception). In Kantian terms, it is the mysterious *schematizing* activity of the imagination that links these.[39] In keyword classification, the human annotator performs this mediating role, judging which concepts are applicable to each image. The software merely *archives* the interpretive system produced by this schematizing activity, but does not perform it. This is how it restructures the semantic. ALIPR, on the other hand, aims to replicate and automate the *capacity* for schematization. The concept model – as an image schema representing the likely visual features of an image tagged x – should allow the correlation of a new set of extracted features with a predefined verbal concept. Right now, the system is not particularly good at this.[40] Solutions the authors propose include using larger

---

Pictures', *IEEE Transactions on Pattern Analysis and Machine Intelligence*, 30/6 (2008): 985–1002. An online demonstration of ALIPR is available at http://alipr.com, accessed July 2008, where users are invited to help the system learn by correcting its annotations and suggesting more appropriate terms.

37   The images were taken from Corel stock photography databases.

38   Researchers in semantics have proposed various understandings of what a concept is. I draw this loose definition from the discussion of these positions in John I. Saeed, *Semantics* (Oxford, 2003), especially chapter 2.

39   Immanuel Kant, *Critique of Pure Reason* (London, 1978), pp. 180–87.

40   As a point of comparison, I entered the stock photograph of a couple on a sofa with a laptop, whose keyword terms are cited above, into ALIPR for annotation. It offered the following: 'indoor, animal, wildlife, landscape, art, grass, tree, drawing, history, antique, bath, kitchen, firearm, gun, elephant'. Although results are reported to be reasonably accurate, with most users of the website checking at least one term as correct, the presence of highly generic terms such as people, landscape and man-made may over-determine this assessment of accuracy. In my example, only 'indoor' is accurate, but many of the other suggested labels directly contradict this.

training sets for each concept, and the incorporation of 3D, shape and contextual information into the learning process.

The fundamental problem, however, is that aesthetic regularities are modelled into schema *without* the determination of concepts. Schema are tagged with words, but words are only arbitrary symbols for concepts. Where schema link image information directly to verbal designations of concepts, there is no actual mediation of a referential concept. This is strikingly close to what Kant described in purely aesthetic judgements, where the free play of the imagination lies in its 'schematizing without a concept'.[41] Despite its claims, ALIPR does not in fact build a model of a concept, and does not bridge the semantic gap programmatically; it merely attributes verbal designations to purely aesthetic features, thus extending a model of aesthetic formalism.[42]

This is hardly, however, the radically de-territorialized formalism of Ernst's anarchival fantasies – at least in its ambitions. His utopian moment of the anti-semantic image archive has already been overtaken by the orientation towards user-friendly applications. The challenge for the future, it seems, will be the restructuring of the mysterious schema; but for the time being, verbal labelling remains key to image retrieval.

---

41   Kant, *Critique of Judgement* (Indianapolis, 1987), p. 151.

42   This is probably why greater success seems to have been achieved in modelling and replicating the capacity for judgements on photographic aesthetics by correlating visual feature extraction with peer ratings. See Ritendra Datta et al., 'Studying Aesthetics in Photographic Images Using a Computational Approach', *Proceedings of the European Conference on Computer Vision* (2006).

Plate 4.1   A QTVR object movie

Plate 5.1   General view of the theatre interior in the computer
reconstruction of the existing Teatro Olimpico. Architect:
Andrea Palladio (1508–1580)

Plate 5.2   View of the *proscenium* in the computer reconstruction of the
existing Teatro Olimpico. Architect: Andrea Palladio (1508–
1580)

Plate 5.3   View of the *auditorium* in the computer reconstruction of
the existing Teatro Olimpico. (a) View of the auditorium and
part of *proscenium*. (b) Aerial view of the auditorium with
removed ceiling. Architect: Andrea Palladio (1508–1580)

Plate 5.4   View of the theatre interior in the computer reconstruction of
the unbuilt design version of Teatro Olimpico

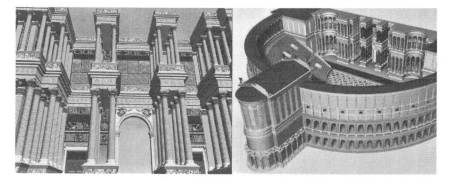

Plate 5.5   Three-dimensional computer reconstruction of the Theatre
of Pompey (dedicated 55 BC) after plan and section drawings
from the restored theoretical reconstruction (1848) of Luigi
Canina (1795–1856). (a) Detail from the *proscenium*. (b) Aerial
view of the theatre

Plate 9.1   Hard copies of books (made for exhibition in IAS Seoul)
             originally manifest as *Classics of net.art*, http://www.ljudmila.
             org/~vuk/books (1997) by Vuk Cosic

Plate 9.2   Duchamp detail from *The History of Art for Airports*, http://
www.ljudmila.org/~vuk/history (1997) by Vuk Cosic

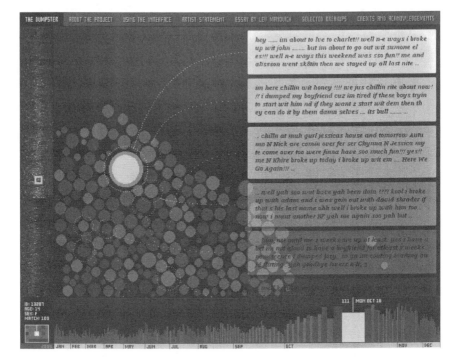

Plate 10.1   *The Dumpster* (2006, Golan Levin in collaboration with
Kamal Nigam and Jonathan Feinberg). Co-commissioned by
Tate Online and artport, the Whitney Museum of American
Art's portal to net art

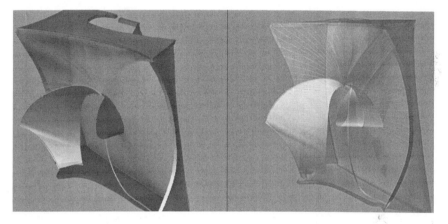

Plate10.2 *Construction in Space 'Crystal'* (1937, Naum Gabo) coloured to show the different sections from which this sculpture has been constructed (2007)

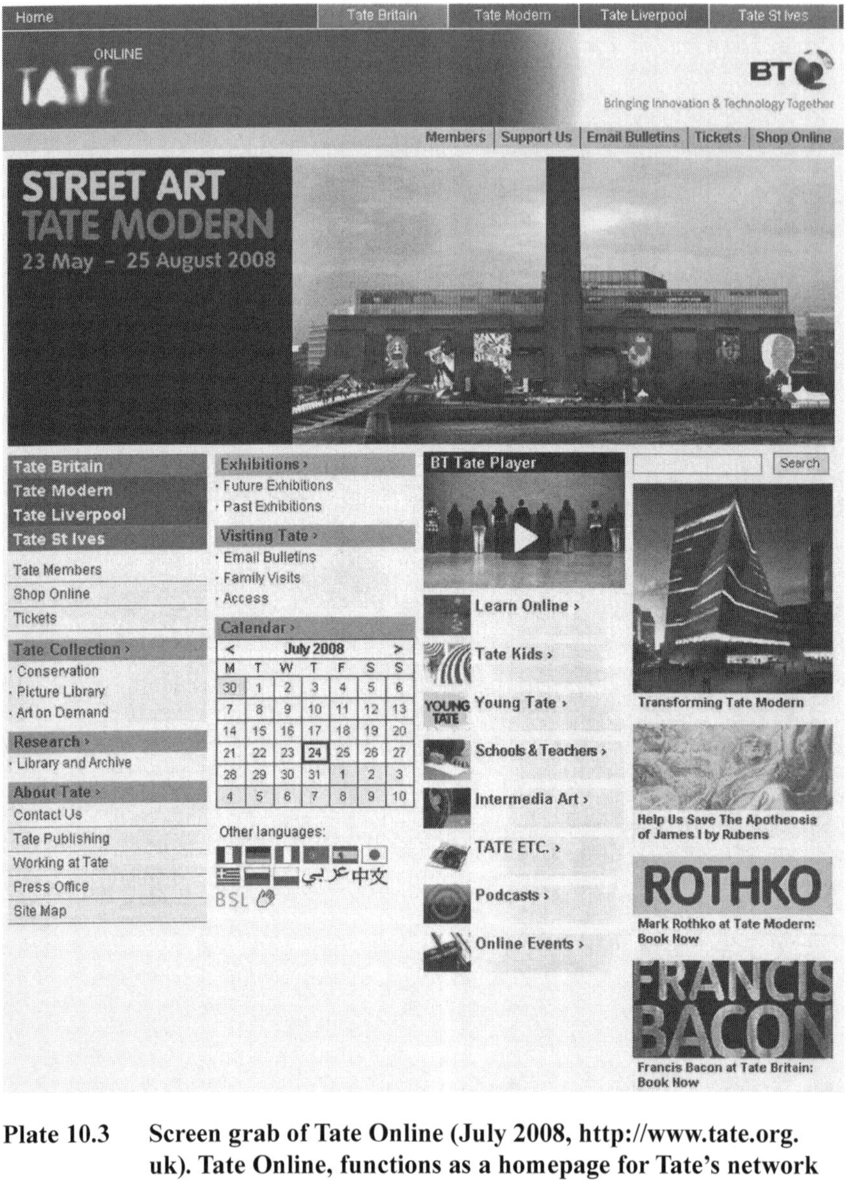

Plate 10.3 Screen grab of Tate Online (July 2008, http://www.tate.org.
uk). Tate Online, functions as a homepage for Tate's network
of real and virtual spaces, as well as an archive for the ideas
generated within the Tate system

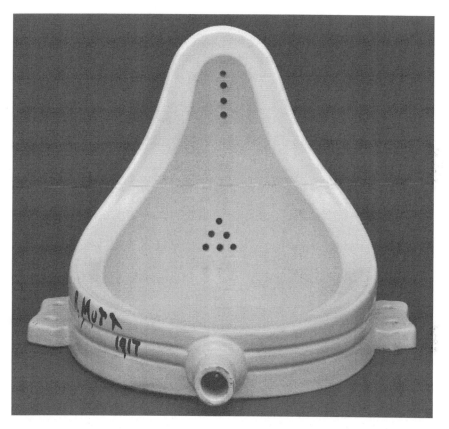

Plate 11.1   *Fountain*, 1917, replica 1964. Marcel Duchamp © Tate, London
2008

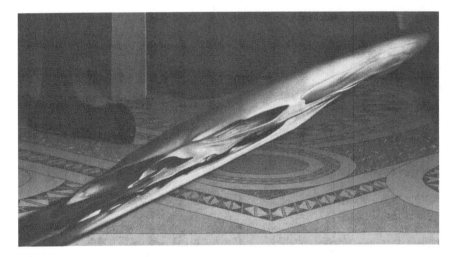

Plate 11.2   *The Ambassadors* (Jean de Dinteville and Georges de Selve), 1533, Hans Holbein the Younger

Chapter 7

For One and All:
Participation and Exchange in the Archive

Sue Breakell

> An archive stands not as a set of things or even a set of statements, but rather a set of relations.[1]

Archives have become an increasingly well-known and used resource, not only for many academic disciplines but also for a more general audience. From being perceived as an unfamiliar specialist field, archives have now acquired both greater currency and a more diverse range of meanings. A significant catalyst for this has been developments in digital technology and the frequent use of the term 'archive' in this context. This chapter considers how the developments of Web 2.0 are affecting, and may go on to affect, the practices of archives, as they endeavour to open up their collections in new ways, to meet a range of user needs and embrace the possibilities of new technology.

Having stated that the meaning of the word 'archive' has become diffused and ever less fixed over recent years, it is perhaps worth starting by setting out what is (and is not) meant by archives in the context of this chapter. The accepted professional definition of the archive is twofold, as expressed in this dictionary definition:

1. A collection of historical records relating to a place, organization or family
2. A place where historical records are kept[2]

In the context of Tate Archive (itself fulfilling the second definition) the first definition would cover the archive of a particular artist, comprising a body of material generated by one person's life, and which therefore has a collective identity. This might include correspondence, sketchbooks, diaries, photographs, business papers, writings and source material, for example. The shape and content of that body of material is in itself part of its evidential value. This may or may not include a particular original order in which it was arranged, reflecting the processes that created it; significance may lie in the interrelationships between the component parts of the archive, which can also imbue one another with authenticity.

---

1 Geoff Cox, 'Notes on Archives' (3 October 2007), see http://project.arnolfini.org.uk/?t=3&a=r&p=project/&f=20071003172428-notes_on_archives, accessed July 2008.

2 Oxford Paperback Dictionary (Oxford: OUP, 1988).

This is distinct from a situation where a single document (such as a sketchbook) has become detached from the original context of its production, and is gathered with other single documents into a Special Collection; a collection of individual, decontextualized 'treasures' or small groups of papers. Such a collection is not generated by any activity other than collecting. An archive is a set of traces of actions, the records left by a life – drawing, writing, interacting with society on personal and formal levels. In an archive, ideally, the sketchbook would be part of a wider body of papers, including correspondence, diaries, photographs – all of which can shed light on each other with a significance which the sketchbook alone cannot access. For example, a diary can locate the artist in a particular place at a particular time, which can help date the contents of the sketchbook.

Thus we can see the difference between, for example, the photographs of John Piper, which, although acquired separately from his main 'paper' archive, fulfil the professional definition of an archive, having a discrete provenance as a group, and a 'photographic archive' of individual images collected together, which, while fulfilling the definition of 'a place where historical records are stored', is actually functioning as an image bank of largely decontextualised images. This distinction explains something about the nature of archives and the importance of the specific way in which they are approached through professional archive practice and knowledge.

While the primary focus of this chapter is the visual arts archive, it should be noted that, as this means primary sources which inform the study of the art object, its scope comprises much non-visual material, as even visual arts archives include a large proportion of text-based documents such as correspondence and notebooks.

Motivated by the twin aims of preservation and access, archives, like museum and library collections, use automated descriptive catalogues as finding aids to allow users to locate and call up specific resources for their research in the reading room. Such activities seek, as far as possible, consistent descriptions, retaining the evidential value of the original context and characteristics of an archive or document. Increasingly, archives digitize selected content to allow greater and remote access to the non-specialist, whilst preserving the original items safely.

Archives were traditionally described in paper catalogues. They would be arranged as a collection – thus you would find a paper list describing the contents of the Piper archive, with a hierarchical structure progressing from the collection-level description to the specific individual items (or units of description). The user could then call up particular items, or runs of items, using the catalogue reference numbers – so, for example, they might ask to see all the letters from John Betjeman to Piper; or Piper's notebooks from the 1950s. When computerized cataloguing really began to take off in the 1980s, the standard approach was to map the paper process onto a database. Libraries made better progress in this area, partly owing to the fact that their contents were 'flat file' (each book a card index entry) and therefore the database could take the same format, and did not need to be relational. Programmers/developers struggled to create systems which accommodated the hierarchical structure of archive catalogues and their one-to-many relationships. So, for example, when first automating its catalogues in the early 1990s, Tate Archive initially used a Library system, UNICORN, whose developers constructed a version that attempted to meet the hierarchical requirements of the archive and to create the one-to-many relationships which this required. This was in the absence of custom-designed products for archives. When such products emerged, at a later point, Tate Archive migrated to a system called CALM, a widely-used proprietary archive system. Initially such catalogues were only available for use in Tate Archive's reading room, but in 2005 they were launched online.[3]

As well as the flexibility of searching options, one of the aims of automated catalogues was to allow standardization of content so that information could easily be exchanged between institutions, and to facilitate consistency of researcher experience. As automated cataloguing developed, so did standards and the quest for interoperability, not just between archives, but across the heritage sectors of museums and libraries.[4] However, many archives have been impeded in their aim to open up their collections and achieve greater visibility by the sheer volume of material they contain: appropriately researched and written catalogues are time-intensive to produce, so many archives still have considerable holdings without full catalogue descriptions. As such, full disclosure remains the prime objective of many institutions.

Existing digitization activities

Given that archive cataloguing is a bedrock on which other activities such as digitization can be built, digitization of holdings has tended to be selective, and based on the model of the 'online gallery' of images, again a flat-file approach, usually selected by theme. Another popular approach is the 'learning package', aimed more at a general user and providing grouped and interpreted material, again around a theme or a group of papers.

There are a number of examples on the Tate website of this kind of approach, drawing on Tate Archive's holdings. A New Opportunities Fund supported project in the early 2000s created three 'Archive Journeys' – which functioned as 'guided tours' through specific parts of archive holdings, with interpretive text and selected digitized material, as well as chronologies. The subjects were the history of the Tate; the Bloomsbury Group; and the art historian Barbara Reise.[5]

---

3   See http://www.tate.org.uk/research/researchservices/researchcentre/, accessed July 2008.

4   The main archive standard for data entry is ISAD (G), the International Standard for Archival Description, which provides a template of fields for data entry. See http://www.ica.org/sites/default/files/isad_g_2e.pdf, accessed July 2008.

5   http://www.tate.org.uk/archivejourneys/, accessed July 2008.

Otherwise, the main motivation for digitization has been in relation to funded programme activities, usually gallery displays, for which a microsite might be developed, allowing the display to have a longer life beyond its installation in the gallery. A number of issues of *Audio Arts* magazine were digitized for a gallery display and are now available on an online microsite. For the Prunella Clough gallery display in 2007, a browsable selection of archive items was created, selected to illuminate Clough's creative process and shed light on the works in the Gallery display.[6]

For Tate, like many other archives, such activities have tended to be somewhat *ad hoc* and opportunist, on the back of other activities. Tate Archive is now seeking a more strategic approach to digitization across its collections (while still not total digitization). A search for models in the archive community for innovative new ways of presenting material demonstrates that this is still a developing area.

One early and well-known example of innovative digitization is the Turning the Pages software, pioneered by the British Library, which allows the online user to turn virtual pages of a manuscript volume or sketchbook.[7] Produced by Armadillo Systems, the latest version of the software, Turning the Pages 2.0™, provides a wire-frame 'book' into which scanned images of individual pages, and their metadata, are called up for presentation at run time, i.e. on the request of the user.

The early work stages of Turning the Pages demonstrated the sheer scale of the problem that lay ahead – each book might take several weeks to produce, including preparation, page-by-page scanning, checking, and data entry, before uploading each book onto a web page interface – each volume costing a couple of thousand pounds. A sense of the scale of the task that lies ahead is given by the fact that only a tiny proportion of the British Library's vast holdings have so far been included. While Google and a number of US libraries (usually academic libraries driven by demand and with the aim of increasing student access to their holdings) are making great progress in speeding up (and reducing the cost of) the digitization of text volumes using more automated processes, the fastest processes involve breaking up books and pulping them after scanning, because the value is not in the item itself but in the contents. This can allow up to 3,000 books a week to be scanned. But this is clearly not feasible for rare books or manuscripts, which remain more labour-intensive and therefore far more costly.

Another innovative example can be found on the website of the Andy Warhol Museum in Pittsburgh, US. Among the museum's online projects is an application which presents one of Warhol's 'Time Capsules', Time Capsule 21.[8] After Warhol's death, the full extent and significance of his time capsules was discovered. Over the period of a month, Warhol would drop 'stuff' – correspondence, papers, and all kinds of other items – into a cardboard box, which was then sealed and sent

---

6   Both microsites are available at http://www.tate.org.uk/research/researchservices/ archive/archiveonline.htm, accessed July 2008.

7   See http://www.bl.uk/onlinegallery/ttp/ttpbooks.html, accessed July 2008.

8   See http://www.warhol.org/tc21/index.html, accessed July 2008.

to storage. These now form a central part of Warhol's archive and one capsule has been digitized and presented online in such a way as to seek to recreate the experience of looking at and browsing through the contents of the original box. Users can click on thumbnail images of various items, which can also be grouped and presented by theme or material type, such as 'photographs' or 'Mother'. The descriptive and interpretive information about each item includes links to related material outside the immediate context of the box itself, enhancing the many-to-many relationships of each item. The user can browse and explore up and down (from the box level to the individual piece within) but also across links to other similar items in the archive (e.g. other telephone messages) or to other works by Warhol for which these might be source material.

While capturing something of the experience of using original material, the application highlights the problem of scale and the inevitability of some kind of selection process: this is just one of over six hundred boxes, and its contents are inventoried in 123 item descriptions, some of which have sub-pieces. The sheer scale of the challenge of archive digitization means that few institutions have made major inroads into the task ahead – indeed, many are still considering how to respond to the challenge – should the approach be selective or complete digitization? If selective, how are those selection decisions taken without ghettoizing parts of our collections? For the territory of the archive has been the location of debates not only around the nature and meaning of archives, but the place and function of physical archives in the digital age.

The postmodern archive

The archive is now a carrier for many signifiers, depending on perspective. Postmodern discourse has found in the archive a fertile ground for discussion: artists, historians and critical theorists of all kinds are intrigued by its facility to reflect much about the modern condition.[9] For the very process of an archive's re-housing within an institution may enact changes on the material and its resonances; that institution is a product of history and the biases of history in terms of the principles and motivations behind its origins and its selection processes, and the nature of archive material itself is fragmentary and unfixed, a paradigm of the postmodern quest to look beyond the document and consider the context and processes of its creation. Certain fundamental principles which underpin archive theory and practice – authenticity and context of the record – are eminently compatible with discussions about the notional archive of critical theory, though archivists have tended to be somewhat diffident about entering these discussions, and have allowed their profession to suffer from a pervasion of stereotypes about gatekeepers, secrecy and dust.

---

9   Among critical theorists, Jacques Derrida, Michel Foucault, Walter Benjamin, Allan Sekula and many others have written about the archive. Charles Merewether's anthology *The Archive* (London and Cambridge, MA, 2006) provides a selection of introductory texts.

Archives are also fertile territory for artistic production, artists perhaps being attracted by the latent ambiguity of the archive: the potential layers of meaning, tales and enactments beyond the immediate informational content. Hal Foster describes the nature of archives as at once 'found yet constructed, factual yet fictive, public yet private'.[10] He describes an archive-inspired 'desire to turn belatedness into becomingness, to recoup failed visions in art, literature, philosophy, and everyday life into possible scenarios of alternative kinds of social relations, to transform the no-place of the archive into the no-place of utopia … [a] move to turn "excavation sites" into "construction sites".'

Creative collaborations between artists and archives may have many motives and take many forms, but their proliferation is indicative of an impulse on the part of the archive to open up holdings to new interpretations. The potential for such multiple and individual responses highlights that there is not one fixed 'archive', frozen as in the popular stereotype; indeed, from an archivist's perspective, the archive which we keep and maintain in its current arrangement is only one of the infinite permutations of and perspectives on that material. The roles of researcher, archivist and creator are now far less distinct, and the boundaries between them more blurred.

Although less well known, archival theorists have responded to the critical discourses of the late twentieth and twenty-first centuries, pointing the way for the archive of the digital age. Erik Ketalaar and Terry Cook have affirmed and developed the notion of what Ketalaar describes as 'Archives of the People, by the People, and for the People',[11] archives which are more responsive, transparent and participative, not only made available for infinite interactions, but added to by users. In this way the network of archival descriptive nodes can be a foundation for other outputs, built by users, and researchers' discoveries, ideas and interpretations can be shared.

Web 2.0 and beyond

There has been much discussion of the possibilities of Web 2.0 for the democratization of information sharing of all kinds, including archives. In this, debate about archives has become conflated with discussions about the associations of the institution and its inevitable selection processes. Does Web 2.0 offer a 'bottom-up' solution to these dilemmas, and those of the apparently rigid structures and imposed orders of the archive?

---

10   Hal Foster, 'An Archival Impulse', *October*, (Fall 2004): 5.

11   Eric Ketelaar, 'Being Digital in People's Archives', http://cf.hum.uva.nl/bai/home/eketelaar/BeingDigital.doc, p. 6. This article originally appeared in *Archives and Manuscripts*, 31/2 (November 2003): 8–22. See also Terry Cook, 'Archival Science and Postmodernism: New Formulations for Old Concepts', http://www.mybestdocs.com/cook-t-postmod-p1-00.htm, accessed February 2008, p. 14, fn 20. This article originally appeared in *Archival Science*, 1/1 (2000): 3–24.

Web 2.0 appears to offer a solution to the perennial problems of selection of material for the archive – either before or after its reception into the institution. For selection depends on the available physical space, a situation which does not arise in the digital environment until much further down the line. The idea of the organic, unregimented, all-inclusive archive, where all things are equal and no value judgements need be made, is seductive. Archivists too aspire to more representative archives, while feeling that keeping everything is not the answer. This chapter does not propose to assess questions of digital utopianism, but from the perspective of the archivist, the web offers tremendous potential, with several key concerns: what are the implications of not knowing the sources for material found online? Who is responsible for ensuring the preservation of our digital heritage, which carries intrinsic obsolescence and auto-destruction, and a need for active preservation, in its very format? These are key arguments for the need for traditional archive principles and professional expertise to be represented in the online community.[12]

Today our lives are endlessly documented in ways unimaginable to previous generations, not only in official records but in those which we create ourselves and share online, as if by doing so we have a voice, a presence, exist more fully. Pierre Nora has written that 'our whole society lives for archival production'.[13] We at once crave and feel overwhelmed by information, by our own tracks and traces and the responsibility of their supply and maintenance.

What will the sheer volume of material mean for researchers in the future? Ben Highmore has written of the (paper) Mass Observation archive – perhaps an interesting model here – 'by inviting everyone to become the author of their own life, by letting everyone speak about everything, the vast archive of documents became literally unmanageable'.[14] In a digital environment, the potential is still more enormous. The internet offers an illusion of permanence by using terms such as 'autoarchiving', but this is not the case – it needs to be actively captured and preserved. Archives that survive must inevitably be kept in some kind of houses of memory, whether real or virtual – because the act of remembering involves both storing and retrieving: it is not a passive process, especially in the digital age. The very quality that makes material so infinitely accessible in that context – the lack of structure and the possibility for anonymity and even

---

12   There are also particular implications in managing archive material which is born digital, be it digital documents or digital images. The very different considerations for the management of these are addressed in the writings of the archive theorists Eric Ketalaar and Terry Cook, for example.

13   Cited in Eric Ketalaar, 'Being Digital in People's Archives', p. 4.

14   Ben Highmore, 'Walls Without Museums: Anonymous History, Collective Authorship and the Document', *Visual Culture in Britain*, 8/2 (2007): 1–20, 16. For the Mass Observation Archive, see http://www.massobs.org.uk/index.htm, accessed July 2008.

deception – means that to be able to confirm the original context and provenance of archives will become more important than ever.[15]

In maximizing the potential of new technology, we must ensure that we build a resource that can be trusted (in that we know its source and the context of its production) and that it can and will be preserved (both in terms of quantity and technology). There is still a tension between the 'professional' urges to standards, which allow the authentification and exchange of data and its compatibility with formats that can be migrated and preserved,[16] and the more free-form, organic activities which support the creation of each person's own tags and taxonomies, and of information customized to the individual's needs. Yet these are not necessarily incompatible.

The Utopian vision for archives is of a participative, more representative model, which does not merely represent the perspective of those in authority but also minority groups and interests. The 'long tail' model, used by Chris Anderson to describe how the internet will widen the availability of resources for minority interest areas, can be applied here.[17] For the archivist, professional expertise would still be represented in the model, as facilitator, whose interest is just one of many, curating bedrock catalogue data on which other tools and applications can be built. Archives can thus have not only the one-to-many relationship of their original context, safely captured in the archive catalogue and structure, but a many-to-many, infinitely repeatable nodal or rhizomatic structure, where, in the user's personal environment, connections can be made and shared in ways which were previously unimagined.

Amid a general rise in the expectations of archive users, and the rise of social networking tools, the art research community, like others, is exploring the possibilities of this new environment, with imaginative archive/content systems built on the specific needs of particular projects, producing an extraordinary array of customized applications, characterized by infinite possibilities of order, interaction and personalization – essentially research-driven self-curation. There is also a strong interest in notions of Creative Commons and open source software.

Tate Online's approach to developing its collections database (distinct from the archive database) reflects such current thinking. While the core descriptive data about each work in the collection remains essentially unchanged, divided between

---

15   This chapter does not address the implications of users' separation from the original document, for example in relation to Walter Benjamin's notion of the aura of the original, as described in his essay 'The Work of Art in the Age of Mechanical Reproduction' (1936).

16   See, for example, the Digital Curation Centre (DCC), http://www.dcc.ac.uk/; the Digital Preservation Coalition (DPC), http://www.dpconline.org/graphics/; the Joint Information Systems Committee (JISC), http://www.jisc.ac.uk/; and the Technical Advisory Service for Images (TASI), http://www.tasi.ac.uk/, and the web magazine ARIADNE, http://www.ariadne.ac.uk/information/#about, among others (all accessed July 2008).

17   See Chris Anderson, *The Long Tail: How Endless Choice is Creating Unlimited Demand* (London, 2007).

fields so that distinct elements of information are available for manipulation, what is being developed is a series of content-rich interfaces which allow a vastly extended range of possibilities for the user to both manipulate and re-present the data. Of course the problem with such applications is that they take time and money to build and develop. Imagine how that scales up from 68,000 works (in Tate's Collection) to potentially millions of documents held in the Archive.

Two key issues for online archival resources are what we might call 'findability' and 'browsability'. The former – visibility – is discussed by Seb Chan in his online blog.[18] If people cannot find your data, it is pointless for it to be on the web. General users may not think to search an institutional website. One solution to this is tools for cross-searching or sharing search results. Seb Chan's institution, the Powerhouse Museum in Sydney, is one of a number of museums which participate in Flickr Commons, where image resources are shared and cross-searched. Flickr Commons thus provides a resource portal which does not require the user to go to the institutional website, but can then lead to the user following a link to the institutional website and the discovery of further resources from its collections. It can attract users who might otherwise never think to visit the institution's website. While the information may be decontextualized, it can be traced back to the location at which its context is recorded.

As Seb Chan writes, 'quality matters, but only when findability issues are solved first. Findability issues are different for expert users and for those who understand museums, and this is largely why we feel comfortable writing and designing content for them. These expert users are also less likely to go elsewhere. But it needs to be stressed that they are in the absolute minority'.[19]

Browsability – or encouraging people to stay on your site once they are there – can be achieved by developing interesting ways to move through the material which are not purely about up-and-down hierarchies and which can encourage intuitive or unexpected connections between materials. AquaBrowser Library is one example of how this can be achieved. It presents existing structures of terminology control in a non-hierarchical way, allowing users to follow links to material both expected (e.g. from 'Warhol' to 'Factory') and unexpected (from 'Warhol' to 'Superstar').

Turning the Pages 2.0™ also includes a 'note-taking' facility, which allows users to place 'post-it' notes on the pages, which can either be kept private to the user, or shared with other users. Armadillo are using this as part of an information-gathering project (working with libraries) to explore user habits and requirements for participative software among more specialist academic researchers. The company have noticed that the needs of the general access/interpretation audience and the research community are slightly different, but identify both as important areas of future development.

18 Seb Chan's blog, fresh+new(er), is at http://www.powerhousemuseum.com/ dmsblog/, accessed July 2008.

19 Seb Chan, fresh+new(er).

The National Archives' (TNA) wiki package, Your Archives, uses open-source Media Wiki software, to offer a parallel to TNA's catalogue, where, as in Wikipedia, users can share their own research information and comment on the contents of the main site. One of a number of experimental applications always under development at TNA, this particular product was created in response to a demand from users which came in the form of an increased number of comments and requests to share or add information. It is also used by staff to store notes and work in progress (material which is not designated for the main catalogue), rather like a note-taking and storage facility where the notes can be developed either by the creator or by other users. Thus the facility serves the function of both capturing and sharing information which might otherwise be lost or unusable, gradually building a knowledge base. The site has not been widely promoted yet, and its users tend to have found the site by chance through other searches. Users range in age from retired academics to research students at a much earlier stage of their career, as well as non-specialist users who might be carrying out family history research.

Characteristic of this project is an experimental approach which sees the facility very much as a work in progress, without the predefined parameters and specific aims of an online catalogue; one which seeks to engage with user needs and interests, and create a resource which is more of a dialogue than a statement; an example of a collaborative approach. This kind of interactivity has enormous advantages for both user and archivist in developing additional content and context.

Meanwhile the research community is developing applications to meet its research needs. Because of their smaller scale and focus, these can create quite rich and complex functionality allowing an incredible range of flexibility in manipulating and re-presenting data. One such example has been produced by the research centre Creative Research into Sound Art Practice (CRiSAP) at the London College of Communication, part of the University of the Arts, London. This focuses on archive material relating to the London Musicians' Collective, dating from the 1960s and 1970s. A selection of about two hundred items has been scanned and the system allows them to be searched, grouped and arranged according to a mind-boggling array of possibilities, including their visual content. For example, all the letter As from the home-produced posters can be presented and arranged (which has proved to be of great interest to graphic design researchers, although this was not the purpose of the application); even the shades of the papers' colours can be presented in order. Users can make their own journeys through the holdings, tagging their selections as they wish, creating their own taxonomies and leaving their selections and commentaries for others to follow, use and build on.

This application offers an extraordinary range of ways to interrogate and re-present the material. However, the question is how such a detailed and specialist application could be applied to a much larger archive; one holding many millions of items. The feasibility of such a scale-up must be considered. It would also be vital to consider whether the quality of the application might be lost if scaled up, in that the sheer volume of potential results might drown the value of those results.

The solution seems to be to find some way for these different approaches to meet, combine and learn from one another, so that the archive can meet its obligation to provide a level of access and interpretation to its general user, while working collaboratively on more specialist applications focusing on a particular area of research, which have the possibility of attracting funding. These applications could of course then be made available more widely across and outside the research community.

One area in which the arts community excels is cross-disciplinary discussions, and within this, the arts archive community can learn from, and participate in, new approaches stimulated by the demands of non-paper-based technologies. Non-standard areas of practice have encouraged and fostered innovative projects, because of the lack of more official attention to the challenges they present. One such area is the documentation of contemporary art, which Adatabase (AD),[20] an initiative of the AFoundation,[21] is seeking to address. It states that contemporary art and associated materials have been 'the poor relations of the art world, vulnerable not only through the intrinsically ephemeral nature of many contemporary art forms – installation, performances, live art – but also to dispersal into private collections, dismantling, destruction and disappearance'.[22] Describing itself as 'no less than a new Manifesto for Artists in the age of the digital revolution' and 'a pioneering open-source research engine and digital archive for contemporary visual culture',[23] AD is a database of contemporary art resources, including images and documents. It is searchable by 'Who' (artist, collector, curator), 'What' (painting, sculpture, performance, etc.), 'When' and 'Where' (venue, town/city). AD provides digitization and digital preservation facilities for a number of smaller institutions that could not otherwise establish equivalent resources alone.

The online Project Arnolfini[24] site considers the theory and the practice of documenting performance art, materials which by their very nature are particularly pertinent to and paradigmatic of the archive. Paul Clarke refers to Rebecca Schneider's argument that 'the archive is founded on loss; its logic emphasizes disappearance and forgetting in order to justify the project of conserving remains – material traces, objects that it can "regulate, maintain and institutionalise"'.[25] It is perhaps this intrinsic ephemerality of this area of practice, and the critical debates surrounding it, which has encouraged the Project Arnolfini team to foster and encourage an experimental and critical approach to the practices of the

20   http://www.adatabase.org/, accessed July 2008.

21   http://www.afoundation.org.uk/, accessed July 2008.

22   http://www.adatabase.org/adatabase/static/A_Database_History.pdf p2, accessed July 2008.

23   http://www.adatabase.org/adatabase/static/A_Database_History.pdf p2, accessed July 2008.

24   http://www.project.arnolfini.org.uk, accessed July 2008.

25   Paul Clarke on 'Between Archival Objects and Events', Arnolfini Performing the Archive Wiki http://project.arnolfini.org.uk/?t=3&st=2, accessed July 2008.

archive in relation to performance. They have posited a range of experimental approaches and online facilities drawing on social networking and ideas of a more participative archive such as those outlined here. These include, for example, blogs, wikis and uphone. On the blog, Geoff Cox offers a vision of an archive that engage[s] practices that derive from network cultures that utilize relational processes that challenge existing hierarchical structures and the social relations that derive from these ... this is the working principle for the archive – one that engages both vertical and horizontal axes and that offers participatory potential but also systematic organizational structures (for example, an archive that uses both standard classification and user-generated systems).[26]

In this vision of the archive, collaboration becomes more important than ever, with archivists, researchers and artists working together in an exchange of information and ideas. The archive will exist as a trusted source of information with its bedrock of catalogue data upon which richer interfaces and user-driven content can be built, moving with changing interests and evolving technologies. This bedrock data will meet the standards required for preservation and exchange. This model places the archivist more in the role of a facilitator, one whose practices are transparent and open for discussion as much as the archives themselves. The challenge for archives within arts institutions is to find partners (for building specialist tools) and funding (for creating data) to be able to meet this challenge.

In a large volume of material, some data will always be privileged over others, and we cannot keep everything. Material which is not associated with formal archival processes and principles may be 'self-selected' by the online community, which might be seen as an organic process, but such an activity will reflect the prejudices of the time and the limitations of the system of its production, just as much as the archivists and historians of the nineteenth century were influenced by their own context in the material they chose to preserve.

Acknowledgements

I would like to thank the following people for their advice and sharing of knowledge and ideas: Paul Clarke, Live Art Archives, University of Bristol; Neil Cummings, Critical Practice, Chelsea College of Art, University of London; Guy Grannam, The National Archives; Cathy Lane and colleagues at CRiSAP, London College of Communication, University of London; John Stack, Head of Tate Media; Michael Stocking, Armadillo Systems Ltd; Simon Tanner, Kings Digital Consultancy Services; Julian Warren, Arnolfini; Neal White; and especially Victoria Worsley.

---

26   Geoff Cox, 'Notes on Archives'.

Chapter 8

The User-Archivist and Collective (In)Voluntary Memory: Read/Writing the *Networked Digital Archive*

James MacDevitt

Binaries abound in Euro-American philosophical traditions: mind/body, subject/object, signifier/signified. Despite the fact that each of these dualities has been repeatedly questioned and/or disrupted in the recent past, theorists of the digital humanities have yet to deconstruct the binaries that inf(l)ect the foundational structure of our own disciplinary practice: user/archive, read/write, data/metadata. As the location of culture becomes indistinct from the location of data, however, it is increasingly important to understand 'how computation participates in the world it represents', and that means exploring the transactional inter(dis)course between these arbitrarily dichotomous categories and the impact of their dialogical permeability on cultural studies in the age of globally distributed flows of information.[1]

Nowhere is this introspection more imperative than in the humanist disciplines that take culture as their focus of study and in the institutions that have, historically, disciplined those disciplines. As Donald Preziosi presciently points out, the archival collections held by, and (equally importantly) ordered by, museums – not to mention the representational photographic *archives* invoked in countless university lecture halls and survey textbooks – 'made the visible *legible*, thereby establishing what was worthy to be seen, whilst teaching museum users how to read what is to be seen: how to activate social memories'.[2] In the age of *Networked Digital Archives*, however, the notion of a *user* can, and often does, take on new associative meanings. The model of an institutionally ensconced *archivist* or *curator* selecting works for canonical inclusion and arranging them in a fixed, canonical order is, if nothing else, problematic when overloaded by the funicity of so-called Web 2.0 paradigms, continuously assembled through algorithmic processing, and collaboratively filtered through rhizomatic pathways made possible by the dynamic spatialized patterns of online search engines. There

---

1 Paul Dourish, *Where the Action Is: The Foundation of Embodied Interaction* (Cambridge, MA, 2004), p. 20.

2 Donald Preziosi, 'The Art of Art History', in Donald Preziosi (ed.), *The Art of Art History* (Oxford, 1998), p. 509.

are, no doubt, many within the centralized structures of archiving institutions who would prefer to sanitize their practices to protect them from the viral effects of new participatory tools such as internal folksonomic labelling and external data mash-ups. But there are also others (both within those organizations and outside them) who recognize the possibilities that these new applications open up for disrupting the power traditionally associated with those very institutions.

What has been less discussed, however, is how such a systematic shift not only fragments age-old notions of disciplinary power, but also remediates traditional concepts of critique. One notable exception is Irit Rogoff, who, in place of critique, with all its oppositional connotations, suggests that cultural historians, in part owing to new technologies of display, are entering an era of criticality, an ambiguous *space of appearance* that allows us to 'engage increasingly with the performative nature of culture, with meaning that *takes place* as events unfold'.[3] Within this dynamic unfolding, resistance to dominant power structures, as such, does not occur from outside those structures, but arises from within them instead. As Kathleen Stewart posits, resistance now 'takes the form of making further inscriptions on the landscape of encoded things – inlays on the existing inscriptions – in an effort to fragment the enclosing, already finished order and reopen cultural forms to history'.[4]

On the surface, concepts such as criticality and institutionalized institutional critique may seem hopelessly paradoxical. However, both notions stem from the ongoing tension between the collapse of oppositional distance provided by distributed information technologies and the entrenched social discourses (such as art history, modernity or late capitalism) that have traditionally relied upon the fantasy of a disembodied, and therefore disinterested, Kantian subject to maintain their authority. As Amelia Jones points out:

> These new ways of thinking and making propose an embrace of a kind of representation that both maintains the body as a locus of subjective meaning, interpretation, and cultural experience and engagement and takes place without the guarantee of a transcendental signifier, and without the firm boundaries between sign and referent. Without this guarantee and without these boundaries, centralized power is no longer possible in its modern (totalitarian) formulations.[5]

Of course, as Alexander Galloway posits in his seminal analysis of network protocols, control can, and does, exist after decentralization.[6] In addition, the

---

3   Irit Rogoff, 'Smuggling – An Embodied Criticality', http://eipcp.net/dlfiles/rogoff-smuggling (2006), p. 1.

4   Kathleen Stewart, 'Nostalgia: A Polemic', *Cultural Anthropology*, 3/3 (1988): 232.

5   Amelia Jones, *Self/Image* (London, 2006), p. 21.

6   Alexander R. Galloway, *Protocol: How Control Exists After Decentralization* (Cambridge, MA, 2004).

potential to dislocate previous modes of power must be understood as being tempered by the asymmetrical access to those new technologies, which are, in fact, a very real vestige of historical economic and political inequities. It is with these caveats in mind, and perhaps even because of them, that I would like to suggest complicating the dualities (of user and archive, reading and writing, and data and metadata) that are liberally sprinkled throughout the discourse of the digital humanities. In order to open up these binaries to new constitutive possibilities, we need to define first how these concepts have traditionally been framed by that discourse and how, in turn, these concepts encircle and engender each other.

The *User* and/in the *Archive*

Like the now ubiquitous term the *Body*, the *Archive* is a theoretical construct that allows for philosophical investigations around, and through, a set of social practices. In point of fact, there is no singular, transcendental *Archive*; there are only multiple *archives*. Leaving this Platonic debate aside, however, it is useful to imagine that all *archives* are functionally equivalent and therefore partake in a kind of *archive-ness*, recognizing, of course, that we are doing so only immediately to dismantle this imaginary construction. The *Archive*, as both a theoretical entity and in its numerous actualized manifestations, is typically understood as the dead space of tangible objects that are forced to lie orderly or, as Preziosi cleverly suggests, 'lie, orderly'.[7] This model, however, which formulates *the Archive* as a tool, an object to be used, implies that subjects exist that put this object to use and are defined by their temporal and authorial relationship to it. The *Archivist* is understood as anterior to the *Archive*, while the *User* is posterior to it. The *Archivist* produces the *Archive*; the *User* consumes it. What both subjectivities have in common is their perpetual exteriority to, and alienation from, this object of their use. As Jacques Derrida posits, 'there is no archive without a place of consignation, without a technique of repetition, and without a certain exteriority. No archive without outside.'[8] At the same time, however, as mutually constituted – inside and outside, object and subject – the *Archive* and its *Users* are systematically intertwined. What this seems to imply is that the *Archive* is not a thing, nor a series of things, nor even a site containing things, but rather an activity or, simply, a desire. From this perspective, the *Archive* is neither the sum-total of the actual material within its collection nor the potential material yet to be absorbed. It is, instead, the abstracted tension between them, the mutual desire to produce and consume.

As such, *archives* exist to expand, to conquer and colonize that which is outside them, including, as we shall see, the material traces of their *archivists* and *users*. Where, after all, does an *archive* stop? The Rosetta Stone is certainly part of the

---

7   Donald Preziosi, *Rethinking Art History: Meditations on a Coy Science* (New Haven, 1989), p. 59.

8   Jacques Derrida, *Archive Fever: A Freudian Impression* (Chicago, 1995), p. 11.

British Museum's *archive*. But what about the replica of the Rosetta Stone, also physically within the museum's walls, to which visitors flock for the requisite souvenir photograph? What about the photographic postcard of the Rosetta Stone sold in the gift shop or the digital photograph of it on the museum's website? What about the paperwork maintained to prove the object's provenance, or descriptive text in the museum's collection database? What about the brochures and maps handed out to visitors, or audio recordings that guide them through the collection? What about records of purchases at the museum café, including visitors' credit card information, or surveillance footage of the various galleries through which visitors traverse every day? It would not be a stretch to suggest that all of these items are material (even digital photographs take up space on a physical hard drive) and that the institution has a vested interest in organizing and preserving them. In this regard, even supposing that the British Museum foregoes acquiring any new *artefacts*, its *archive* will continue to grow.

If *archives* are inherently colonial and cancerous, *networked digital archives* are even more insatiable. As processing speed accelerates, storage space increases, and bandwidth availability improves, *networked digital archives* are growing at an almost unimaginable rate, often becoming functionally interconnected with each other. Ironically, this could be seen as a dystopian return to a singular, universal *Archive*, as manifest in the (hopefully) aborted programme chillingly labelled Total Information Awareness, coordinated through the research wing of the United States military, the Defense Advanced Research Projects Agency. Of course, total information awareness, this 'dark side of the database imaginary',[9] as Steve Dietz calls it, would only be feasible if all *networked digital archives* had access to all other *networked digital archives* and they accessed each other in exactly the same way. This is, in point of fact, impossible, since access is the mechanism by which dispersed subjectivities and algorithmic representations are assembled dynamically through the transactional space of information networks. However, by nature of being connected to a network, and especially to the global network commonly called the Internet, *networked digital archives* are, at least, *selectively accessible*. Closed proprietary database applications once assured that this *selective accessibility* was limited to internal institutional use, connecting the multitude of relational databases within a museological *archive* to each other. However, with the advent of structured transport mechanisms like dynamic XML feeds, as well as parasitic parser scripts that can extract meta/data solely from the template-based patterns of database-driven museum websites, meta/data is increasingly difficult for institutions to isolate from external signification. This means that some, or all, of the meta/data within those *archives* are available to be synthesized (mashed up) with meta/data from other *archives*, folded together to construct *aggregated data representations* that are, in fact, and quite tautologically, *archives* as well.

---

9   Ibid.

The recent phenomenon of trans-institutional museum *archives* is just one testament to the value of reproductive exposure made possible by *selectively accessible* meta/data. For example, like many online *archives*, the Museums and the Online Archive of California[10] (MOAC) database can be dynamically searched and browsed using its web-based front-end portal, an operative transaction that fuses user desire/action and computational code (localized in both the client and server computers). MOAC, however, is actually an *archive* of *archives* that are independently maintained by numerous public and private institutions spread throughout the state of California. The meta/data within these *archives* are functionally accessible to the MOAC servers, or more specifically the coded applications housed on the MOAC servers, only because of the imposition of standardized database fields collectively agreed upon by representatives from MOAC member institutions.[11] As Galloway makes clear, 'the contradiction at the heart of protocol is that it has to standardize in order to liberate. It has to be fascistic and unilateral in order to be utopian.'[12] In order to communicate effectively, computers and databases, like people, need to use the same language, though in a computational environment this actually manifests as a continuous material hierarchy of languages, protocols and/or *archives*.

Along this same line, it should be noted that the HTML code used by the client browser to render MOAC's front-end webpage could also be theoretically understood as an *archive*, in that it contains structural data for ordering digital objects such as text and JPEG images. Of course, the HTML code itself never contains those digital objects per se, but simply points to them. A webpage only comes into being when structure (HTML, CSS), objects (digital files), and interpreter (browser) temporarily intertwine. If *a network* is synonymous with flows of information, a *networked digital archive* is a network of stoppages, a series of informational flows that are momentarily halted and forced to coalesce by computational algorithm and/or user action, a paradoxical event in that a stoppage at any point in the network causes the archive to expand elsewhere. Using this same logic, Google could then be understood as an *archive* of *archives* (of *archives*, etc.), in that it indexes HTML documents and connections between them, temporarily ordering those documents for functional use, and tracking user interaction with that ordering to improve future functionality.

Of course, one may then justifiably inquire as to the relative distinction between the corporate entity of Google and the academic entity of MOAC and/or its member institutions, but doing so is practically futile. Since these institutions, or more specifically their dispersed archival databases, are enacted within *aggregated data representations*, it is clearly impossible to pinpoint a border, a boundary,

---

10   Museums and the Online Archive of California, http://www.bampfa.berkeley.edu/moac/search.html, accessed July 2008.

11   Guenter Waibel, 'MOAC Standards and Specifications' (2003), http://www.bampfa.berkeley.edu/moac/classic/bpg.html, accessed July 2008.

12   Galloway, *Protocol*, p. 95.

between them. Each is simultaneously an independent *archive* and part of another *archive*, though they are performed differently depending on user desire/action, computational code and degrees of access. What might this zone of indistinction do to the supposedly hallowed sanctity of the art-historical and/or museological *archive*? It could certainly be argued that connecting museological *archives* to the global network and making their meta/data accessible for aggregation, via standardized protocols, such as identification numbers, and transport carriers, such as RSS, opens those institutions, and the cultural memory they enshrine, to commercial exploitation and political manipulation. To make such an argument, however, one must completely overlook the extensive, and now well-documented, historic correlation between, for example, museological *archives*, anthropological and art-historical discourses, and colonization. *Archives* have, in point of fact, always been open to exploitation. It is certainly true that, as David Weinberger has pointed out, 'unique identifiers don't just provide a way to pull information together. They also allow information to be dispersed.'[13] However, and especially in the age of *Networked Digital Archives*, this dispersal is open not only to appropriation by dominant powers, as has historically been the case, but also by subaltern and/or diasporic groups looking to reclaim their representation by countering the objectivizing gaze of those institutions and discourses. As bell hooks has asserted, 'the ability to manipulate one's gaze in the face of structures of domination that would contain it, opens up the possibility of agency'.[14]

If, as Steven Nelson has posited, 'representation is the starting point for the construction of the subject', then it must also be the case that agency takes place in, and through, self-representation.[15] Though typically portraiture, or possibly first-person narrative, comes to mind when imagining self-representation, these are by no means the only methods for doing so. As any user of social networking websites could tell you, organizing objects (digital or otherwise) is an equally effective form of self-representation. These ordered objects 'form a syntagmatic array of physical signs in a spatial representation of identity', which Jennifer González calls an *autotopography*.[16] As such, a *Networked Digital Archive* that opens itself to dispersal, making its meta/data available for intra-archival and inter-archival mash-ups, affords the opportunity for constructing newly empowered subjectivities, partly because these new *aggregated data (self-)representations* simultaneously

13   David Weinberger, *Everything is Miscellaneous: The Power of the New Digital Disorder* (New York, 2007), p. 127.

14   bell hooks, *Black Looks: Race and Representation* (Boston: South End Press, 1992), p. 116.

15   Steve Nelson, 'Emancipation and the Freed in American Sculpture: Race, Representation, and the Beginnings of an African American History of Art', in Elizabeth Mansfield (ed.), *Art History and Its Institutions: Foundations of a Discipline* (London, 2002), p. 288.

16   Jennifer González, 'Autotopographies', in Gabriel Brahm Jr and Mark Driscoll (eds), *Prosthetic Territories: Politics and Hypertechnologies* (Boulder, 1995), p. 133.

reach back to incorporate, and therefore revise, imposed subjectivities regulated by disciplinary institutions as manifest by the institutionally controlled meta/data.

To read and to write: Submitting to the *networked digital archive*

The agency to construct and act *through* self-representations, however, is predicated on the ability to write, not just read, meta/data. Therefore, a *networked digital archive*, opened up for dispersal and aggregation, by definition folds together the two archival identities of *Archivist* and *User*. The newly constituted *User-Archivist* does not just consume the meta/data of the *Archive*, but produces them as well. Instead of proceeding or following the *Archive*, the *User-Archivist* simultaneously encapsulates it. The *Archive* is set free from its moorings. It moves. It comes alive. As it does so, the *User-Archivist* is objectified by the newly subjectivized *Archive*. As object, as representation, the *User-Archivist* enters the *Archive*, which has apparently not lost its appetite. Theoretically, this is dangerous territory. Extropian dreamers have long proposed a trans-human upload of a disembodied subject into the mainframe of the *Network*, as imag(in)ed in numerous cyberpunk novels and films like William Gibson's *Neuromancer* or the Wachowski Brothers' *Matrix*.

This is in no way what I suggest occurs in the transactional exchange between the *User-Archivist* and the *Networked Digital Archive*. In fact, my assertion is not even anything extraordinarily new or innately digital. When, prior to the ubiquitous employment of digital technologies in museum collections, an *archivist* would, using nothing more complicated than a piece of paper and pencil, write an entry in a collection's finding aid (the museological equivalent of a library's card catalogue), that material inscription became a part of the museum's *archive*. Anyone familiar with that *archivist*'s handwriting, could, on future reference, identify the individual who had composed that description. The corporeal world is so bloated with meta/data that involuntary information is always appended to the material products of voluntary actions. The first *archivist* was thus, if involuntarily, represented materially in the *archive*. This is only possible because the *archivist*'s body/self was materially connected to what Maurice Merleau-Ponty calls the '*flesh-of-the-world*'.[17] In other words, to be an *archivist* means to be materially represented in an *archive*. Considering the mediated, some might go so far as to claim virtual, nature of interaction with digital technologies, it is easy to believe that the material continuity between a *user-archivist* and a *networked digital archive* would be disrupted and that, without a shared materiality, representative inscription could not occur. In fact, just the opposite seems to be true. The appetite of the *Networked Digital Archive* is so hyper-voracious that (in)voluntary representations are perpetually absorbed, even if they are only partial and locationally deferred inscriptions. As such, to be a *user-archivist* means to be materially represented in a *networked digital archive* and to have that representation inscribed simply through use.

---

17 Maurice Merleau-Ponty, *The Visible and the Invisible* (Evanston, 1969).

That use, any use, enacts a change within the *Networked Digital Archive* (representationally on the screen, functionally in the code, and physically in the material medium of the computers involved). In the age of informational data flows, any reading of the *Networked Digital Archive* is simultaneously a writing to it; a chiasmic combination of machinic and operator actions. As Anna Munster points out in *Materializing New Media*:

> The more connected one is – through mobile phones that are internet enabled, through wireless technologies accessed via laptops and personal data assistants – the more 'access' one has to the world of information, and concomitantly, the more one is profiled, monitored and available for information itself.[18]

Simply searching or browsing through a *Networked Digital Archive* is likely to leave a digital trace, whether it is a line of digitized text in server logs or, increasingly, a row of meta/data within a relational database (typically to be operated upon in later actions to produce new *aggregated data (self-)representations* – as is the case when *User-Archivists* edit preferences, add items to a virtual cart/basket, create playlists, etc.). As Wendy Hui Kyong Chun has pointed out, 'all this is invisible to the user, whose gaze is focused on the representations before it, rather than on the ways in which it too is represented and circulated'.[19]

Despite the endless and simple recourse to terms such as 'virtual' or 'immaterial' in the popular, and even academic, literature regarding digital representations, it must be emphasized here that, like the shared *'flesh-of-the world'* that allowed an *archivist* to be represented in an *archive*, *User-Archivists* are materially co-spatial with digital technologies and, therefore, with *networked digital archives* and *aggregated data representations*. This phenomenon, called 'continuous materiality' by Kenneth Knoespe and Jichen Zhu, is manifested as:

> a wide spectrum of materiality activated by a hierarchy of codes that moves from 'lower' machine code to 'higher' readable computer languages and to codes in general (structural, legislative, social, cultural, etc). Each level of code engages natural language and the physical world in different ways, varying from the shifting voltage of computer circuits to our everyday activity.[20]

Like Judith Butler or the later Ludwig Wittgenstein, Knoespe and Zhu highlight the way language (signification) is intertwined with the physical world through

---

18   Anna Munster, *Materializing New Media: Embodiment in Information Aesthetics* (Hanover, 2006), p. 36.

19   Wendy Hui Kyong Chun, 'Scenes of Empowerment: Virtual Empowerment and Digital Divides', in *New York University Humanities Graduate Colloquium* (New York, 2001), p. 2.

20   Kenneth J. Knoespe and Jichen Zhu, 'Continuous Materiality: Through a Hierarchy of Computational Codes', *Fibreculture*, 11 (2007), p. 1.

'a hierarchy of codes'. This fusion of language and materiality does not stop at the fuzzy edge of *Networked Digital Archives* or even the information and communication technologies into which they are embedded, but rather augments, and is augmented by, the physical and social worlds with which those technologies are enmeshed. After all, as Butler points out 'the matter of bodies [is] indissociable from the regulatory norms that govern their materialization and the signification of those material effects'.[21]

This ongoing and dynamic bi-directional coupling, between human agent and information machine, has alternately been called *technophenomenology* by Jones and *emerging digital embodiment* by Munster. Either term suffices to describe the increasingly common experience of augmenting reality by experiencing distal phenomena through proximal transactions. Not unlike 'using a stick to feel your way in the dark', operating a computer involves acting *through* the machine, appending it to the embodied self.[22] Paul Dourish effectively explains this pseudo-cyborgian experience:

> Much of the time, I act *through* the mouse; the mouse is an extension of my hand as I select objects, operate menus, and so forth ... Sometimes, however, such as when I reach the edge of the mousepad and cannot move the mouse further, my orientation towards the mouse changes. Now, I become conscious of the mouse mediating my action, precisely because of the fact that it has been interrupted.[23]

Implied in the above example is not just that the human agent acts *through* the physical object of the mouse to move the cursor on the screen, but also that she acts *through* the cursor to operate the menus, and that she acts *through* the menus to navigate and/or activate information. Just as hands become coupled with the mouse or the keyboard, eyes become coupled with the representation(s) on the screen. In other words, 'there is no division between the embodied self and the image over there'.[24] While the *User-Archivist* is acting *through* the digital representations, including those of the objects within the museological *archive*, they are not separate from *the User-Archivist's* body/self, but an extension of their embodied intentionality.

As with any embodiment, this *emerging digital embodiment* can, and does, inscribe itself on the environment in which it lives. As the *User-Archivist* acts in, and *through* digital representation, traces of that activity remain, fixed into place by the very system that brought it into being. The *User-Archivist* is always, and simultaneously, submitting (donating) to, and submitting (surrendering) to, the *Networked Digital Archive*, but is rarely conscious of doing either. From the perspective of the *User-Archivist*, the *Networked Digital Archive* is a site of activity,

---

21   Judith Butler, *Bodies That Matter: On the Discursive Limits of 'Sex'* (London: 1993), p. 2.
22   Dourish, *Where the Action Is*, p. 120.
23   Ibid., p. 109.
24   Jones, *Self/Image*, p. 9.

of coming into presence, not a locus of preservation. Unless purposely performing for the camera, as do the Surveillance Camera Players, a museum visitor caught on CCTV is not trying to create or preserve a record, she is simply living. That doesn't stop her representation, however, from being fixed in the *Archive*. In the *Networked Digital Archive*, these fixations, which Philip Agre calls 'grammars of action', are, by definition, mediated inscriptions, more like tyre tracks than fingerprints.[25]

As with the now ubiquitous CCTV record, these mediated inscriptions are finding their way into museological *archives*. Sebastian Chan has been at the forefront of implementing this kind of integrated system at the Powerhouse Museum in Australia. As he explains, 'when a visitor searches the database, intentional data is recorded – the search term entered and the object selected by the user are recorded in a search table along with a datestamp'.[26] Per his description, a possible record in this search table would look something like these: 'chinese', '127548', '2009-06-20'. As a representation of the complex couplings that take place as visitors to the museum website stroke their keyboards and caress their mice, this set of encoded meta/data leaves much to be desired. It does not even transform action into legibility, as would, say a photograph. Instead, like the inscription itself, and reminiscent of Lisa Gitelman's discussion of Thomas Edison's phonographic records, its legibility is a mediated one.[27]

In the example from the Powerhouse Museum discussed above, it is clear that no *user-archivist* (except perhaps for the server administrator) will ever experience/read the meta/data directly, but rather will (re)experience/(re)read it as it is manifested in *aggregated data representations*. Chan makes this quite clear, in fact, stating that '"frictionless serendipity" is provided by user tracking; the aggregate behavior of visitors to the site is used to make further recommendations based on actual behavior'.[28] This can be seen, for example, in the proportional scale of the text in a tag-cloud, which signifies the popularity of that label as measured by an algorithmic meta-search of the user-aggregated terms. A side-effect of this mediated legibility is that the creation of meta/data for aggregation has as much effect on *aggregated data representations* as computational algorithms. For all intents and purposes, then, the *User-Archivist* could be understood as a co-programmer, or even a hacker.

---

25   Philip E. Agre, 'Surveillance and Capture: Two Models of Privacy', in Noah Wardrip-Fruin and Nick Montfort (eds), *The New Media Reader* (Cambridge, 2003), p. 754.

26   Sebastian Chan, 'Tagging and Searching – Serendipity and Museum Collection Databases', in J. Trant and D. Bearman (eds), *Museums and the Web 2007: Proceedings* (Toronto, 2007), p. 5.

27   Lisa Gitelman, *Always Already New: Media, History, and the Data of Culture* (Cambridge, 2006), pp. 18–19.

28   Chan, 'Tagging and Searching', p. 8.

It may be the case that, as Galloway has suggested, 'code is the only language that is executable.'[29] However, what code executes is simply the layer of code beneath it in the 'hierarchy of codes'. When the source code written in a scripting language such as PHP is activated on a server, it is translated into bytecode, which is then converted into machine code, which is then physically executed by the server's central processing unit. As Galloway himself continues, 'it is wrong to make claims about the relative purity of machine code over source code, for each is equally mediated by the environment of the digital computer'.[30] Might it not also be wrong to make claims about the relative purity of source code over what we might call surface code? As Cindy Cohn and James Grimmelman point out, 'Some people code in C++; others code in HTML – but there are also those who "code" in a language of pull-down menus and icons.'[31] As with all protocols, this coding is constrained by the limitations of the protocol beneath it in the hierarchy. However, by that same logic, it also sets limits on the protocols resulting from its execution, i.e. the *aggregated data representations* produced from the assemblage of dispersed meta/data.[32]

The location of meta/data and access to order

Within such a system, *User-Archivists* are not simply victims of disciplinary, panoptic surveillance. Their actions, bodily produced and representationally enacted, are, through individual and collective repetition, performatively constituted – enframed by, but not necessarily constrained by, the system. Digital inscription in the *Networked Digital Archive* is the process of the subject becoming object in order to become subject again, (re)enacted through *aggregated data representations*. As such, all *User-Archivist* action, filtered through the computer as digital representation, is thus a kind of speech-act, a performative utterance. Importantly, this should not be seen only to include the (in)voluntary inscriptions resulting directly from a *User-Archivist*'s actions, but also the existing inscriptions that are coupled with those actions. Mark Poster makes this clear in his analysis of object digitization, the necessary first step in opening up meta/data (museological or otherwise) for aggregation:

> When cultural objects are digitized, they take on certain characteristics of spoken language. Like an oral sentence or a song, digitized voice is easily and with little

---

29   Galloway, *Protocol*, p. 165.

30   Ibid., p. 167.

31   Cindy A. Cohn and James Grimmelman, 'Seven Ways in Which Code Equals Law (And One in Which It Does Not)', in *Ars Electronica 2003: Code: The Language of Our Time* (Linz, 2003), p. 22.

32   Galloway, *Protocol*, p. 10.

cost reproduced by the networked computer user. We do not say of someone who repeats a sentence out loud that he or she is a consumer of that sentence.[33]

Navigating through the website interfaces that commonly function to connect museum visitors to online representations of archival material is perpetually a phenomenon of the present and of presence. Digitized cultural objects, represented as image and textual meta/data, are simultaneously the product of the viewing subject and the production of that subject as object. A DJ, scratching a pre-recorded music track and/or mixing it with other pre-recorded tracks, produces a new musical object and produces herself as a musician. In this age of *Networked Digital Archives*, Poster asserts 'individuals are now constituted as subjects in relation to these complex information systems: they are points in circuits of language-image flows; they are, in short, textualized agents'.[34]

As textualized agents, writers of meta/data, coders of information flows, the *User-Archivist* exists for others, and for herself, not unlike the Foucauldian Author-Function does, as a subjectivized identity assembled through the *text* assumed to be the product of her actions. Galloway highlights this similarity when he claims:

> On the Internet there is no reason to know the name of a particular user, only to know what that user likes, where they shop, where they live, and so on. The clustering of descriptive information around a specific user becomes sufficient to explain the identity of that user.[35]

Of course, by its very nature, the *Networked Digital Archive* is constantly excluding information from being written and from being read, from being inscribed and from being processed. In this *selective accessibility*, new kinds of normatively visible, and monstrously invisible, identities are constru(ct)ed.

The asymmetry of this accessibility has led Heather Murray correctly to worry, with regard to the machine-readable bodies of biometric technologies, 'what kind of subculture of outcasts might be formed not by those who chose not to participate, but rather by those who are prevented from participating by the technology?'[36] Just taking discrepancies in biometric readings into account, it is clear that the simplistic formula of a sufficiently substitutive *data double* needs to be unpacked. The *User-Archivist* is, after all, by nature of her embodied coupling with digital representations, also an *aggregated data representation* – multiple, dispersed and fragmented by levels of access. The *data double(s)*, then,

---

33   Mark Poster, *Information Please: Culture and Politics in the Age of Digital Machines* (Durham, NC, 2006), p. 244.

34   Mark Poster, 'Textual Agents: History at "The End of History"', in John Carlos Rowe (ed.), *'Culture' and the Problem of the Disciplines* (New York, 1998), p. 204.

35   Galloway, Protocol, p. 69.

36   Heather Murray, 'Monstrous Play in Negative Spaces: Illegible Bodies and the Cultural Construction of Biometric Technology', *The Communication Review*, 10/4 (2007), p. 351.

are projections, as Michel Foucault explains, 'our way of handling texts; in the comparisons we make, the traits we extract as pertinent, the continuities we assign, or the exclusions we practice'.[37]

As such, there is not one singular *data double* produced through these assemblages, but many, each distinctly different depending on levels of access, and each one only momentarily valid while it is assembled. As Kevin Haggerty and Richard Ericson contend, 'Data doubles circulate in a host of different centers of calculation and serve as markers for access to resources, services, and power in ways which are often unknown to its referent.'[38] The impact of this dispersion means that meta/data accumulate in different *Networked Digital Archives* across the *Network* and meta/data accumulate differently at these various sites. Within the *Networked Digital Archive*, access provides what Derrida calls the *différance* through which meaning is, at least temporarily, made manifest.

Due to the dynamic and fragmentary nature of this system, the assumed uni-directional relationship between data and metadata must be challenged. It is common for those working with it to describe metadata as 'data about data'. Such a formula, however, is remarkably similar to the (now generally defunct) structuralist assumptions about the relationship between the significer and the signified. Within the physical space of the museum, it is clear that the old structuralist model reigns supreme. The wall-text describes the object on display, rarely the other way around. However, in the *Networked Digital Archive*, the 'miscellaneous order' as Weinberger calls it, 'the only distinction between metadata and data is that metadata is what you already know and data is what you're trying to find out'.[39] All data is, in effect, meta/data. The museological object, therefore, need not be seen as the static data around which the institutional metadata must gravitate.

Folksonomic tagging, for example, provides much-needed alternatives, or at least augmentations, to the rigid classification structures commonly used in museological *archives*.[40] Objects, and/or their representative data records (ignoring, for a second, that these are typically treated as synonymous), that would never be associated with one another using traditional archival methodologies can be associated *through* the palimpsest of folksonomic tags provided by *User-Archivists*. *User-Archivist*-submitted meta/data does not just connect objects, however. 'These connections define an implicit relationship between resources through the users that tag them; similarly, users are connected by the resources

---

37   Michel Foucault, 'What is an Author?', in Donald Preziosi (ed.), *The Art of Art History* (Oxford, 1998), p. 307.

38   Kevin Haggerty and Richard V. Ericson, 'The Surveillant Assemblage', *British Journal of Sociology*, 51/4 (2000), p. 613.

39   Weinberger, *Everything is Miscellaneous*, p. 104.

40   Jennifer Trant et al., 'The Eye of the Beholder: steve.museum and Social Tagging of Museum Collections', in J. Trant and D. Bearman (eds), *International Cultural Heritage Informatics Meeting (ICHIM07): Proceedings* (Toronto, 2007).

they tag.'[41] In the first instance, the (digital) objects functioned as the data the folksonomic metadata was describing. In the second instance, the (digital) objects were performed as the metadata describing the *User-Archivists* that tagged them. The same contextualized relationships could be deduced from the 'frictionless serendipity' provided by tracking *User-Archivists'* movements through the *Networked Digital Archive* itself. Whether voluntary or not, the *User-Archivist* creates *lines of desire* as she moves through the *Networked Digital Archive*, inscribing associations between digital objects and between those digital objects and herself, and, in the process, disrupting the canonical pathways through the *Networked Digital Archive*.

Practicing the *Archive*, disrupting the *Canon* and (s)mashing up the museum(s)

Unlike the disinterested Kantian viewer, the *User-Archivist* is always already materially connected to the object(s) of her desire within the museological *archive*. Clicking on a link, tagging an image – both are akin to identifying a *punctum* in the *Networked Digital Archive*, establishing a network of attraction. It is through these *punctums*, these holes, that the art-historical canon starts to leak. The Barthesian *punctum* is, after all, as Jones explains, 'a leak that manifests the uncontainability of meaning within the image (and of identity within the body)'.[42] Simply navigating the museological *archive*, then, can be a tactical practice (*à la* de Certeau), a 'resistance from within'. As in the urban environment, where *lines of desire* are 'the routes that people insert into the landscape that amend, oppose, and reconfigure paths designed by planners, bureaucrats, and other city officials', the *User-Archivist's lines of desire* co-opt and reconfigure the established order of things.[43]

If, as Preziosi contends, museological *archives* have traditionally been organized to 'construe the significance of works as a function of their *relative position* in an unfolding historical or genealogical scheme of development', then the museum of the self, the representational *autotopography* assembled from a *Networked Digital Archive*, or (s)mashed up from a combination thereof, inevitably challenges that institutional ordering.[44] As more *User-Archivists* practise the *Networked Digital Archive*, *lines of desire* cross and intertwine, becoming new *aggregated data*

---

41   Cameron Marlow et al., 'HT06, Tagging Paper, Taxonomy, Flickr, Academic Article, ToRead', in *Proceedings of Hypertext 2006* (New York, 2006), p. 2.

42   Jones, *Self/Image*, p. 54.

43   Janna Graham and Shadya Yasin, 'Reframing Participation in the Museum: A Syncopated Discussion', in Griselda Pollock and Joyce Zemans (eds), *Museums After Modernism: Strategies of Engagement* (Oxford, 2007), p. 159.

44   Donald Preziosi, 'Art History: Making the Visible Legible', in Donald Preziosi (ed.), *The Art of Art History* (Oxford, 1998), p. 16.

(collective-)representations, new canonical pathways, new *lieux de memoire*. The leak opened up by *User-Archivist punctums* begins to seep into the system, into the art-historical *archive*. For Irit Rogoff, seepage is the ideal metaphor to describe the theoretical space in which criticality is possible:

> By seepage, we mean the action of many currents of fluid material leaching on to a stable structure, entering and spreading through it by way of pores, until it becomes a part of the structure, both in terms of its surface and at the same time continues to act on its core, to gradually disaggregate its solidity. To crumple it over time with moisture.[45]

The *art-historical archive*, when enacted as the *Networked Digital Archive*, can only be materially resisted and remade from within the archival network itself. In discussing the theoretical entity of the *Archive*, Derrida claimed, 'what is no longer archived in the same way is no longer lived in the same way'.[46] For the *Networked Digital Archive*, the opposite also seems to hold true: what is no longer lived in the same way is no longer archived in the same way either.

---

45   Rogoff, 'Smuggling', p. 5.
46   Derrida, *Archive Fever*, p. 18.

Chapter 9
Internet Art History 2.0

Charlotte Frost

The unwritten can often loom larger than the written, and certainly makes its presence felt in and around the positives to its perceived negative. Giorgio Agamben has it that all writing alludes to its absent other half:

> Every written work can be regarded as the prologue (or rather, the broken cast) of a work never penned, and destined to remain so, because later works, which in turn will be the prologues or the moulds for other absent works, represent only sketches or death masks. The absent work, although it is unplaceable in any precise chronology, thereby constitutes the written works as prolegomena or paralipomena of a non-existent text; or, in a more general sense, as a parerga which find their true meaning only in the context of an illegible ergon. To take Montaigne's fine image, these are the frieze of grotesques around an unpainted portrait, or, in the spirit of the pseudo-Platonic letter, the counterfeit of a book which cannot be written.[1]

Interest in the unwritten has long been a popular critical tool. In the late 1990s net artist Vuk Cosic simulated a set of monographs missing from art history departmental libraries the world over with *Classics of net.art*[2] (1997) (see Plate 9.1). While the fantastical collection of non-existent tomes from 'The Official History of net.art Volume II' included works on many prolific internet (net) artists including Alexei Shulgin, the duo Joan Heemskerk and Dirk Paesmans (better known as Jodi), and Heath Bunting, the tongue-in-cheek 'blurb' for his own 'non-o-graph' read: '[o]ne of the world's most celebrated net.artists, Vuk Cosic, has dedicated much of his life's work to global communication, international understanding, and world peace. This motivation is reflected in imagery that flows throughout his art, and in his numerous contributions of works of art for humanitarian purposes.'[3] In general, this piece has been regarded as a 'one liner' commenting on the art-historical deficit which has on one hand burdened and on the other compelled net art practice from the start. However, by both asking after net art's missing art histories and answering its own question it critiques the hegemony of art-historical

---

1 Giorgio Agamben, *Infancy and History: Essays on the Destruction of Experience* (London, 1993), p. 3.

2 http://www.ljudmila.org/~vuk/books, accessed July 2008.

3 http://www.ljudmila.org/~vuk/books, accessed July 2008.

discourse. By connoting conundrums such as: who needs print when you have hypertext and why write *mono*graphs on artists who work collectively, it troubles the very concept of art history, making it seem antiquated and outmoded in light of online art production and reception.

But there is something more that this work does not say. By demonstrating the *wider* implications of net art's art-historical absenteeism, by 'problematizing' art history, this chapter will address the question of whether net art might be successfully deployed in an exposure of art history's latent problem with technology. By this means it may be possible to demonstrate how net art might be used in order to provoke a deconstruction of art history that will reveal its own art-historical value. To begin, a brief illustration of net art's story so far will be useful.

Net art history

Twenty-five years after the inception of the internet, art and the internet met. Critic Robert Atkins marks the mid-1990s as a seminal moment for art history:

> Future art historians will mark the 1994–5 season as the year that the art world went online. Art buffs with the requisite computer-and-modem hardware and internet access could discuss the Whitney Biennial and Lacanian theory, inspect an international array of museum schedules, search the International Repertory of the Literature of Art (RILA), and peruse auction prices from Sotheby's and Christie's. They could also view artworks – some for sale and others designed for electronic, interactive formats – by artists ranging from paleolithic daubers to Laurie Anderson.[4]

It was also around this time that geographically disparate pockets of artists, activists and interested amateurs discovered the potential inherent in championing cyberspace as a context for artistic practice, and net art was born. Although, as Josephine Bosma notes, focusing entirely on this period as the genesis of net art seems a little short-sighted, in that it drew from a rich history of related art forms. She explains:

> A history of research and development in net art probably should begin long before the development of the internet in the late 1980s. In effect most key issues in net art were dealt with in earlier art practices or disciplines, be it writing, cinema, radio art, sound art, music, kinetic art, conceptual art, the performing arts, mail art, digital art or video art. The novelty of net art lies in the amplification and realization of earlier art concepts in a new, personalized media field.[5]

---

4   Robert Atkins, 'The Art World (and I) Go On Line', *Art in America*, 83/12 (1995): 58.
5   Josephine Bosma, 'Net Art: Building Something out of Nothing: Self Education, Collaboration and Networking' (2005), http://laudanum.net/cgi-bin/media.cgi?action=display&id=1118750062, accessed July 2008.

Yet it remains possible to say that around 1994, early works of net art were being created, including: *The World's First Collaborative Sentence*[6] (1994) by Douglas Davis, *King's Cross Phone In*[7] (1994) by Heath Bunting and *The File Room*[8] (1994) by Antonio Muntadas.

The early phase of net art activity was dominated by a band of artists who used a collective title for their work which replicated protocol for naming computer files, calling their work 'net.art'. The origin of the term has often been credited to Pit Schultz, although net.art mythology has it that Cosic received it in an accidentally encrypted email, as Rachel Greene explains:

> The term 'net.art' is less a coinage than an accident, the result of a software glitch that occurred in December 1995, when Slovenian artist Vuk Cosic opened an anonymous e-mail only to find it had been mangled in transmission. Amid a morass of alphanumeric gibberish, Cosic could make out just one legible term – 'net.art' – which he began using to talk about online art and communications.[9]

As the original source of this story was fellow net.artist Alexei Shulgin,[10] it is likely that it can be considered a piece of net.art in its own right. Despite its dubious origins, however, the name was speedily adopted by a number of artists active at the time including: Rachel Baker, Natalie Bookchin, Heath Bunting, Vuk Cosic, Olia Lialina, Alexei Shulgin and collectives: etoy, Jodi and RTMark (amongst many others). Overall, net.art might be described as the emergent, experimental or 'beta' phase of development (often known, mainly by the self-styled net.artists themselves, as the Heroic Period), which precedes the wider field of 'net art' (which drops the dot), although sometimes the two terms are used interchangeably.

Many discursive online arenas inspired and instigated net art creativity. At first the Bulletin Board System (BBS) was a popular networking tool. This was a result of the parallel and non-ARPANet-based Usenet initiative, set up originally for colleges excluded from ARPANet, and providing remote access to online 'news groups'. In 1991 a BBS entitled THING,[11] which was founded by the artist Wolfgang Staehle, became one of the original art-orientated online discussion arenas. Soon after this, however, email mailing lists or list serves/servs (email-based discussion groups managed by software applications that automate the forwarding of content to subscribers), began to dominate discourse development in the online arts arena. Even though chat rooms were becoming popular with other internet enthusiasts,

---

6   http://artport.whitney.org/collection/davis/Sentence/sentence1.html, accessed July 2008.

7   http://www.irational.org/cybercafe/xrel.html, accessed July 2008.

8   http://www.thefileroom.org, accessed July 2008.

9   Rachel Greene, 'Web Work: A History of Internet Art', *Artforum*, 38/9 (2000): 162.

10   http://amsterdam.nettime.org/Lists-Archives/nettime-l-9703/msg00094.html, accessed July 2008.

11   http://www.thing.net, accessed July 2008.

for the net art community, net culture lists including nettime,[12] founded in 1995; The Syndicate;[13] Rhizome; and the long-defunct 7–11; facilitated the core of the community's communication.

Net art production and discussion were speedily followed by the creation of websites dedicated to consolidating the collective efforts of the net art community through central, well-resourced sites known as portals. The first net art portal – and one which remains integral to the net art network today – was Rhizome.[14] This was founded in the US in 1998 by Mark Tribe, on the back of his successful aforementioned mailing list, which had originated in Berlin two years previously. To develop the portal side of operations, Tribe added the Artbase, an ever-expanding catalogue of net artworks organized via searchable terms (such as title, or thematic keyword); the Textbase, a critical equivalent of the Artbase; and hired several additional members of staff, including Rachel Greene and Alex Galloway. Other versions of the net art portal also setting up cyber-camp included Furtherfield.org,[15] which began in 1997 in the UK and originally operated from the founders' (Marc Garrett and Ruth Catlow's) home in London. Meanwhile, seemingly now defunct portals including hell.com (1995–8),[16] Low-Fi[17] (2001–2008) and Discordia (2003–2004)[18] had also staked their claim on the proliferation and presentation of net art and net art discourse.

Offline art and technology centres and discursive arenas were also forming and engaging with net art. Large centres such as Der Zentrum fur Kunst und Medientechnologie (ZKM) in Karlsruhe, Germany, opened in 1989, and Tokyo's Intercommunication Centre (ICC), opened in 1997. Smaller venues, equally instrumental in net art's ascent, such as Postmasters and Eyebeam, both in New York, and production venues like Backspace in London and Ljudmila in Ljubljana also arrived on the scene. Relevant conferences began to be held across the globe, such as The Next 5 Minutes (N5M), which was first held in Amsterdam in 1993, and Beauty and the East, held in 1997 in Ljubljana, which united the nettime community for 'f2f' (face to face) discussion. In fact, net art was increasingly an element of the conference/festival – and soon even the biennale – scene. Ars Electronica, held since 1979 in Linz, Austria, and the globe-trotting International Symposium on Electronic Art – now the Inter-Society for Electronic Arts (ISEA), enthusiastically added it to their line-up in the mid-1990s, and in 1997 even Documenta took it on.

There was also a short-lived period in which art galleries and museums were amenable to net and new media art curators. In 1996 Beryl Graham curated 'Serious

---

12 http://amsterdam.nettime.org, accessed July 2008.
13 http://sympa.anart.no/sympa/info/syndicate, accessed July 2008.
14 http://www.rhizome.org, accessed July 2008.
15 http://www.furtherfield.org, accessed July 2008.
16 http://www.hell.com, accessed July 2008.
17 http://www.low-fi.org.uk, accessed July 2008.
18 http://www.discordia.us/scoop, accessed July 2008.

Games: Art, Interaction, Technology' at the Laing Art Gallery (Newcastle) and Barbican Art Gallery in London. This was followed in 1998 by 'Beyond Interface', curated by Steve Dietz at the Walker Art Center in Minneapolis. Later, in 2001, Tate Britain hosted 'Art Now: Art and Money Online' in London, an exhibition devised and curated by Julian Stallabrass. Of more renown perhaps, were the exhibitions 'net_condition', at the ZKM in 1999, '010101: Art in Technological Times', held in 2001 at the San Francisco Museum of Modern Art, and 'Bitstreams', also in 2001, at the Whitney Museum of American Art in New York. Although as critic Tilman Baumgartel noted: 'these exhibitions only showed a small portion of ... a lively Net art scene'.[19]

As a safer and easier foray into net art, some institutions introduced their own online arts portals. The Walker Art Center in Minneapolis operated a new media arts portal from 1997 to 2003 known as Gallery9,[20] which was curated by Steve Dietz. The Whitney Museum of American Art followed suit and set up Artport[21] in 2001, under the management of curator Christiane Paul, and in 2003 the New Museum of Contemporary Art, also in New York, added a net art portal to their collection by acquiring Rhizome. In the UK, Tate Modern's approach was somewhat different, beginning in 2000 when they commissioned a member of the Mongrel collective, Graham Harwood, to create a piece of net art for the opening of Tate Modern and the Tate website. The controversial work: *Uncomfortable Proximity* (2000), also known as *Tate Mongrel*,[22] became something of a 'net art baptism of fire' given its critique of the organization, but it pushed Tate curators into grappling with the field and they have continued this commitment.[23]

In 1999, however, the niche of net.art was pronounced dead by many of its central figures. In an article called 'net.art Year in Review: State of net.art 99',[24] Alex Galloway stated:

> Net.art (the jodi-vuk-shulgin-bunting style) was the product of a particular technological constraint: low bandwidth. Net.art is low bandwidth through and through. We see it in ASCII art, form art, HTML conceptualism – anything that can fit easily through a modem. As computers and bandwidth improve, the primary physical reality that governed the aesthetic space of net.art begins to fall away.[25]

---

19 Tilman Baumgartel, *net.art 2.0: New Materials Towards Net Art* (Nuremberg, 2001), p. 10.

20 http://gallery9.walkerart.org, accessed July 2008.

21 http://artport.whitney.org, accessed July 2008.

22 http://www.tate.org.uk/netart/mongrel, accessed July 2008.

23 http://www.tate.org.uk/intermediaart, accessed July 2008.

24 Alex Galloway, 'net.art Year in Review: State of net.art 99', *Switch*, 5/3 (1999).

25 Ibid.

This period was not characterized by a decline in net art activity per se, but rather (as the above quotation also implies), the maturing of the technologies involved and the emergence of a more varied aesthetic. Access to technology also improved and another main feature of this period of change was a sharp increase in artists working within or tangentially to the field. While this may in part have caused the disbanding of the group of artists most associated with the movement of net.art, whose monopoly on the field was crowded out, there was certainly no abrupt end to internet-based art activity. In fact, world events, such as the war in Yugoslavia, and the events in New York on 11 September 2001, had a significant impact on online artists' communities. This was coupled with a global economic down-turn which forced art institutions to be more frugal – with non-commercial art hardest hit. The Walker Art Center responded, for example, by making new media curator Steve Dietz redundant, while Rhizome introduced a highly controversial membership fee. So, although the late 1990s and early 2000s witnessed the end of the glory days of net.art, net art remained active.

Until very recently, however, net art appeared to have been entirely omitted from the history of art in terms of published literature. In 2001, artist and critic Walter van der Cruijsen noted that while the internet was receiving a great deal of attention, its relation to art history had gone largely unannounced:

> Over the last few years an incredible range of books, readers, syllabi, zines and other printed media have been published on the rise of the internet. However, only a few have been publishing what we refer to as net.art. The new forms of art that come with technology still have to be described, not only from an art-historical perspective, but also within the context of media culture itself.[26]

Indeed, despite its huge output, net art has failed to engage art historians. Although this situation is gradually changing, material remains sparse.

The earliest collection of print-published net art history can be found in the UK-based publication *Mute*. Originally subtitled the 'art and technology newspaper', it has featured a range of articles focusing on net art history, including those by critics Josephine Berry and Josephine Bosma.[27] At the same time that *Mute* introduced net art critique, critic Tilman Baumgartel was engaged in compiling a set of interviews with net artists such as Douglas Davis, John F. Simon Jnr, Jodi, Lisa Jevbratt and 0100101110101101.org (01.org). Although many of these interviews had originally been created and circulated online, they were soon published as a compendium in German in 1999, and in English and German in an

---

26   Walter van der Cruijsen, 'Working Conditions', in Peter Weibel and Timothy Druckrey (eds), *net_condition: Art and Global Media* (Cambridge, MA, 2001), p. 367.

27   Josephine Berry, 'Art is Useless', *Mute*, 13 (1999): 52–7; Josephine Berry, 'Do As They Do, Not As They Do', *Mute*, 16 (2000): 22–3; Josephine Berry, 'Repeat and Win', *Mute*, 22 (2001): 58–9; Josephine Bosma, 'Is it Commercial? Noooo … Is it Spam? Nooo – its net.art!', *Mute*, 10 (1998): pp. 73–4.

extended version in 2001, under the title *net.art 2.0: New Materials Towards Net Art*.[28] Baumgartel's book was followed by Rachel Greene's 2000 article on the history of net art for *Artforum*,[29] which went on to form the basis of her own book, *Internet Art*,[30] which Greene was commissioned to write as part of the Thames and Hudson 'World of Art' series of introductory texts to art movements. Just prior to this, art historian Julian Stallabrass and Tate Press released an account of net art, entitled *Internet Art: The Online Clash of Culture and Commerce*.[31] There has also been a scattering of publications dealing with the wider field of new media art that address net art to some degree.[32]

Although the charge that net art might simply be too young to be *historicized* as such has weight, the question of whether net art's apparent absence in the annals of art history might be used to indicate something about art history itself should be considered. For example, 'absent art history' is a concept that has been addressed in the work of art historian Linda Nochlin as a means to analyse the nature of art-historical discourse.

The 'absent art history' approach

In her 1971 essay 'Why Have There Been No Great Women Artists?',[33] Nochlin used the situation compounding a distinct lack of accounts of women artists in the history of art to reason that art-historical discourse had been structured in such a way as to facilitate the disavowal of women artists. She explained, for example, that art history had relied upon the idea that great art was produced by people who were somehow genetically predisposed to producing work of an exceptionally high standard, and that this genetic predisposition was allegedly located in men only. But she went on to demonstrate how this notion, which she termed the 'golden-nugget theory of genius',[34] papered over the reality of the situation, which was that high standards of art were actually produced by artists who had been heavily trained, and that such training had only been available to men. In order that women artists should no longer be subordinate to a system that automatically devalued their output, Nochlin set out to devalue the art-historical systems instead.

---

28   Baumgartel, net.art 2.0.

29   Greene, 'Web Work', pp. 162–7, 192.

30   Greene, *Internet Art* (London, 2004).

31   Julian Stallabrass, *Internet Art: The Online Clash of Culture and Commerce* (London, 2003).

32   These have included: Christiane Paul, *Digital Art* (London, 2003); Tom Corby (ed.), *Network Art: Practices and Positions* (London, 2005); Joline Blais and Jon Ippolito, *At the Edge of Art* (London, 2006); Mark Tribe and Reena Jana, *New Media Art* (Cologne, 2006); Oliver Grau (ed.), *MediaArtHistories* (Cambridge, MA, 2007).

33   Linda Nochlin, 'Why Have There Been No Great Women Artists?' (1971), in Linda Nochlin, *Women, Art and Power and Other Essays* (London, 1989), pp.145–78.

34   Nochlin, pp. 155–6.

To do this, she showed how a question concerning a shortfall of women's art could actually be turned into a question about the shortfalls of historical discourse. She described how the technique might unfold:

> Even a simple question like 'Why have there been no great women artists?' can, if answered adequately, create a sort of chain reaction, expanding not merely to encompass the accepted assumptions of the single field, but outward to embrace history and the social sciences, or even psychology and literature, and thereby, from the outset, can challenge the assumption that the traditional divisions of intellectual inquiry are still adequate to deal with the meaningful questions of our time, rather than the merely convenient or self-generated ones.[35]

That is, she claimed that the answer to the question 'Why have there been no great women artists?' lay in challenging the very criteria used in determining art's historicity.

In a paper entitled 'Why Have There Been No Great Net Artists?',[36] which he gave as a talk at San Jose State University in 1999, Steve Dietz adopted some of Nochlin's ideas to compare net art's art-historical absence with that, formerly, of women artists. He found, for example, that networked practice challenges the still prevalent belief that art originates from a 'golden nugget' of lone (male) genius and encountered some of the reasons why net art had been ignored:

> The problem with net.art is that it is so opaque. The problem with net.art is that it is so obvious. The problem with net.art is that not everyone can see it. The problem with net.art is that it takes too long. The problem with net.art is that it's ephemeral. The problem with net.art is that it's too expensive. The problem with net.art is that anyone can make it. The problem with net.art is no one supports it. The problem with net.art is that it is being usurped. The problem with net. art is that it's boring. The problem with net.art is that it's too challenging. The problem with net.art is all those plug-ins. The problem with net.art is that it is so reliant on industry standards. The problem with net.art is that it's old hat. The problem with net.art is that it's too new. The problem is that there is no great net.art.[37]

Over all, Dietz's point, as in Nochlin's original essay, was that we should stop asking why some art does not fit into accounts of art history and continue to question exactly what it is we are trying to fit it into. As he put it: 'Rather than trying to assimilate net.art into our existing understanding of art history, there may

---

35   Ibid., pp. 146–7.

36   Later published as Steve Dietz, 'Why Have There Been No Great Net Artists?', in Lucy Kimbell (ed.), *New Media Art: Practice and Context in the UK 1994–2004*, (Manchester, 2004), pp. 74–82.

37   Ibid., p. 78.

be a way that it can be understood to problematize many of the very assumptions we take to be normal, if not natural.'[38] Therefore, for Dietz, net art also appeared to trouble art history, and missing net art, like missing art by women artists, offered a tool for undoing and examining aspects of its practice and processes. However, even taking the above into account and also asserting that net art can be used to determine the parameters of the discipline, the theory is not exactly a perfect fit.

Experiencing technical trouble

Net art (as shown by *Classics of net.art*)[39] is partly based on the original aim of interventionist, so-called 'new', and feminist art historians (among others) to test the belief systems bound by art institutions – and indeed tease academics. Therefore, although it does disenfranchise those without access to technology, its sphere of operation can hardly be described in the same exclusive terms as an art world before feminist intervention. Unlike the very literal lack of women artists Nochlin was referring to, net art represents a field absolutely bursting with artists; by widening the remit of what counts as art and championing techniques that require little to no formal training, the field of net art can be described as decidedly *in*clusive. But perhaps the most important reason Nochlin's ideas cannot be seamlessly transferred to the situation compounding a distinct lack of accounts of net artists in the history of art is because the web itself offers an abundance of net art contextual materials. Through mailing lists, portals, blogs, wikis and many other systems, the net art network has spawned a wealth of net art 'histories'. Thus, it is not that net art is under-analysed, but rather that its forms of art *and* context remain *equally* ignored.

Does Nochlin's approach uncover a much more fundamental way in which net art problematizes art history? It is surely in art history's failure to fully accommodate or analyse not just net art, but adjunct activities providing interpretation, documentation, curation, preservation, legitimization and critique, that yet another exclusive convention in art history can be revealed. It seems that net art indicates something much greater than its own overlooked oeuvre and that is art history's trouble with technology.

Thus far the art-historical system has encouraged the omission of art not just by women or net artists, for example, but a great deal of art involving any new or increased level of technology has also regularly been ignored. In her paper 'Art, Technology, and Postmodernism: Paradigms, Parallels, and Paradoxes',[40] art and technology theorist Margot Lovejoy explains that, on the whole, technological art has been disregarded in art-historical scholarship. She states:

---

38   Ibid., p. 75.

39   http://www.ljudmila.org/~vuk/books, accessed July 2008.

40   Margot Lovejoy, 'Art, Technology, and Postmodernism: Paradigms, Parallels, and Paradoxes', Art Journal, 49/3, *Computers and Art: Issues of Content* (1990): 257–65.

Although technological change and new tools have always influenced art, no mention of technology appears in most standard art history texts. In those by E. H. Gombrich, H. W. Janson, and H. H. Arnason, for example, the word is not even indexed.[41]

Charlie Gere, another theorist of the art and technology nexus, echoes Lovejoy's claim:

Since the beginning of the last century some artists have attempted to come to terms with the technological developments of their time, including those involving information-communication technologies; and, since the 1960s, artists have engaged seriously in the possibilities of real-time technologies for the making of art under various banners, including computer art, art and technology, new media art, and, most recently, net.art and internet art. On the whole such work has been ignored or marginalized by the mainstream art world and gallery system.[42]

While conferences such as 'Refresh!', held in Banff, Canada (and billed as the 'First International Conference on the Histories of Media Art, Science and Technology') and publications including *MediaArtHistories*[43] represent a growing interest in rectifying this situation, it remains the case that many of these attempts appear to build little more than a ghetto outside the main gates of art history proper.

Likewise, but even less noted, is the fact that the technologies of art history itself have remained almost completely invisible. That is, historiographical surveys of the discipline tend on the whole to describe the theories used and supported by art historians who have made a specific impact on the discipline. Art historian and historiographer Donald Preziosi describes what histories of art history generally entail:

Existing histories of art history have either been biographical and genealogical accounts of influential professionals, narrative accounts charting the evolution of theories of art (either in a vacuum or as unproblematic reflections of some broader spirit of an age, people, or place), or accounts of the development of various interpretative methodologies.[44]

So far, such accounts have failed to address the material technologies involved in making and recording these art-historical judgements in any sense other than as transparent, naturalized, pseudo-scientific instruments. The main reports on

---

41   Ibid., p. 257.

42   Charlie Gere, *Art, Time and Technology* (Oxford, 2006), p. 2.

43   Ed. Oliver Grau.

44   Donald Preziosi (ed.), *The Art of Art History: A Critical Anthology* (Oxford, 1998), p. 15.

the discipline, including: those by Vernon Hyde Minor,[45] Preziosi himself,[46] Eric Fernie,[47] and Michael Hatt and Charlotte Klonk,[48] also follow this trend and all but ignore the tools of the art historian's trade.

But if one considers the fact that it is not until the invention of photography, for example, that the discipline of art history as we generally understand it today was truly formed, such exemptions seem incongruous to say the least. In fact, despite later perpetuating the exclusion of art-historical technology from his own anthology of art-historical texts, in his earlier book *Rethinking Art History: Meditations on a Coy Science*, Preziosi emphatically opined how photography was responsible for art history:

> The powerful network of apparatuses constituting the modern discipline of art history presupposes the existence of photography. Indeed, art history as we know it today is the child of photography: From its beginnings as an academic discipline in the last quarter of the nineteenth century, filmic technologies have played a key role in analytic study, taxonomic ordering, and the creation of historical and genealogical narratives.[49]

Echoing this, in his essay addressing the impact of photography on the discipline, art historian Fredrick N. Bohrer has asked: '[c]ould there be art history without photography? Photography has arguably been *the* indispensable technology of modern art history.'[50] Robert S. Nelson, who concerned himself with the effect of slides on the lecturing system has noted:

> Art history is about two hundred years old, but only since the end of the nineteenth century have its practices begun to coalesce into normative patterns. Certainly an art lecture in 1900 was utterly different from one given a century before, the principal difference being the speaker's ability to illustrate and thus make present the work of art.[51]

45　Vernon Hyde Minor, *Art History's History* (New York, 1994).

46　Preziosi (ed.), *The Art of Art History*.

47　Eric Fernie (ed.), *Art History and Its Methods: A Critical Anthology* (London, 1995).

48　Michael Hatt and Charlotte Klonk, *Art History: A Critical Introduction to its Methods* (Manchester, 2006).

49　Donald Preziosi, *Rethinking Art History: Meditations on a Coy Science* (New Haven, 1989), p. 72.

50　Frederick N. Bohrer, 'Photographic Perspectives: Photography and the Institutional Formation of Art History', in Elizabeth Mansfield (ed.), *Art History and Its Institutions: Foundations of a Discipline* (London, 2002), p. 246.

51　Robert S. Nelson, 'The Slide Lecture, or the Work of Art History in the Age of Mechanical Reproduction', *Critical Inquiry*, 26/3 (2000), p. 422.

Yet such comments remain rare and despite their ubiquity, photographs (alongside other technical developments in the interpretation of artworks) have, in effect, been written out of art history.

Therefore it seems that the presence of technology has been successfully suppressed across the discipline of art history. Given the time, this finding might occasion a delve into the theories surrounding technics by Jacques Derrida, Friedrich A. Kittler and Bernard Stiegler,[52] to mention but a few. Suffice it here to say that in varying manners, these theorists have opined that technicity is a necessary element of historicity and they have sought to initiate technical accounts of the nature of being. What is being invoked here, however, is the possible link between the disavowed role of photography, for example, in art history, and net art's art-historical non-realization – while hinting at the eventual use of such theories in a technical assessment of the history of art. Like many a net artist, I want to abort the traditional trajectory of art history.[53]

net.art.history

Of course it was precisely the lack of net art history that catalysed much net.art. Indeed, it has often been claimed that net.artists specifically set out to aggrandize their work and argue their way into art history books. So here again, not saying may be seen to be as powerful as saying. Much of the work of Vuk Cosic, for instance, provides (net) art-historical commentary. *The History of Art for Airports*[54] (see Plate 9.2) from 1997, conveys a narrative of the history of art in basic symbols like those used to transcend language barriers and provide simple visitor information in public buildings such as airports and stations. Thus, the work renders arguably 'great' moments in the history of art as though they were lavatory signs or danger warnings, while undermining disciplinary systems by using images, rather than language, to narrate the history of art. Berry explains:

> In one of his best known net art works, The History of Art for Airports, Cosic compresses thousands of years of art history, from the caves of Lascaux to the net art of Jodi, into a few images of recombinant toilet people interacting with cocktail glasses and other airport fare (eat your heart out Ernst Gombrich!).[55]

Yet for the most part, these art (historical) interventions have been ignored!

---

52   Jacques Derrida, *Archive Fever: A Freudian Impression*, trans. Eric Prenowitz, (Chicago, 1995); Friedrich, A. Kittler, *Discourse Networks 1800/1900* (Stanford, 1990); Bernard Stiegler, *Technics and Time, 1: The Fault of Epimetheus*, trans. Richard Beardsworth and George Collins (Stanford, 1998).

53   This paragraph sets up the area of enquiry I embark upon in my doctoral thesis: Internet Art History 2.0.

54   http://www.ljudmila.org/~vuk/history, accessed July 2008.

55   Josephine Berry, 'Art is Useless', *Mute*, 13 (1999): 53.

If art history could be retuned to accept and analyse technological innovation, a vantage point might be achieved from which arenas for the reception of net art (that have thus far fallen under its radar, like mailing lists, portals, blogs, wikis etc.) might be assessed as art-historical. It seems that it is in the recognition of emergent, online approaches to art interpretation as an art-historically inspired activity, that net art's missing art history can be located. Could it be that in the process of recognizing the potential of net art as a way of *deconstructing* the discipline and of *reinserting* appraisals of art history's originary technicity that net art's *true* place in the history of art might be discovered?

Chapter 10

Museum Migration in Century 2.08

Jemima Rellie

The impact that digital technologies are having on fine art museums is both complex and profound. Everything, from the creation of art to its circulation and reception is being transformed by digital technologies. This transformation requires a reassessment of the structure and logic of art museums. It offers art museums a range of new opportunities, which, if identified and embraced, will result in a radically modified notion of what such institutions are and what they do.

In order to consider the impact that digital technologies are having on art museums as fully as possible, it is necessary to keep in mind the whole art museum ecosystem. Fine art is at the centre of the system and the practice of art-making itself is evolving in the digital age. Indeed digital technologies are transforming every step in the creative process. Artists working with more traditional media such as painting or sculpture now regularly use digital technologies to research their subjects. Artists whose work might be considered to be based firmly in the tradition of producing unique objects will also now frequently employ both electronic software and hardware in the physical production of their work.

One such artist is Fiona Rae, who since the 1990s has used computer software to work out her abstract painterly applications before projecting them onto a canvas to trace. Rae describes her painting as 'a series of edits'.[1] She goes on to suggest that 'To edit is to shape something and adjust it and cut things out'. The reason that artists like Rae employ digital technologies in their practice is that such methods have made this editing process significantly easier.

The transformation of art-making by digital technologies is not confined to artists making use of these technologies as tools to research or to make work. Rather, these digital technologies increasingly actually make up the materials or media which twenty-first-century artists now employ in the work itself. A whole generation of new media artists has emerged making work ranging from installation art to internet art, whose very existence is dependent on new media. What is more, these artists, such as Golan Levin (see Plate 10.1), Jodi, Thompson and Craighead and Cory Arcangel, are increasingly finding institutional acceptance and commercial success.

---

1   Fiona Rae, *Art and Culture*, http://www.artandculture.com/cgi-bin/WebObjects/ ACLive.woa/wa/artist?id=642, accessed July 2008.

Where once new media art was confined to the art and technology festivals such as Ars Electronica[2] and ISEA (Intersociety for Electronic Arts),[3] digital artists have, since the turn of the twenty-first century, started appearing more regularly in major art museum exhibitions. Two of the most notable early exhibitions in this respect were *010101: Art in Technological Times*[4] at SFMoMA, and *Bitstreams*[5] at the Whitney, both shown in 2001. Neither of these marked the first time that art which is explicitly and inherently dependent on technology was shown in an art museum, but they were significant for their scale and can be said to signal a point when new media art migrated into the mainstream.

That said, while it is no longer a shock to discover new media artists within the walls of a museum, they have yet to make more than a fleeting appearance within art museum collections. One reason for this is the difficulty art museums still face in determining a conservation policy for these pieces. Progress is, however, being made, arguably most noticeably in the efforts of the Variable Media Network,[6] which articulates and promotes a range of preservation strategies including storage, migration, emulation and re-interpretation. While art museums continue to struggle with the issues surrounding the preservation of new media art, they run the real risk of failing to collect and conserve a body of work which is highly specific to this time and which would be of great value to future art-historical researchers.

Somewhat ironically, all this is happening at a time of crisis for various non-digital works within art museum collections, as revealed in a conference at the Getty Conservation Institute on 'The Object in Transition' in 2008.[7] A year earlier, a workshop at Tate Modern brought together a group of international, interdisciplinary professionals to focus more specifically on the challenges of decay and replication in relation to sculpture of the last hundred years.[8] The catalyst for the workshop was the degradation of certain Naum Gabo sculptures

---

2   Ars Electronica, http://www.aec.at, (Linz, 1979), accessed July 2008.

3   Inter-Society for the Electronic Arts (ISEA), http://www.isea-web.org (Amsterdam, 1990) accessed July 2008.

4   010101, http://010101.sfmoma.org, SFMoMA (San Francisco, 2001), accessed July 2008.

5   Bitstreams, http://www.whitney.org/bitstreams, Whitney Museum of American Art (New York, 2001), accessed July 2008.

6   The Variable Media Network, http://variablemedia.net (New York, 2001), accessed July 2008.

7   The Object in Transition: A Cross Disciplinary Conference on the Preservation and Study of Modern and Contemporary Art, Getty Center (Los Angeles, January 2008), http://www.getty.edu/conservation/publications/videos/object_in_transition.html, accessed July 2008.

8   'Inherent Vice: The Replica and Its Implications in Modern Sculpture Workshop', Tate Papers, 8 (London, 2007), http://www.tate.org.uk/research/tateresearch/tatepapers/07autumn/, accessed July 2008.

in the Tate Collection, specifically those incorporating cellulose materials.[9] Among the activities underway to conserve these works is 3D modelling of the sculptures (see Plate 10.2). This is nominally a documentation effort as opposed to a preservation strategy, although the project team do not rule out the possibility of using these computer software models in the future as a basis for highly precise replicas, assuming of course that the philosophical and legal obstacles can also be negotiated.

The Chinese are arguably ahead of the curve with respect to surpassing the philosophical hurdles in utilizing copies in public exhibitions and displays. In China it is not only considered acceptable to use a photograph to represent a work which is too fragile to be displayed, but it is also common practice to substitute a masterpiece with a copy (digital or material) when the original is not available, without necessarily acknowledging the nature of the replica to museum visitors.[10] It is possible to speculate that such an approach will become increasingly acceptable to future Western audiences, raised on digital culture, in which images are infinitely malleable and reproducible, and the traditional art historical notions of 'original' and 'authenticity' are challenged.

As meaningfully as digital technologies are altering the creative and conservation process, so too are they affecting how the visual arts are both accessed and received by the audience. The internet and the World Wide Web have empowered the audience and changed expectations. It is possible to find multiple reproductions, albeit of varying quality, of many canonical works of art online today. Many art museums are well under way with the process of digitizing their collections and regularly offer free access to photographic reproductions on their websites. Broadband technologies support more media-rich applications which can better reproduce 3D works and physical spaces. These efforts vary from virtual simulations of room-sized installations, to efforts to reveal the subtle, textured surface of paintings, as demonstrated in the range of Tate's 'Special imaging treatments'.[11]

The impact of these efforts is enormous, not least on the opportunities now afforded to engage with time-based art. The potential now exists for visitors to watch video art in its entirety at a time and place that suits them best – a potential which Tate, and others are increasingly taking advantage of. For example, all the films included in Pierre Huyghe's *Celebration Park exhibition at* Tate Modern in

---

9   Jackie Heuman and Lyndsey Morgan, 'Recording Changes in Naum Gabo's Plastic Sculptures', Tate Research (London, 2005), http://www.tate.org.uk/research/tateresearch/majorprojects/naum_gabo.htm, accessed July 2008.

10   Holland Cotter, 'China's Legacy: Let a Million Museums Bloom', *The New York Times*, July 2008, http://www.nytimes.com/2008/07/04/arts/design/04museums.html?page wanted=2&sq=chinese%20musuems&st=cse&scp=1, accessed July 2008.

11   Special Imaging Treatments, Tate Online, http://www.tate.org.uk/collections/ptm/default.htm (London, 2001–2003), accessed July 2008.

2006[12] were made available on the Tate website for the duration of the exhibition. This allowed time-poor visitors to the physical gallery to watch the films in their entirety at a later stage, as well as affording those who were unable to visit the offline exhibition an opportunity to experience the work, albeit in an alternative context.

Museum digitization efforts are increasingly moving beyond the fine art collection boundaries and into art museum libraries and archives. Visitors can now browse through a range of works in Tate's Archive Online[13] without having to make a reservation or don white gloves; while virtual visitors to the Getty Research Library can now consult thousands of digitized books, without applying for special reader privileges, thanks to an ongoing collaboration with the Internet Archive.[14] The general public can dip into this new wealth of material as frequently as they like, while an academic researcher can pore over works for as long as needed. Explicit links can be made between related items, from either within the organization or beyond, as long as best practice standards (namely the use of persistent URLs) are deployed in the implementation of the resources. These developments empower audiences of all motivations.

In pre-internet times, an institutional mission such as Tate's, 'to increase knowledge, understanding and appreciation' of art, was primarily considered to be linear and one-way: the dissemination of a coherent canon from a small number of revered art historians ensconced in the collection to the homogenous general public beyond the institution. This position is untenable if art museums wish to continue to thrive. For, as Maxwell Anderson has noted in his essay on museum content:

> While previous generations sought authoritative information, today's young audiences make minimal investments in traditionally authoritative sources. A trinity of features – 'do-it-yourself' claims for attention, familiar/gossipy tone, and room for the end-user's interaction, is overwhelming traditional ways of reaching an audience, with profound effects on art museums to come.[15]

---

12   Pierre Huyghe, *Celebration Park, Tate Modern/Tate Online,* http://www.tate.org. uk/modern/exhibitions/pierrehuyghe/default.shtm (London, 2006), accessed July 2008.

13   Tate Archive Collection Online, http://www.tate.org.uk/research/researchservices/ archive/archiveonline.htm (London 2002), accessed July 2008.

14   Digitized Library Collections, The Getty Research Institute, http://www.getty.edu/ research/conducting_research/digitized_collections/ (Los Angeles, 2008), accessed July 2008.

15   Maxwell Anderson, 'Who Will Own Art Museums' Content?', http://www. maxwellanderson.com/WhoWillOwnArtMuseumsContent.htm (October 2005), accessed July 2008.

While the effects envisioned by Anderson are yet to be fully realized or understood, what is already clear is that digital technologies have accelerated the shift from a focus on art museum collections to an equal interest in audiences.

In the UK this shift is both evident in, and partly the result of, the evolving policies of government departments (namely the Department for Culture, Media and Sport (DCMS), the Department for Children, Schools and Families (DCSF), the Department for Innovation, Universities and Skills (DIUS) and the old Department for Education and Skills (DCFS)) and museum funders (be they charitable or corporate). However, it is digital technologies that are responsible for the speed and recent intensity of this shift. Digital technologies have provided the perfect catalyst for the change in focus from objects to access that has taken place in the previous few decades. Similarly, they are now largely responsible for the switch in perspective from access to participation that is likely to dominate the museum agenda for the next decade.[16]

Supporting this shift in focus is a shift in the use of resources. Art museums now need funds to support the activities that are associated with their increasing concern with audience development and emergent interest in audience participation. These activities emanate most obviously from marketing, education and web teams rather than the curatorial departments who have traditionally been centre stage.

In the process of moving, at least sporadically, centre stage, each of these departments is also being transformed. They are no longer tasked in simple support roles, facilitating access and interpretation of the exhibitions and collections programmes. Rather the web, education and marketing teams are themselves creating (or curating?) media-rich content which is central to the visitor's museum-going experience. Tate again serves as a useful model here, having, as Charlie Gere has described, expanded:

> its remit far beyond the normal conception of the gallery's role, even if as far as most people are concerned its primary business is still physically displaying works of art. Much of what it now does is closer to the kind of activities traditionally associated with schools, art schools, universities, or institutions such as the Institute for Contemporary Arts; lectures, seminars, webcasts, publications, on-line forums and so on. In a sense, like the paradigmatic post-industrial company, Tate is transforming itself from an institution concerned primarily with things to one concerned with information and knowledge.[17]

Tate has expanded in this way because the proliferation of digital technologies have enabled it to do so. Tate has also expanded like this because it has had to, owing to

---

16   Jemima Rellie, 'The Disruptive Decade (1995–2005): The Impact on Museums', Personal visions – Inspire, OMNi, Open Media Network, http://www.openmedianetwork. org.uk/contentandvision/inspire.htm (London, 2007), accessed July 2008.

17   Charlie Gere, 'Network Art and the Networked Gallery', Tate Online, http://www. tate.org.uk/netart/networkgallery.htm (London, 2006), accessed July 2008.

the proliferation of digital culture. In the digital age Tate has metamorphosed, both practically and conceptually, from being a physical space, to being a network, of 'real' and virtual spaces, ultimately interested in ideas (see Plate 10.3).

Research remains crucial to art museums in the digital or information age, but once again the nature of the research they undertake is being reshaped by digital technologies. Research agendas are changing in a number of ways. For one thing, they are no longer limited to analysis of the artworks in the collection. Accompanying the shift in the relative status of art museum departments is an emphasis on new areas of art museum research, focused firmly on the audience and their interactions with art.

Tate's research strategy is currently divided into three primary areas: 'collections; exhibitions and displays; and experimental or exploratory research'.[18] Although it has yet to elaborate publicly on the scope of the third category, it is likely to include non-art-centred research such as audience research, thereby formalizing its status. As previously mentioned, research is no longer confined to those staff charged with curating or preserving art. Instead, it is now acknowledged as a crucial part of both the education and the communications teams' remit.

In addition to focusing on new areas of research, Tate is also considering whether research should in principle start as a partnership with other institutions from the outset. This is already increasingly the case, as is evident in two recent Tate research projects: the art work-focused *The Sublime Object: Nature, Art, and Language*;[19] and the audience-focused *Tate Encounters*,[20] both of which engaged university scholars as principal project partners from the start. This is an interesting development because it illustrates Tate's reliance on outside research expertise and a willingness to let research flow in different directions, both out of and into the museum.

Of course art-historical scholarship has never been confined to the art museum but rather has always been a web that centres on the artwork and extends well beyond the gallery walls. Digital technologies have simply made this reality more explicit and easy to facilitate. A networked approach to research is greatly enabled via the use of internet technologies, and going further, it can be argued that it is internet technologies that are providing the impetus to embrace this approach to an extent which was previously impractical.

The impact of digital technologies on art museum research is multi-faceted. Digital technologies allow research to be undertaken in a distributed way, but

18   Minutes of the Meetings of the Trustees of the Tate Gallery, http://www.tate.org. uk/about/governancefunding/boardoftrustees/tatetrustees_minutes_2007-11.pdf, (London, November), p. 8, accessed July 2008.

19   *The Sublime Object: Nature, Art and Language*, Tate, http://www.tate.org.uk/ research/tateresearch/majorprojects/sublimeobject.htm (London, 2007–10), accessed July 2008.

20   Tate Encounters, Tate, http://www.tate.org.uk/research/tateresearch/majorprojects/ tate-encounters, (London 2007–10), accessed July 2008.

equally importantly, they allow the process to be far more iterative and immediate than it has been ever before. Research used to be all about product – the exhibition or the catalogue – but it is now increasingly about process. Digital technologies have the potential to accelerate research. They facilitate the mass distribution of information (though digitization and electronic networks) as well as the potential for mass access to and enhancement of that information.

The audience for a curator's lecture is no longer restricted by space and time to the audience aggregated in the presentation venue. Instead, a lecture can now easily be disseminated to equally large numbers, online, using (should you choose) only simple, free software and platforms that currently make no charge for hosting and promoting this content. As the audience then uses the same set of tools to re-mix and re-distribute that content, so research becomes an increasingly iterative process, whereby an ever larger matrix of knowledge provides additional context around the art work – be it object, or idea – at the focus.

Art museums now acknowledge, embrace even, the diversity within their audiences and are increasingly using digital technologies to incorporate their voices back into the mix. This content may live on the museum's website, but it will also extend beyond it onto the wider network, creating an ever richer, more nuanced body of knowledge and source of inspiration. The single biggest threat to this potential new wisdom of crowds[21] is copyright laws and international intellectual property rights. The copyright policy on many art museum websites restricts the reproduction of any content, in any way. Tate's policy, for instance, while encouraging personal 'viewing, interacting or listening', prohibits:

- Any form of reproduction whatsoever, including without limitation, the extraction and/or storage in any retrieval system or inclusion in any other computer program or work.
- Any reproduction whatsoever of details, alterations and adaptations of works.[22]

This sweeping policy includes artwork on the website which is in the public domain. It curtails the use of Tate content for homework by schoolchildren (on- or offline) as forcefully as it impedes the use of Tate content for commercial ends. At the other extreme, the Victoria and Albert Museum should be applauded as one of the museums leading efforts to try to ensure that as much of its content as possible is made freely available for non-commercial, academic and educational use.[23]

Existing copyright law presents hurdles to art museums as well as to individuals. Despite owning a work of art, a UK museum is required to seek

---

21 James Surowiecki, *The Wisdom of Crowds* (London, 2004).

22 Tate's Copyright Policy, Tate Online, http://www.tate.org.uk/about/media/ copyright/, accessed July 2008.

23 Martin Bailey, 'V&A to Scrap Academic Reproduction Fees', *The Art Newspaper*, 175, http://www.theartnewspaper.com/article.asp?id=525, accessed July 2008.

additional clearance from the artist or artist's estate when that artist is alive or has been dead for less than seventy years, as well as from the photographer of the work. Furthermore, details of works of art, or anything that is considered to distort the original image, such as cropping it or marking it to illustrate a point, are open to claims of copyright abuse.

Art museums face further copyright challenges when attempting to compile comprehensive online resources that might best benefit their audiences. Art museums' physical collections are at least partially arbitrary and the result of what artists' works were available to them, when, and for what price. In an age where information and knowledge are an art museum's primary concern, it is obvious that art museums will not want to restrict their online content to the physical objects within their own collections. Instead they will want to use digital technologies to fill the gaps in their collection virtually. UK copyright law makes this time-consuming and costly.

The situation is similar in other parts of the world. Rights for books in a print world are still usually negotiated by territory. While this is harder online, it is now a possibility as evidenced in the online offerings of television networks. It is possible to access the BBC's website from America, and for Americans to listen to BBC radio online. It is not, however, possible to access BBC's televisual content from outside the United Kingdom – a trend which could eventually become the norm for UK art museums' content too.

The argument is that UK tax-payers fund the BBC's content and distribution through the licence fee, and that they should not pay for the bandwidth used by people in other countries accessing this content online. As long as UK art museums continue to be partially funded by the state, and to create increasingly large amounts of rich-media content, it seems highly plausible that the time will come when those not paying UK taxes will be expected to pay to access this content. This may well prove acceptable, but at its extreme this is a trend which will result in less freedom to enjoy art and more barriers to access culture than we take for granted today.

It should be remembered that much contemporary art practice is now being framed as 'research' (as recognized in the establishment of The Centre for Practice-Led Research in the Arts (CePRA) in 2006), in that it is process-based, performative and iterative; building explicitly on the cultural production that has preceded it.[24] This type of practice is jeopardized if the artist's access is restricted or denied even before the challenges of integrating their practice within the logic and structure of the art museum are properly explored.

Initiatives such as Creative Commons[25] offer some hope but there remains a real risk that much of the content currently available on art museum websites internationally will one day, sooner or later, be destroyed as the associated rights become simply too difficult to manage or too costly to maintain. As more and

---

24 CePRA, Leeds University, http://www.leeds.ac.uk/cepra/, accessed July 2008.
25 http://creativecommons.org, accessed July 2008.

more of our creative heritage falls under corporate stewardship, and for-profit organizations assert and extend copyright protections, the debate has intensified in art institutions over what constitutes fair usage.

An organization like Tate, with limited funds and not-for-profit status, can adopt a relatively risk-friendly approach to fair usage. While concerted attempts will be made to secure clearance, if an image is complicated or hard to clear but considered low risk then that work will be included in the online resource until a complaint is made. If and when, on a rare occasion, a complaint is forthcoming, then so too is an apology and the image is quickly removed. This is obviously trickier territory for any institution with deeper pockets such as the Getty with its multi-billion-dollar endowment. With these deep pockets comes the associated threat of compensation being sought for any breach of rights, necessitating a far more diligent – and laborious – approach to rights negotiations.

Fortuitously perhaps, attempts by art museums to track digital rights have made little headway. While digital usage rights are now routinely requested in perpetuity by museums, the permanent rights are frequently denied by rights owners, uncomfortable predicting the future and taking a gamble on a possible loss of additional revenue. What occurs more regularly is that a counter offer is made by the rights holder for something like five years' usage. This is acceptable, but because of the difficulty that museums face in tracking large numbers of images on their websites, they must put the onus for remembering to remove the image on the rights holder. In other words the rights holder is given the comfort of knowing that they can request the removal of an image at any point after the five-year term is up, on the assumption that they are unlikely to do so at that stage.

Processes such as those pertaining to copyright clearance still need fine-tuning, but this should not diminish the very clear fact that digital technologies provide the impetus, as well as the tools, to transform the way museums disseminate knowledge, share understanding and stimulate appreciation. Put quite simply, digital technologies make it easier to augment, map and share the matrix of knowledge that surrounds and electrifies museum objects. Acknowledging that most of this knowledge, or value, exists outside the institution, Greg Dyke, the former Director General of the BBC, updated the Reithian mantra, suggesting that the public service broadcaster's role is now to 'inform, educate, entertain ... and connect'.[26]

The BBC's and Tate's missions have long been similarly worded but their outputs were perceived quite differently in the analogue age. With the advent of digital technologies, however, both the missions and the outputs of not-for-profit museums and public sector broadcasters blur. Like universities, libraries and publishers, they are all in the content business, and brought closer together, both conceptually and competitively, as that content is digitized or is born digital. For as David Green succinctly put it:

---

26   John Arlidge, 'Dyke's New Mantra for the Future BBC: Only Connect', *The Observer*, http://www.guardian.co.uk/media/2002/jan/06/bbc.broadcasting1 (London, 6 January 2002), accessed July 2008.

> While the techniques of mechanical reproduction might be said to have
> problematized the relationship that had previously existed between notions of
> the original and the copy, the techniques of computer simulation have effectively
> rendered void the very notions of the original and the copy.[27]

The flip-side of this new reality is that various functions within art museums
have been noticeably threatened by digital technologies. Traditional commercial
revenue generators based on content dissemination such as book publishing and
image licensing are slowing at best, while visits to free but inherently reproducible
collections such as art museum libraries are in near terminal decline. While
arguably tangential to the core museum programmes of collecting and exhibiting
fine art, the challenges faced in these tangential areas have repercussions beyond
these activities. Indeed, when considered alongside the challenges faced at the
start of this chapter, when art becomes digital, these challenges collude to threaten,
fundamentally, the very *raison d'être* of the art museum itself.

Academic art book publishing requires heavy subsidies. In an age when museum
funding is increasingly self-generated through commercial activities such as ticket
sales and memberships, or is reliant on patronage, as evident in recent outspoken
support for tax breaks for nom-domiciles by British art museum leaders,[28] heavily
subsidizing printed books simply does not make sense. As Maxwell Anderson has
described, 'Today's flying fingers on keyboards 24 hours a day from time zone to
time zone are toying with the fate of the $65 exhibition catalogue that costs $11 to
ship and sits on a shelf as eyes are glued to screens.'[29]

Despite the economic imperative for this switch to electronic publishing, it
must also be noted that digital distribution is far better suited to supporting the
core art museum objective of furthering knowledge. A better alternative to printing
the catalogue is to put the content online, where it is cheaper to distribute and
can reach far larger audiences. Hybrid solutions offering print-on-demand can be
implemented to satisfy those reluctant to read extensive text on screen. Future
art-book publishing should focus on the creation of profitable, populist lists, with
plenty of coffee-table books which function in part as an object themselves.

This trajectory for art-book publishing has already been witnessed with
university presses, many of whom now offer electronic imprints and some of which
have either ceased to operate or have gone entirely electronic. One such example
is the Rice University Press, which was abolished in 1996, but revised in 2006 as

---

27   David Green, 'Painting as Asporia', *Critical Perspectives on Contemporary
Painting: Hybridity, Hegemony, Historicism* (Liverpool, 2003), p. 100.

28   'Cruel Britannia', *The Times*, http://www.timesonline.co.uk/tol/comment/leading_
article/article3359700.ece (London, 13 February 2008), accessed July 2008.

29   Maxwell Anderson, 'Who Will Own Art Museums' Content?', http://www.
maxwellanderson.com/WhoWillOwnArtMuseumsContent.htm (October 2005), accessed
July 2008.

an electronic-only operation.[30] *The Ithaka Report*[31] on new models of publishing for university presses clearly advised universities to be more strategic about the relationship of publishing to other organizational objectives. The authors of the report describe publishing succinctly as 'scholarly communications', suggesting that 'By publishing we mean simply the communication and broad dissemination of knowledge, a function that has become both more complex and more important with the introduction and rapid evolution of digital and networking technologies.' They go on to explain that:

> Formal scholarly publishing is characterized by a process of selection, editing, printing and distribution of an author's content by an intermediary (preferably one with some name recognition). Informal scholarly publication, by comparison, describes the dissemination of content (sometimes called 'gray literature') that generally has not passed through these processes, such as working papers, lecture notes, student newsletters, etc. In the past decade, the range and importance of the latter has been dramatically expanded by information technology, as scholars increasingly turn to preprint servers, blogs, listservs, and institutional repositories, to share their work, ideas, data, opinions, and critiques. These forms of informal publication have become pervasive in the university and college environment. As scholars increasingly rely on these channels to share and find information, the boundaries between formal and informal publication will blur. These changes in the behavior of scholars will require changes in the approaches universities take to all kinds of publishing.[32]

It is not a question of whether museum book publishers should take heed of the lessons learnt and conclusions drawn in the *Ithaka Report*, but how quickly. To their credit many art museums have already started to consider these issues. Several art museums have ceased print publishing their collection catalogues, conference proceedings and annual reports, instead sharing them for free online. What is more, discussions are beginning to take place at some organizations, such as Tate, which speculate on redefined job roles for collection curators which would see one of their functions as the use of new media technologies to support the dissemination of knowledge.[33] Put bluntly, a future has been imagined that could

---

30   New Model for University Presses, Inside Higher Education, http://www. insidehighered.com/news/2007/07/31/ricepress (Washington, July 2007), accessed July 2008.

31   Laura Brown, Rebecca Griffiths and Matthew Rascoff, 'University Publishing in A Digital Age', *Ithaka Report*, http://www.ithaka.org/strategic-services/Ithaka%20Univers ity%20Publishing%20Report.pdf (New York, 2007), accessed July 2008.

32   Brown, Griffiths and Rascoff, *Ithaka Report*, p. 3.

33   Minutes of the Meetings of the Trustees of the Tate Gallery, http://www.tate.org. uk/about/governancefunding/boardoftrustees/tatetrustees_minutes_2007-11.pdf, (London, November 2007), p. 8, accessed July 2008.

see all art curators obligated to spend at least part of their time producing digital content for access on the web.

It is clear that the introduction of digital technologies has had, and continues to have, disruptive ramifications for art museums. It is difficult to isolate these ramifications from the impact of other changes in culture and society, but this chapter has sought to demonstrate how intertwined, complicated and simultaneously profound these ramifications are. Digital technologies impact on everything from the mission, to the objectives and the future plans of art museums. Art museums fulfil their mission through a variety of means, including the collection, exhibition and preservation of art; as well as through research, education and outreach, each of which has been affected in multiple ways by digital technologies. Furthermore, these technologies are also transforming allied sectors such as libraries, universities and public sector broadcasters, bringing them all into closer competition. For art museums to maintain credibility – and to maintain their status in contemporary visual culture – much more time and effort needs to be spent analysing the impact of digital technologies on art museums and considering how these institutions can and should remain distinct in the digital information age.

Chapter 11
Slitting Open the Kantian Eye

Charlie Gere

My father was Keeper of the Prints and Drawings Department at the British Museum. He had an eye. Not just any eye, but 'a better eye ... than anyone else alive today'.[1] This last comment was made, in conversation with a friend of my father's, by the art historian Kenneth Clark. The comment was presumably inspired by conversations between the two about the works of art on the walls of Clark's apartment. Taken at face value, Clark's comment perfectly encapsulates a certain kind of art history and the assumptions of elitism and superiority it embodied. In case this sounds overly critical, these are qualities that both Lord Clark and my father would have fully endorsed and supported. By 'anyone else alive today' Clark of course did not mean literally the full complement of living humanity, but rather the few score connoisseurs of art, among whom he counted both himself, and on the evidence above, my father. By 'a better eye' he meant a capacity to look carefully at works of art, drawings especially, and in particular to be able to make attributions on the grounds of style. To be a connoisseur was to be part of a tradition established 'without the aid of photography, teams of graduate students, Witt libraries and other modern amenities now taken for granted' which involved the 'scientific and methodical study of an artist's drawings considered as essential elements in the construction and assessment of his work as a whole'.[2] The last two quotations come from my father's introduction to the catalogue of an exhibition at the Fitzwilliam Museum, devoted to the connoisseurial achievement of his mentor and colleague Philip Pouncey, but they can also stand as a self-portrait of a self-confessed connoisseur and even a manifesto of connoisseurship. To possess an eye, as my father reputedly did, required, according to my father's own prescription, 'a particular combination of qualities of mind, some more scientific than artistic and others more artistic than scientific: a visual memory for compositions and details of compositions, exhaustive knowledge of the school or period in question, awareness of all the possible answers, a sense of artistic quality, a capacity for assessing evidence, and a power of empathy with the creative processes of

---

1   C. White, 'John Arthur Giles Gere 1921–1995', in *Proceedings of the British Academy, 90: 1995 Lectures and Memoirs* (London, 1996), p. 373.

2   J. Gere, 'Introduction' to J. Stock and D. Scrase, *The Achievement of a Connoisseur: Philip Pouncey* (Cambridge, 1985).

each individual artist and a positive conception of him as an individual artistic personality'.[3]

In his essay 'From Blindness to blindness: Museums, Heterogeneity and the Subject' the sociologist Kevin Hetherington discusses what he calls the 'Kantian gaze of the connoisseur'. This essay is extraordinarily useful for understanding some questions about the eye and subjectivity in relation to art and the museum and in this chapter I will refer to it extensively. For Hetherington the emergence of this way of looking involves a disavowal of the heterogeneity of the world of things. The 'Kantian eye' is disinterested and seeks to make it possible to 'make claims about the beauty of [an] object that can be taken as universal and communicated to an aesthetic community'.[4] According to Hetherington the emergence of the Kantian gaze is part of a longer history of 'material heterogeneity' through which 'subjectivity is constituted'.[5] Hetherington follows the history of such spaces from the princely palaces of the Northern Italian Renaissance, to the seventeenth-century cabinets of curiosity through to the 'modern, Kantian disciplinary museum'. His essay is also a 'history of the eye and what it sees' and of the gaze, as well as revealing the 'blind spots of the museum', which also demonstrate that 'the more we think we see in totality the less that is actually before our eyes'.[6]

Hetherington suggests that there is a close connection between the kind of seeing that was developed in the Renaissance with the development of linear perspective and the types of object collections that emerged at the time.[7] As has been pointed out by many commentators, linear perspective, for all its apparent realism, differs quite markedly from how we actually perceive space. Instead of the saccadic, embodied, binocular, temporal experience of seeing with our own eyes, linear perspective presents a static, abstracted, monocular, disembodied model of vision, or what Martin Jay calls the 'Albertian-Cartesian perspectivalism', one of the principal 'scopic regimes of modernity'. This is the way of seeing and representing the world in terms of 'three-dimensional, rationalized space of perspectival vision' that 'could be rendered on a two-dimensional surface by following all of the transformational rules spelled out in Alberti's *De Pittura* and later treatises by Viator, Dürer, and others'.[8] Jay points out that this technique of rendering was based on a static, unblinking, single eye, looking through a peephole, rather than the binocular, shifting vision that actually typifies human visual perception. Jay quotes Norman Bryson to the effect that vision adheres to the logic of the gaze

---

3   Ibid.

4   K. Hetherington, 'From Blindness to blindness: Museums, Heterogeneity and the Subject', in J. Law and J. Hassard (eds), *Actor Network Theory and After* (Oxford and Malden MA, 1999).

5   Ibid., p. 52.

6   Ibid., p. 54.

7   Ibid.

8   M. Jay, 'Scopic Regimes of Modernity', in H. Foster (ed.), *Vision and Visuality* (Seattle, 1988), p. 6.

rather than the glance which in turn arrests 'the flux of phenomena' to produce a static, disembodied, eternalized vision.[9] This is the model of what Richard Rorty calls the 'mirror of nature', the basis of Descartes' modern epistemology, in which 'the intellect inspects entities modeled on retinal images'.[10]

> Cartesian perspectivalism was ... in league with a scientific world view that no longer hermeneutically read the world as a divine text, but rather saw it situated in a mathematically regular spatio-temporal order filled with natural objects that could only be observed from without by the dispassionate eye of the neutral researcher'.[11]

Hetherington, following the work of Brian Rotman, connects the development of linear perspective to the discovery of the idea of infinity and its representation by the number zero, adopted from Hindu mathematics via the Muslim world. As a character able to signify nothing, zero is both a sign within the system of mathematical notation and a meta-sign that can stand for the principle of numbering itself, and thus enables infinity to be represented. Zero represents infinity in the number system much as the vanishing point does in linear-perspectival images. The viewer of the image is positioned as standing outside of it, mirroring the position of the vanishing point in the picture, much as zero is outside the system of integers. Thus the 'subject, perhaps for the first time stands outside and separate from the material world, able to look in on it from a privileged position'.[12]

> Linear perspective establishes a unique relationship between the human subject as subject and the object world as something separate that is seen as if through a window ... Perspective constitutes 'the miraculous', the subject of many Renaissance paintings, as a world of heterogeneous objects separate from the viewing subject and allows the subject, rather than God, the privileged role of being able to give that heterogeneity a sense of order, just like zero does to the numbers one to nine. The subject, a Christian subject, is no longer a part of God's multiplicitous and miraculous world, but a secular objectivised subject who can look in on that world, not from on high perhaps, but at least from a privileged position outside the frame of things.[13]

However, the diversity of objects in Renaissance collections 'did not represent heterogeneity in the sense of anomaly and difference but hidden and secret forms of connection that linked them as a totality'.[14] Following Foucault, Hetherington

---

9   Ibid., p. 7.
10 R. Rorty, *Philosophy and the Mirror of Nature* (Princeton, NJ, 1980), p. 45.
11 Jay, 'Scopic Regimes of Modernity', p. 9.
12 Hetherington, 'From Blindness to blindness', p. 56.
13 Ibid., p. 57.
14 Ibid., p. 58.

points out that Renaissance orderings of the material world were governed by various means by which correspondences and similitudes between objects could be ascertained. 'Chains of resemblance, an endless and multiple ordering was constituted in the space of these collections' with the subject (firstly the prince and later the connoisseur, artist and scholar) standing outside as an 'appreciative eye located at the point of infinity'.[15]

By contrast, the next stage in the ordering of heterogeneity is represented by the seventeenth-century cabinets of curiosity and Dutch art of the same period. By contrast with the earlier princely collections, material heterogeneity is understood as something *other* to the viewing subject.[16] Francis Bacon in particular argues that, in Hetherington's words, only by 'understanding the anomalous and monstrous, the heteroclites ... will we be able to discern the true natural history'.[17] In place of the viewer at the vanishing point of infinity a different kind of gaze emerges, now scrutinizing the world as if separate from it and not heterogeneous to it. Heterogeneity is no longer synonymous with eye, but separate from it. It is seen by and helps constitute the eye. In this mode of viewing, the world is laid out on a table 'to be viewed and classified by the viewer who can now hope to attain the position of God by viewing that world as a picture'.[18] This is an allusion to Heidegger's notion of the 'Age of the World Picture'. In the essay of that name Heidegger characterizes scientific modernity as being capable, unlike the Greek and medieval worlds, of enabling the world to be thought of as a picture, owing to the emergence of 'man' as a subject, who sets himself in front of, and separate from, the world of objects. This in turn enables an instrumental relationship towards the world, which can be treated as 'standing reserve' for use and exploitation. As Heidegger puts it:

> Where the world becomes picture, what is, in its entirety, is juxtaposed as that for which man is prepared and which, correspondingly, he therefore intends to bring before himself and have before himself, and consequently intends in a decisive sense to set in place before himself ... Hence world picture, when understood essentially, does not mean a picture of the world but the world conceived of and grasped as a picture.[19]

Hetherington discusses the third mode of viewing, that of the Kantian gaze of the connoisseur, by way of Foucault's famous invocation of Bentham's Panopticon, his model of an ideal prison, in which every cell is visible to a central watchtower, but the guards in the tower cannot be seen by the prisoners. Since a prisoner can

---

15   Ibid., p. 59.

16   Ibid., p. 61.

17   Ibid.

18   Ibid., p. 63.

19   M. Heidegger, *The Question Concerning Technology and Other Essays* (New York, 1977), p. 129.

never tell if he is being watched at any moment he will continually regulate his own behaviour just in case he is.[20] For Foucault, the Panopticon is the model for our contemporary 'disciplinary society'.[21] Hetherington points out that, though the panoptic apparatus bears some resemblance to the geometry of linear perspective, it is in reverse. In the latter the objects are ordered around the vanishing point and the viewing subject occupies the space mirroring that point on the other side of the picture plane. In the Panopticon it is the object, the watchtower that occupies the viewing point, and the subject, the prisoner, at the vanishing point.[22]

Thus, in a reversal of the paradigm of linear perspective, it is the subject who becomes heterogeneous and it is in his or her interior self that heterogeneity is to be found, and '[G]azing at the outside world becomes only a means to inner reflection.'[23] For Hetherington this is exemplified in the modern museum, and its corresponding type of gaze, that of the Kantian connoisseur. As Hetherington puts it:

> For Kant, aesthetic judgment is the product of a disinterested eye ... The object before our eyes is of no real interest to Kant, what is of interest is a person's reaction to that object and their ability to make claims about the beauty of that object that can be taken as universal and communicated to an aesthetic community. Heterogeneity takes the form of sense perceptions and the process of ordering them, of making sense of that heterogeneity, is one that is internal to the subject and not to be revealed in the object itself.[24]

Thus, like the prisoners becoming aware of their 'internal heterogeneity', their crimes and deviances, the gaze of the connoisseur orders the chaotic and heterogeneous sense impressions generated through the categories of beauty and taste. In turn, the Kantian connoisseur can train the public to look at the beautiful and noble objects in the museum in a proper disinterested manner and thus to be constituted as an appreciative aesthetic community.

The sociologist Tony Bennett has written a subtle analysis of nineteenth-century museums and exhibitions, or what he calls the exhibitionary complex, in which he steers a path between spectacular and panoptic analyses of its operation. He defines the exhibitionary complex as 'a set of cultural technologies concerned to organize a voluntarily self-regulating citizenry'.[25] Like Foucault's Panopticon, it was a response to 'the problem of order, but one which worked differently in seeking to transform the problem into one of culture'.[26] It worked:

---

20 Hetherington, 'From Blindness to blindness', p. 65.
21 M. Foucault, *Discipline and Punish: The Birth of the Prison* (New York, 1979).
22 Hetherington, 'From Blindness to blindness', p. 66.
23 Ibid.
24 Ibid.
25 T. Bennett, *The Birth of the Museum* (London, 1995).
26 Ibid., p. 63.

through the provision of object lessons in power – the power to command and arrange things and bodies for public display ... to allow the people, and en masse rather than individually, to know rather than be known, to become the subjects rather than the objects of knowledge. Yet, ideally, they sought also to allow the people to know and thence to regulate themselves to become, in seeing themselves from the side of power, both the subjects and objects of knowledge, knowing power and what power knows, and knowing themselves as (ideally) known by power, interiorizing its gaze as a principle of self-surveillance and, hence, self-regulation.[27]

What is noticeable in this analysis is that the visitor to the museum is an observer, whose role is to look at the display of power, as well as observing themselves as power might observe them. According to Jonathan Crary, the nineteenth century produced a particular kind of observer, one appropriate to the emerging mass culture.[28] Crary sees this observer as one aspect of the emerging subject of the nineteenth century described by Foucault. This was the free-floating subject of the industrial revolution, torn away from the agrarian communities and family arrangements of pre-industrial society, and who needed to be regulated and controlled.[29] Crary is interested in particular in the many technologies of vision, such as photography and stereoscopy, which were developed in the early nineteenth century, which 'codified and normalized the observer within rigidly defined systems of visual consumption'.[30]

Through Bennett's analysis it is possible to see the museum also as a technology of vision, operating in a similar manner as such technologies. It is a place of visual consumption that presumes and addresses a particular kind of observer. It is therefore precisely a medium, a system of display through which messages are communicated, and which mediates those messages. The historian of early cinema Mark B. Sandberg has studied the relation between folk museums in Scandinavia at the end of the last century and cinema spectatorship.[31] He points out how the way that such museums were experienced was through 'composite viewing habits from a variety of late nineteenth-century attractions, habits usually identified with modernity (a taste for distraction. mobile subjectivity, panoptic perspectives, and voyeuristic viewing)'.[32] He suggests that the late nineteenth century, through the development of optical and recording

---

27   Ibid., p. 64.

28   J. Crary, *Techniques of the Observer* (Cambridge, MA and London, 1992), pp. 6–7.

29   Ibid., p. 15.

30   Ibid., p. 18.

31   M. Sandberg, 'Effigy and Narrative: Looking at the Nineteenth Century Folk Museum', in L. Charney and V.R. Schwartz (eds), *Cinema and the Invention of Modern Life* (Berkeley, 1995).

32   Ibid., p. 321.

technologies, the circulation of mass-produced images and new institutionalized forms of viewing created the conditions for a 'roving patronage of the visual arts', which encompassed the museum as well as the early cinema.[33]

It is perhaps the greater mobility of images made possible by photography and cinema that, in enabling the irruption of the heterogeneous other into the spaces of modernity, made possible challenges to the regime of the Kantian gaze. Hetherington suggests that though some might cite Freudianism, which reveals 'the inner heterogeneity of the subject under the name of the unconscious', the first such challenge came from Duchamp, Dada and the Surrealists' project 'fundamentally to restore heterogeneity to the object world by challenging its taming within the disciplined assumptions about exhibitionary spaces and their associated positioning of the viewing subject'.[34] Most famously of course this was achieved by Duchamp's ready-made piece, the urinal he exhibited as 'Fountain' under the name R. Mutt at an exhibition organized by the Society of Independent Artists, which had declared that they would exhibit any piece submitted (see Plate 11.1). As Hetherington puts it.

> A piece of porcelain that one urinated in, displayed in a museum, mocks the idea of formal and disinterested judgement, one can only be shocked or laugh at the idea established by the spatial location of such an item and the idea that such an object can have beauty. Such an object is heterogeneous and one can only behave in an undisciplined way before it.[35]

As such the urinal 'performs a blind spot before the eye'.[36] (In an earlier unpublished version of his paper he then suggests it 'gets up and pisses all over the museum floor'.) He continues that '[T]he ready-made cannot be seen by the modern eye without that eye being revealed to itself as an artifice' and suggests that '[O]ne is hardly encouraged to discipline one's inner heterogeneity in the face of such unassimilable heterogeneity.'[37] Perhaps the best representation of this for Hetherington is the moment in Luis Buñuel and Salvador Dali's film *Un Chien Andalou* when a young woman's eye appears to be slit open. This is the slitting open of the Kantian eye, that allows all the heterogeneity to spill from within the subject into the material world of things.[38]

Near the end of his paper Hetherington presents a challenge; that the next issue will be to:

---

33   Ibid., p. 322.
34   Hetherington, 'From Blindness to blindness', p. 68.
35   Ibid.
36   Ibid., p. 69.
37   Ibid.
38   Ibid.

reveal the unbounded and fluid character of the object, dissolved into a similitude of signification with no attachment to a subject at all ... That is perhaps the project for the next type of museum. Perhaps the museum is already here but we have yet to be able to fully see it and identify its location. It is unlikely to be found in the social space of the modern museum but somewhere else.[39]

One answer to this might be that the new location of the next type of museum is to be found online, in the reciprocal participatory spaces of the internet and the World Wide Web. As in the cinema the traditional museum message goes only one way. It goes out from the museum to the people, but they cannot communicate back. Thus, if understood in terms of media, the museum is a one-to-many, unidirectional medium. In this it is similar to the twentieth-century mass-media technologies: film, the radio, and television which were developed out of nineteenth-century technological advances, and, more to the point, manifest nineteenth-century ideologies of the spectator.

This uneven reciprocity of communication in the media has been a cause of concern for commentators, particularly from the Left, from the Frankfurt School onwards. Adorno and Horkheimer wrote of a monolithic entity they called the 'culture industry', in which radio, for example, turns 'all participants into listeners and authoritatively subjects them to broadcast programs which are all exactly the same. No machinery of rejoinder has been devised, and private broadcasters are denied any freedom.'[40]

Pessimistic analyses such as those of Adorno and Horkheimer have been criticized for their reductive simplification of a set of complicated phenomena. There are, arguably, different kinds of relations within the apparently monolithic media industries, and possibilities for reciprocation. Their analyses also depended on a characterization of the receiving subject as entirely passive. They failed to engage with the ways that messages may be received and used in ways other than those intended by their senders. Yet they are right in seeing most media in terms of being concerned only with distribution, rather than communication, the messages going only one way, from a single transmitter to many receivers. Perhaps, more controversially, they suggest that the technologies themselves are deliberately developed to exclude, as far as possible, the possibilities of reciprocal communication. Following them, Hans Magnus Enzensberger suggests that this is merely a technological problem:

> Electronic techniques recognize no contradiction in principle between transmitter and receiver. Every transistor radio is, by the nature of its construction at the same time a potential transmitter – it can interact with other receivers by circuit reversal. The development from a mere distribution medium to a

---

39   Ibid., p. 70.
40   T. Adorno and M. Horkheimer, *Dialectic of Enlightenment* (London and New York, 1979), p. 122.

communication medium is technically not a problem. It is consciously prevented for understandable political reasons.[41]

Enzensberger suggested that it is merely a matter of political will to enable reciprocal communication in mass media. He also saw it as a duty of the radical Left to effect such reciprocity.[42]

In Enzensberger's analysis there is one medium which has from the beginning maintained the capacity for two-way communication: the telephone. But the telephone differed from other media by being a one-to-one medium, or at best one-to-a-few. Though developments such as party lines, faxes and so on may have increased its potential for sending a message to more than one receiver, it was not a useful way of disseminating messages widely. Thus it might be argued that its capacity for far-reaching reciprocal communication was tolerable to the powers that be because of its ineffectiveness as a mass medium. Even so Enzensberger, among others, saw that telephone networks represented a model of media that contained, immanently, the potential for free and liberatory forms of mass communication.

Enzensberger was writing when the internet barely existed. Nevertheless, his essay anticipates such a network, without being able fully to imagine what it might be like and how it might work. While he was imagining the possibilities of, among other things, two-way radio networks and 'electro-libraries', the American Defense Department had already set up a network of computers in government departments, universities and businesses, based on a structure that would link communications systems in such a way that if any part was disabled by a nuclear strike, the rest could continue to communicate. This network, known as ARPAnet was, ironically, given its origin in the military-industrial complex, the beginnings of the internet, the communications system which has come closest to realizing Enzensburger's and others' ideas.

To begin with the internet was limited mainly to enabling messages, email, to be sent from one user to another. In this it was little more than a textual variation of the telephone. Soon, however, interested parties began to develop ways of using the technology to broadcast messages through bulletin boards. In the late 1980s scientists at the European nuclear research laboratory, CERN, were looking for a way to disseminate their findings and papers to colleagues more quickly than conventional paper methods. They developed a way of publishing material of various sorts on the internet. Later developments enabled the inclusion of pictures, sound and video as well as text. Anyone with the right equipment and software could view this material. With a little more equipment people could publish their own material. Though at first limited to a few users this subsystem has recently achieved wide dissemination and popularity, and has became known as the World Wide Web.

---

41   H.M. Enzensberger, 'Constituents of a Theory of the Media', in J. Hanhardt (ed.), *Video Culture: A Critical Investigation* (New York, 1987), p. 98.

42   Ibid., pp. 98–9.

The internet seems to be precisely the emancipatory reciprocal mass medium dreamt of by Enzensberger. In addition to the practical opportunities made possible by its existence it also offers a powerful model of communication and knowledge dissemination. One place, I suggest, it has started to resonate is in discussions of the museum. As a network of decentralized communication it counters the centralized and hierarchical model of knowledge dissemination that the museum represents. But it also presents an opportunity for the museum to be rethought in ways that may be more appropriate to this postmodern, post-colonial age.

But this is in turn begs another question; how will the act of seeing the material contents of such a museum work, especially if it is to realize the 'unbounded and fluid character of the object, dissolved into a similitude of signification with no attachment to a subject at all', and also go beyond the provocative gestures of the avant-garde in merely disrupting a space still ordered according to the regime of the Kantian gaze. To answer this I turn to another discussion of the gaze, this time by Norman Bryson, from the symposium on 'vision and visuality' held at the Dia Art Foundation in New York in 1988, and published as a short book of that name in the same year. Bryson's contribution is entitled 'The Gaze in the Expanded Field'.[43] He starts with an account of some of the conceptions of the gaze in twentieth-century continental thought, in particular those of Jean-Paul Sartre and Jacques Lacan, which are in some ways the theoretical equivalents to the Duchampian, Dadaist and Surrealist strategies described above. Bryson acknowledges that both Sartre and Lacan were unmistakeably concerned with a radical decentring of the subject, but also suggests that in crucial respects their thinking 'remains held within a conceptual enclosure, where vision is still theorized from the standpoint of a subject placed at the center of the world'.[44] Bryson recounts two of the most common scenarios concerning vision put forward by these thinkers; Sartre's scenario of the watcher in the park and Lacan's exchange with a Brittany fisherman about a sardine can.

In Sartre's story, he enters a park where he is, at first, alone, and thus at the centre of the visual field, unchallenged 'master of its prospects, sovereign surveyor of the scene'. But this reign ends when another person enters the park and suddenly Sartre is no longer the sole seer but also the seen, and the lines of force which had converged on him now reconverge on the intruder, making Sartre a tangent rather than a centre.[45] Bryson compares this to the vanishing point in perspectival painting that implies the position of the viewer in a corresponding vanishing point mirrored on the other side of the picture plane. 'The self-possession of the viewing subject has built into it, therefore, the principle of its own abolition: annihilation of the subject as center is a condition of the very moment of the look.'[46] In Lacan's

43   N. Bryson, 'The Gaze in the Expanded Field', in H. Foster (ed.), *Vision and Visuality* (Seattle, 1988).

44   Ibid., pp. 87–8.

45   Ibid., pp. 88–9.

46   Ibid., p. 91.

story he is with some fisherman out on the open sea near Brittany. One of the fishermen indicates a sardine can floating on the surface of the sea, and says to Lacan 'You see that can? Do you see it? Well it doesn't see you?' Yet for Lacan this observation is in some senses untrue. As Bryson puts it 'the world of inanimate objects to some extent always looks back at the viewer'.[47] This is because the visual field is interrupted, not in this case by another viewer, but by the Signifier.

> When I look, what I see is not simply light but intelligible form: the *rays* of light are caught in a *rets* [fr: trap, snare], a network of meanings, the same way that flotsam is caught in the net of the fishermen. For human beings collectively to orchestrate their visual experience together it is required that each submit his or her retinal experience to the socially agreed description(s) of an intelligible world.[48]

He continues that '[B]etween retina and world is inserted a screen of signs, a screen consisting of all the multiple discourses on vision built into the social arena.'[49] When we look through this screen what we see is 'caught up in a network that comes to outside from the outside' a 'visual discourse that saw the world before I saw it and will go on seeing after I see no longer'. What I see 'exists independently of my life and outside it' and is 'indifferent to my mortality'. The network of signifiers 'cuts into' my visual field and the screen 'casts a shadow of death', which Bryson compares to the anamorphic skull in Holbein's painting *The Ambassadors*.[50] (see Plate 11.2). Thus for Bryson the seeing subject is as decentred as the speaking subject. What he or she sees is as formed by paths and networks laid down in advance of their seeing, just as much as what the speaking subject says follows paths or networks that he or she has neither created or controlled.

For the Japanese philosopher Keiji Nishitani, to whom Bryson now turns, Sartre's nihilism is 'half-hearted'. Having fully understood the death of God and the consequent field of nihility in which it exists, and refused the possibility of an ethics imposed on the outside, the Sartrean *je* 'reacts by falling back on itself, and by struggling to locate an authenticity of the self from which ethical action can emanate directly'. This is intended to overcome the nihility in which everything is cast into doubt as a result of the death of God. Yet treating the field of nihility as something against which the self reacts merely reinforces the subject's position at the centre of its experience. Thus the experience of being seen by another in the park, and therefore being objectified by the other's gaze, does not fundamentally challenge the status of either as a subject. Instead of embracing a full decentring of the position of the subject, Sartre and Lacan both react to such

---

47   Ibid.
48   Ibid.
49   Ibid., p. 92.
50   Ibid., pp. 92–3.

a possibility as a threat and a menace.[51] Nishitani is also concerned to deconstruct the Cartesian subject, but to do so he turns to an intellectual resource from his own cultural background, the Buddhist concept of *śūnyatā*, which can be translated as 'emptiness', 'radical impermanence', 'blankness' and 'nihility'.[52]

In the field of *śūnyatā* neither subject nor object can be sustained as separate. Only by screening out the rest of the universe and by cutting into the field can a stable entity persist as a fixed form with a bounded outline. Otherwise all entities, all objects, exist only as part of a mobile continuum. Any entity is part of the universal field of transformations, and cannot be stabilized or separated out. It 'cannot enjoy independent self-existence, since the ground of its being is the existence of everything else'. Thus objects' presence can only be defined in negative terms, and an object is really only the difference between what appears as it and everything else.[53] This is close to Saussure's description of the operations of language in terms of difference, and because entities are also changing and differentiating over time, also close to Derrida's radicalization of Saussurean difference in terms of *différance*, meaning both spatial difference and deferral in time.[54] Bryson's example is that of a flower, which is only a 'phase of incremental transformations between seed and dust, in a continuous exfoliation or perturbation of matter'.[55] He also quotes Nishitani's two aphorisms, that 'fire does not burn fire' and 'water does not wash water', meaning that both fire and water only become distinctly what they are when they meet and are interpenetrated by other entities, such as when wood is burned or fields are flooded.[56]

It can be argued that the various gazes from that of the prince in the Renaissance to the Kantian gaze in the eighteenth century are products of the culture of printing and linear perspective. The challenges to these gazes offered by Duchamp, Dada and Surrealism are the products of mass media and mechanical reproduction. If this is so, then it might also be suggested that the model of the gaze and of subjectivity that Bryson finds in Nishitani's use of the idea of *śūnyatā* is appropriate for a new media paradigm, that of digital networks such as the internet. As is well known the internet is based quite literally on a decentred structure. Its distributed system means there is no, indeed there can be no centre. Furthermore, being both binary and digital, what it contains is in the end nothing but pure difference; the difference between 0 and 1. The extraordinary reach and massive interconnectivity of the internet and the World Wide Web also mean that it is almost impossible for anyone to imagine they occupy any kind of central point within its *rets*. And since every page on the World Wide Web is implicitly or explicitly connected with so many others, the idea of the autonomous subject seems largely irrelevant here.

---

51 Ibid., pp. 94–6.
52 Ibid., p. 97.
53 Ibid.
54 Ibid., p. 98.
55 Ibid., p. 97.
56 Ibid., p. 99.

Thus it might be on the web, understood as a 'space' of radical impermanence and emptiness that Hetherington's search for a 'new type of museum' in which to express 'the unbounded and fluid character of the object, dissolved into a similitude of signification with no attachment to a subject at all' might be found. But what might it look like? Not at all like the various attempts to build 'virtual museums' would certainly be one answer. A more plausible response might be something a bit like Flickr, the Web 2.0 application that allows anyone to upload photographs and videos and, increasingly, do a lot more besides. As of November 2007 there were two billion images on Flickr.[57] The sheer scale of such an archive suggests not just that it will be necessarily extraordinarily heterogeneous in terms of subject matter, style and type of image, but also that no attempt by any individual to master that heterogeneity is possible. There is no subject position, no central point from which such a vast array of images can be grasped and judged, no table on which it could be laid and organized, and no singular aesthetic community to which it could speak and by which it could be subject to judgements. The very means of gaining access to the images is necessarily opaque. They are hidden somewhere sublimely inaccessible behind the computer screen. The most any individual subject can do is to glimpse the possibility of an infinite number of different images from seeing what they could of what is so far available. When Buñuel and Dali slit open the Kantian eye to empty out the heterogeneity contained within they could not have imagined the sheer amount of stuff that from all the subjects would be disgorged. This is no longer Sartre's park in which the solipsism of the solitary subject is disturbed by the intrusion of a single other, but a crowd of subjects stretching to the horizon, each separate but connected to his or her neighbours. At the end of 'From Blindness to blindness' Hetherington suggests that

> [N]ow the fluid of heterogeneity that was once inside the eye is placed outside, the eye no longer attains the privileged position of being able to represent the subject ... Where once we were Blind to our subjectivity, now blindness is the character of our subjectivity. The object itself begins to see. Our response to the 'seeing' object becomes increasingly blind. Our knowledge becomes situated ... and partially connected ... Perhaps we have to rely on senses other than sight to explore this new space.[58]

Between October 1990 and January 1991 the Louvre in Paris held an exhibition in the Napoléon Hall entitled *Memoirs of the Blind*. The first of their *Parti Pris* series selected by guest curators; it was organized by Derrida and featured a series of drawings from the Department of Graphic Arts (the equivalent of my father's department at the British Museum) of the blind, including one by Federico Zuccaro, upon whom, along with his brother Taddeo, my father wrote a major

---

57   http://www.flickr.com/photos/88646149@N00/2000000000/.
58   Hetherington, 'From Blindness to blindness', p. 71.

study. The accompanying book by Derrida of the same name[59] engages in a brilliant series of analyses and considerations of the drawings that, unsurprisingly, go way beyond the normal connoisseurial concerns, all around the theme of blindness. Hetherington ends his essay with a quotation from *Memoirs of the Blind*.

> The theme of drawings of the blind is, before all else, the hand. For the hand ventures forth, it precipitates, rushes ahead, certainly, but this time in place of the head, as to precede, prepare and protect it.[60]

Perhaps the hand here is the hand on the computer mouse, venturing forth into the ungraspable world of images behind the computer screen.

---

59   J. Derrida, *Memoirs of the Blind: The Self-Portrait and Other Ruins* (Chicago and London, 1993).

60   Ibid., p. 4.

Bibliography

Addis, Matthew, Hafeez, Shahbaz, Prideaux, Daniel et al., 'The eCHASE System for Cross-border Use of European Multimedia Cultural Heritage Content in Education and Publishing', in *AXMEDIS 2006: 2nd International Conference on Automated Production of Cross Media Content for Multi-channel Distribution*, Leeds, UK, (2006).

Addis, Matthew et al., 'New Ways to Search, Navigate and Use Multimedia Museum Collections over the Web', in *Museums and the Web 2005* (Vancouver, 2005).

Adorno, T. and Horkheimer, M., *Dialectic of Enlightenment* (London and New York, 1979), p. 122.

Agamben, Giorgio, *Infancy and History: Essays on the Destruction of Experience*, trans. Liz Heron (London, Verso, 1993).

Agre, Philip E., 'Surveillance and Capture: Two Models of Privacy', in Noah Wardrip-Fruin and Nick Montfort (eds), *The NewMediaReader* (Cambridge: MIT Press, 2003).

AHDS, 'Note of Expert Seminar: Strategic Approaches to Developing the e-infrastructure for Arts and Humanities Research, 1 April 2008, Wellcome Institute, London', unpublished (2008), p. 20.

AHDS Digital Images Archiving Study, <http://ahds.ac.uk/about/projects/archivingstudies/ digital-images-archiving-study.pdf>.

Andersen, Peter Bøgh, *A Theory of Computer Semiotics* (Cambridge: Cambridge University Press, 1999).

Anderson, Chris, *The Long Tail: How Endless Choice is Creating Unlimited Demand* (London: Random House Business Books, 2007).

Anderson, S. and Heery, R., *Digital Repositories Review* (2005), para. 4.1, p. 15.

Appadurai, A., *Globalization* (Durham, NC: Duke University Press, 2001), p. 10.

Aroyo, Lora, Stash, Natalia, Wang, Yiwen et al., 'CHIP Demonstrator: Semantics-Driven Recommendations and Museum Tour Generation', in *The Semantic Web. 6th International Semantic Web Conference, 2nd Asian Semantic Web Conference, ISWC 2007 + ASWC 2007, Busan, Korea, November 11–15, 2007. Proceedings* (Berlin: Springer, 2008).

Atkins, Robert, 'The Art World (and I) Go On Line', *Art in America*, 83/12 (1995): 58–65.

Bailey, C., 'Rapporteur's Report', AHRC ICT Methods Network Expert Seminar on Visual Arts: From Pigments to Pixels (2006), http://www.methodsnetwork.ac.uk/redist/pdf/es5rapreport.pdf: 1.

Baines, A. and Brophy, K. 'What's Another Word for Thesaurus? Data Standards and Classifying the Past', in P. Daly and T.L. Evans (eds), *Digital Archaeology: Bridging Method and Theory* (London: Routledge, 2006).

Bakewell, E., Beeman, W.O., and Reese, C.M., *Object Image Inquiry: The Art Historian at Work*; Report on a Collaborative study by the Getty Art History Information Program (AHIP) and the Institute for Research in Information and Scholarship (IRIS), Brown University (Santa Monica, CA.: AHIP, 1988), p. 72.

Baumgartel, Tilman, *net.art 2.0: New Materials Towards Net Art* (Nuremberg: Institut fur Moderne Kunst, 2001).

Beacham, Richard, *The Roman Theatre and Its Audience* (London: Routledge, 1991).

Beacham, Richard, 'Reconstructing Ancient Theatre with the Aid of Computer Simulation', *Crossing the Stages: The Production, Performance, and Reception of Ancient Theater, Syllecta Classica*, 10 (1999): 189–208.

Beacham, Richard and Denard, Hugh, 'The Pompey Project: Digital Research and Virtual Reconstruction of Rome's First Theatre', *Computers and the Humanities*, 37/1 (2003), 129–39.

Beagrie, N., 'The JISC Digital Preservation Focus and the Digital Preservation Coalition', *New Review of Academic Librarianship*, 6 (2000): 257–67.

Benjamin, Walter, 'The Work of Art in the Age of Mechanical Reproduction' (1936), trans. Harry Zohn, in W. Benjamin, *Illuminations* (London: Jonathan Cape, 1970).

Bennett, T., *The Birth of the Museum* (London, 1995).

Benveniste, Emile, 'A Semiology of Language', in Robert E. Innis (ed.), *Semiotics: An Introductory Anthology* (Bloomington: Indiana University Press, 1985), pp. 228–46.

Berners-Lee, Tim, Hendler, James and Lassila, Ora, 'The Semantic Web', *Scientific American*, May (2001).

Berry, Josephine, 'Art is Useless', *Mute*, 13 (1999): 52–7.

Berry, Josephine, 'Do As They Do, Not As They Do', *Mute*, 16 (2000): 22–3.

Berry, Josephine, 'Repeat and Win', *Mute*, 22 (2001): 58–9.

Blais, Joline and Ippolito, Jon, *At the Edge of Art* (London: Thames and Hudson, 2006).

Boast, Robin, Bravo, Michael and Srinivasan, Ramesh, 'Return to Babel: Emergent Diversity, Digital Resources, and Local Knowledge', *The Information Society*, 23/5 (2007).

Bohrer, Frederick, N., 'Photographic Perspectives: Photography and the Institutional Formation of Art History', in Elizabeth Mansfield (ed.), *Art History and Its Institutions: Foundations of a Discipline* (London: Routledge, 2002), pp. 246–59.

Bolder, David Jay and Grusin, Richard, *Remediation: Understanding New Media* (Cambridge: MIT Press, 1999).

Bosma, Josephine, 'Is it Commercial? Noooo ... Is it Spam? Nooo – its net.art!', *Mute*, 10 (1998): 73–4.

Bosma, Josephine, 'Net Art: Building Something out of Nothing Self Education, Collaboration and Networking' (2005), http://laudanum.net/cgi-bin/media. cgi?action=display&id=1118750062.

Bowker, Geoffrey C. and Star, Susan Leigh, *Sorting Things Out: Classification and Its Consequences* (Cambridge, MA: MIT Press, 1999).

Brooks, F.P., 'No Silver Bullet – Essence and Accident in Software Engineering', *Proceedings of the IFIP Tenth World Computing Conference*, 1986, pp. 1069–1076.

Brown, Frank Edward, *Roman Architecture* (New York: G. Brazilier, 1961).

Brown, Laura, Griffiths, Rebecca and Rascoff, Matthew, 'University Publishing in a Digital Age', *Ithaka Report*, http://www.ithaka.org/strategic-services/Ithaka %20University%20Publishing%20Report.pdf (New York, 2007).

Bryson, N., 'The Gaze in the Expanded Field', in H. Foster (ed.), *Vision and Visuality* (Seattle, 1988).

Burdea, Grigore and Coiffet, Philippe, *Virtual Reality Technology*, 2nd edn (Hoboken: Wiley-Interscience, 2003).

Burford, Bryan, Briggs, Pamela and Eakins, John P., 'A Taxonomy of the Image: On the Classification of Content for Image Retrieval', *Visual Communication*, 2/2 (2003): 123–61.

Butler, Judith, *Bodies That Matter: On the Discursive Limits of 'Sex'* (New York: Routledge, 1993).

Canter, David, *The Psychology of Place* (London: The Architectural Press, 1977).

CEDARS, *Long-term Access and Usability of Digital Resources: The Digital Preservation Conundrum* http://www.ariadne.ac.uk/issue18/cedars/.

Chan, Sebastian, 'Tagging and Searching – Serendipity and Museum Collection Databases', in J. Trant and D. Bearman (eds), *Museums and the Web 2007: Proceedings* (Toronto: Archives and Museum Informatics, 2007).

Chun, Wendy Hui Kyong, 'Scenes of Empowerment: Virtual Empowerment and Digital Divides', in *New York University Humanities Graduate Colloquium* (New York: New York University, 2001).

Cohn, Cindy A. and Grimmelman, James, 'Seven Ways in Which Code Equals Law (And One in Which it Does Not)', in *Ars Electronica 2003: Code: The Language of Our Time* (Linz: Hatje Cantz Publishers, 2003).

Condron, F., Richards, J., Robinson, D. et al., *Strategies for Digital Data* (York: Archaeology Data Service, 1999).

Content-based image retrieval: http://en.wikipedia.org/wiki/CBiR.

Cook, Terry, 'Archival Science and Postmodernism: New Formulations for Old Concepts' *Archival Science*, 1/1 (2000): 3–24.

Corby, Tom (ed.), *Network Art: Practices and Positions* (London: Routledge, 2005).

Crary, J., *Techniques of the Observer* (Cambridge, MA and London, 1992), pp. 6–7.

Cripps, Paul, Greenhalgh, Anne, Fellows, Dave et al., 'Ontological Modelling of the Work of the Centre for Archaeology' (Centre for Archaeology, English Heritage, 2004).

Crofts, Nicholas, 'Combining Data Sources – Prototype Applications Developed for Geneva's Department of Historical Sites and Monuments Based on the CIDOC CRM' (2004).

Crofts, Nicholas et al., 'Definition of the CIDOC Conceptual Reference Model. Version 4.2.4' (2008) http://cidoc.ics.forth.gr/docs/cidoc_crm_version_4.2.4_March2008_.pdf.

Daniel, Sharon, 'The Database: An Aesthetics of Dignity', in Victoria Vesna (ed.), *Database Aesthetics: Art in the Age of Information Overflow* (Minneapolis: University of Minnesota Press, 2007).

Datta, Ritendra, Ge, Weina, Li, Jia et al., 'Toward Bridging the Annotation-Retrieval Gap in Image Search by a Generative Modelling Approach', *Proceedings of the ACM International Conference on Multimedia* (2006).

Datta, Ritendra, Joshi, Dhiraj, Li, Jia et al., 'Image Retrieval: Ideas, Influences, and Trends of the New Age', *ACM Computing Surveys*, 40/2 (2008).

Derrida, Jacques, *Margins of Philosophy* (Chicago: University of Chicago Press, 1982).

Derrida, Jacques, *Memoirs of the Blind: The Self-Portrait and Other Ruins* (Chicago and London, 1993).

Derrida, Jacques, *Archive Fever: A Freudian Impression* (Chicago: University of Chicago Press, 1996).

Derrida, Jacques, *Paper Machine* (Stanford, CA: Stanford University Press, 2005).

Dietz, Steve, 'Why Have There Been No Great Net Artists?' in Lucy Kimbell (ed.), *New Media Art: Practice and Context in the UK 1994–2004* (Manchester: Arts Council England/Cornerhouse, 2004), pp. 74–82.

Dietz, Steve, 'The Database Imaginary: Memory_Archive_Database v 4.0', in Victoria Vesna (ed.) *Database Aesthetics: Art in the Age of Information Overflow* (Minneapolis: University of Minnesota Press, 2007).

DigiCULT, 'DigiCULT Issue 3: Towards a Semantic Web for Heritage Resources' (2003).

Dix, A., *Called xxxxx while Waiting for a Title*, Position paper, HCI, the Arts and Humanities, Kings Manor, York, July 2003, http://www.comp.lancs.ac.uk/~dixa/papers/xxxxx-2003/.

Doerr, Martin, 'The CIDOC Conceptual Reference Module: An Ontological Approach to Semantic Interoperability of Metadata', *AI Magazine*, 24/3 (2003).

Doerr, Martin and Iorizzo, Dolores, 'The Dream of a Global Knowledge Network: A New Approach', *Journal on Computing and Cultural Heritage*, 1/1 (2008).

Doerr, Martin, Schaller, Kurt and Theodoridou, Maria, 'Integration of Complementary Archaeological Sources', paper presented at CAA 2004, Prato, Italy.

Dourish, Paul, *Where the Action Is: The Foundation of Embodied Interaction* (Cambridge: MIT Press, 2004).

Dunning, A. and Pringle, M., *Ban All Digital Cameras?*, http://ahds.ac.uk/news/ban-digital-cameras.htm.

Eide, Oyvind, Felicetti, Achille, Ore, Christian-Emil, et al., 'Encoding Cultural Heritage Information for the Semantic Web. Procedures for Data Integration through CIDOC-CRM Mapping', in David Arnold, Franco Niccolucci, Daniel Pletinck et al. (eds), *Open Digital Cultural Heritage Systems, EPOCH Final Event Rome, February 2008* (EPOCH, 2008).

Enzensberger, H.M., 'Constituents of a Theory of the Media', in J. Hanhardt (ed.), *Video Culture: A Critical Investigation* (New York, 1987), p. 98.

Ernst, Wolfgang, 'Dis/continuities: Does the Archive Become Metaphorical in Multi–Media Space?', in Wendy Hui Kyong Chun and Thomas Keenan (eds), *New Media, Old Media: A History and Theory Reader* (New York: Routledge, 2006), pp. 105–23.

Ester, M., *Image Use in Art – Historical Practice* (1993), http://arl.cni.org/symp3/ester.html.

Featherstone, Mike, 'The Archive', *Theory, Culture and Society*, 23/2–3 (2007). 591–6.

Fernie, Eric (ed.), *Art History and Its Methods: A Critical Anthology* (London: Phaidon Press Limited, 1995).

Fleischmann, M. and Strauss, W., 'Images of the Body in the House of Illusion', first published in C. Sommerer and L. Mignonneau (eds), *Art and Science* (Berlin, 1998), pp. 133–147.

Forsyth, D.A. et al., 'Finding Pictures of Objects in Large Collections of Images', in *Object Representation in Computer Vision II, Lecture Notes in Computer Science*, vol. 1144 (1996), pp. 335–60.

Foster, Hal, 'An Archival Impulse', *October*, 110 (Fall 2004): 3–22.

Foster, N.F. and Gibbons, S., 'Understanding Faculty to Improve Content Recruitment for Institutional Repositories', *D-Lib Magazine*, 11/1 (2005), http://www.dlib.org/dlib/january05/foster/01foster.html.

Foucault, M., *Discipline and Punish: The Birth of the Prison* (New York, 1979).

Foucault, M. 'What is an Author?', in Donald Preziosi (ed.), *The Art of Art History* (Oxford: Oxford University Press, 1998).

Frosh, Paul, *The Image Factory* (New York: Berg, 2003).

Galloway, Alex, 'net.art Year in Review: State of net.art 99', *Switch*, 5/3 (1999).

Galloway, Alexander R., *Protocol: How Control Exists After Decentralization* (Cambridge: The MIT Press, 2004).

Gere, Charlie, *Art, Time and Technology* (Oxford: Berg, 2006).

Gere, Charlie, 'Network Art and the Networked Gallery', Tate Online, http://www.tate.org.uk/netart/networkgallery.htm (London, 2006).

Gere, J., 'Introduction' to J. Stock and D. Scrase, *The Achievement of a Connoisseur: Philip Pouncey* (Cambridge, 1985).

Getty Vocabulary Program, http://getty.edu/research/conducting_research/vocabularies/.

Gitelman, Lisa, *Always Already New: Media, History, and the Data of Culture* (Cambridge: MIT Press, 2006).

Godfrey, J., 'A Digital Future for Slide Libraries?', *Art Libraries Journal*, 29/1 (2004): 10–22.

Gonzalez, Jennifer, 'Autotopographies', in Gabriel Brahm Jr and Mark Driscoll (eds), *Prosthetic Territories: Politics and Hypertechnologies* (Boulder: Westview Press, 1995).

Graham, Janna and Yasin, Shadya, 'Reframing Participation in the Museum: Syncopated Discussion', in Griselda Pollock and Joyce Zemans (eds), *Museums After Modernism: Strategies of Engagement* (Oxford: Blackwell Publishing, 2007).

Graham, M.E. and Bailey, C., 'Digital Images and Art Historians', *Art Libraries Journal*, 31/3 (2006): 23.

Grau, Oliver (ed.), *MediaArtHistories* (Cambridge, MA: MIT Press, 2007).

Green, K., 'More-accurate Video Search', *Technology Review*, 12 June 2007.

Greene, Rachel, 'Web Work: A History of Internet Art', *Artforum*, 38/9 (2000): 162–7, 192.

Greene, Rachel, *Internet Art* (London: Thames and Hudson, 2004).

Gruber, Thomas R., 'Towards Principles for the Design of Ontologies Used for Knowledge Sharing', in Nicola Guarino and Roberto Poli (eds), *Formal Ontology in Conceptual Analysis and Knowledge Representation*, Special issue of the *International Journal of Human and Computer Studies* (Deventer: Kluwer Academic Publishers, 1995).

Haggerty, Kevin D. and Ericson, Richard V., 'The Surveillant Assemblage', *British Journal of Sociology*, 51/4 (2000): 605–22.

Harm, Deborah, 'Motion Sickness Neurophysiology, Physiological Correlates and Treatment', in Kay M. Stanney (ed.), *Handbook of Virtual Environments: Design, Implementation, and Applications* (Mahwah: Lawrence Erlbaum Associates, 2002), pp. 637–61.

Hatt, Michael and Klonk, Charlotte, *Art History: A Critical Introduction to Its Methods* (Manchester: Manchester University Press, 2006).

HEFCE, Zipped pdf file, Unit 3 Art and Design, RAE 2008 Subject Overview Report (2009), http://www.rae.ac.uk/pubs/2009/ov/: 2.

Heidegger, M., *The Question Concerning Technology and Other Essays* (New York, 1977), p. 129.

Heron, Michal, *Digital Stock Photography: How to Shoot and Sell* (New York: Allworth Press, 2007).

Hetherington, K., 'From Blindness to blindness: Museums, Heterogeneity and the Subject', in J. Law and J. Hassard (eds), *Actor Network Theory and After* (Oxford and Malden, MA, 1999).

Hildebrand, Michiel, van Ossenbruggen, Jacco and Hardman, Lynda, '/facet: A Browser for Heterogeneous Semantic Web Repositories', *The Semantic Web – ISWC 2006* (2006): 272–85, http://dx.doi.org/10.1007/11926078_20.

Holt, B. and Hartwick, L., '"Quick, Who Painted Fish?": Searching a Picture Database with the QBIC project at UC Davis', *Information Services and Use*, 14 (1994): 79–90.

hooks, bell, *Black Looks: Race and Representation* (Boston: South End Press, 1992).

House of Commons Education and Skills Committee, *UK e-University: Third Report* (2004–2005), summary, p. 3.

Hyde, Vernon, Minor, *Art History's History* (New York: Harry N. Abrams, 1994).

Hyperbolic trees, <http://www.thebrain.com/>.

Hyvönen, Eero et al., 'MuseumFinland – Finnish Museums on the Semantic Web', *Web Semantics: Science, Services and Agents on the World Wide Web*, 3/2–3 (2005).

Hyvönen, Eero, Ruotsalo, Tuukka, Häggström, Thomas et al., 'CultureSampo – Finnish Culture on the Semantic Web: The Vision and First Results', in *Information Technology for the Virtual Museum* (Berlin: LIT Verlag, 2007).

Iconclass, <http://www.iconclass.nl/index.html>.

'Inherent Vice: The Replica and its Implications in Modern Sculpture Workshop', *Tate Papers*, Issue 8 (London, 2007), http://www.tate.org.uk/research/tateresearch/tatepapers/07autumn/.

INSCRIPTION, <http://www.fish-forum.info/inscript.htm>.

International Semantic Web Conference, ISWC 2006, Athens, GA, USA, November 5–9, 2006. Proceedings (Berlin: Springer, 2006).

Iqbal, Q. and Aggarwal, J.K., *Combining Structure, Color and Texture for Image Retrieval: A Performance Evaluation*, 16th international Conference on Pattern Recognition (ICPR), Quebec City, QC, Canada, 11–15 august 2002, vol. 2, pp. 438–43.

Jay, M., 'Scopic Regimes of Modernity', in H. Foster (ed.), *Vision and Visuality* (Seattle, 1988), p. 6.

Jeffrey, S. *Three Dimensional Modelling of Scottish Early Medieval Sculpted Stones*, unpublished PhD Thesis, University of Glasgow, 2003.

Jones, Amelia. *Body Art: Performing the Subject* (Minneapolis: University of Minnesota Press, 1998).

Kalay, Yehuda and Marx, John, 'The Role of Place in Cyberspace', in Hal Thwaites and Lon Addison (eds), *Seventh International Conference on Virtual Systems and Multimedia (VSMM'01)* (Berkeley: IEEE Computer Society, 2001), pp. 770–79.

Kant, Immanuel, *Critique of Pure Reason* (London: Macmillan, 1978).

Kant, Immanuel, *Critique of Judgement* (Indianapolis: Hackett, 1987).

Ketelaar, Eric, 'Being Digital in People's Archives', *Archives and Manuscripts*, 31/2 (2003): 8–22.

Kim, S., Lewis, P. and Martinez, K., *SCULPTEUR D7.1 Semantic Network of Concepts and their Relationships* – Public version, IAM, ECS, University of Southampton, 2004 at http://www.sculpteurweb.org/html/events/D7.1_Public. zip.

Kittler, Friedrich, A., *Discourse Networks 1800/1900* (Stanford: Stanford University Press, 1990).

Knoespe, Kenneth J. and Jichen Zhu, 'Continuous Materiality: Through a Hierarchy of Computational Codes', *Fibreculture*, 11 (2007).

'Kodak Confirms Plans To Stop Making Slide Projectors': http://www.kodak. com/us/en/corp/pressReleases/pr20030926-01.shtml.

Larson, Kent, *Louis I. Kahn. Unbuilt Masterworks* (New York: Monacelli Press, 2000).

Lavin, M.A., 'Making Computers Work for the History of Art', *Art Bulletin*, 79/2 (1997): 198.

Lew, Michael S., Sebe, Nicu, Djeraba, Chabane et al., 'Content-Based Multimedia Information Retrieval: State of the Art and Challenges', *ACM Transactions on Multimedia Computing, Communications, and Applications* (February 2006).

Li, Jia and Wang, James Z., 'Automatic Linguistic Indexing of Pictures by a Statistical Modelling Approach', *IEEE Transactions on Pattern Analysis and Machine Intelligence* 25/9 (2003): 1075–88.

Li, Jia and Wang, James Z., 'Real-Time Computerized Annotation of Pictures', *Proceedings of the ACM International Conference on Multimedia* (2006).

Linked Data, <http://linkeddata.org/>.

Lovejoy, Margot, 'Art, Technology, and Postmodernism: Paradigms, Parallels, and Paradoxes', *Art Journal*, 49/3, *Computers and Art: Issues of Content* (Autumn, 1990): 257–65.

Machin, David, 'Building the World's Visual Language: The Increasing Global Importance of Image Banks in Corporate Media', *Visual Communication*, 3/3 (2004): 316–36.

McLuhan, Marshall, *Understanding Media: The Extensions of Man* (London: Routledge, 2001).

Malpas, Jeff, *Place and Experience: A Philosophical Topography* (Cambridge: Cambridge University Press, 2007).

Manovich, Lev, *The Language of New Media* (Cambridge: MIT Media Press, 2001).

Marlow, Cameron, Naaman, Mor, boyd, danah et al., 'HT06, Tagging Paper, Taxonomy, Flickr, Academic Article, ToRead', in *Proceedings of Hypertext 2006* (New York: Hypertext, 2006), p. 2.

Merewether, Charles, *The Archive* (Whitechapel, MIT Press, 2006).

Merleau-Ponty, Maurice, *The Visible and the Invisible*, trans. Alphonso Lingis (Evanston: Northwestern University Press, 1969).

Munster, Anna, *Materializing New Media: Embodiment in Information Aesthetics* (Hanover: Dartmouth College Press, 2006),

Murray, Heather, 'Monstrous Play in Negative Spaces: Illegible Bodies and the Cultural Construction of Biometric Technology', *The Communication Review*, 10/4 (2007): 347–65.

Nancy, Jean-Luc, 'Being Singular Plural', in *Being Singular Plural* (Stanford: Stanford University Press, 2000).

Nelson, Robert, S., 'The Slide Lecture, or the Work of Art *History* in the Age of Mechanical Reproduction', *Critical Inquiry*, 26/3 (2000): 414–34.

Nelson, Steve, 'Emancipation and the Freed in American Sculpture: Race, Representation, and the Beginnings of an African American History of Art', in Elizabeth Mansfield (ed.), *Art History and Its Institutions: Foundations of a Discipline* (London: Routledge, 2002).

Nochlin, Linda, *Women, Art and Power and Other Essays* (London: Thames and Hudson, 1989).

Norberg-Schulz, Christian, *Genius Loci. Towards a Phenomenology of Architecture* (New York: Rizzoli, 1984).

The Object in Transition: A Cross Disciplinary Conference on the Preservation and Study of Modern and Contemporary Art, Getty Center (Los Angeles, January 2008), http://www.getty.edu/conservation/publications/videos/object_in_transition.html.

Oceanic art: http://www.oceanicart.com.au/.

Open Archives Initiative Protocol for Metadata Harvesting, <http://www.openarchives.org/pmh/>.

van Ossenbruggen, Jacco et al., 'Searching and Annotating Virtual Heritage Collections with Semantic-Web Techniques', paper presented at Museums and the Web 2007, San Francisco.

OWL Web Ontology Language Overview, http://www.w3.org/TR/owl-features/.

Panofsky, E., 'The History of Art as a Humanistic Discipline', in *Meaning in the Visual Arts: Papers in and on Art History* (Garden City, NY: Doubleday Anchor Books, 1955), p. 7.

Parry, Ross, Poole, Nick and Pratty, Jon, 'Semantic Dissonance: Do We Need (And Do We Understand) The Semantic Web?', paper presented at Museums and the Web 2008, Montreal, Canada.

Paul, Christiane, *Digital Art* (London: Thames and Hudson, 2003).

Poster, Mark, *Information Please: Culture and Politics in the Age of Digital Machines* (Durham: Duke University Press, 2006).

Poster, Mark, 'Textual Agents: History at "The End of History"', in John Carlos Rowe (ed.), *'Culture' and the Problem of the Disciplines* (New York: Columbia University Press, 1998).

Prensky, M., 'Digital Natives, Digital Immigrants', *On the Horizon*, 9/5 (2001), http://www.marcprensky.com/writing/default.asp.

Preziosi, Donald, 'The Art of Art History', in Donald Preziosi (ed.), *The Art of Art History: A Critical Anthology* (Oxford: Oxford University Press, 1998).

Preziosi, Donald, *Rethinking Art History: Meditations on a Coy Science* (New Haven: Yale University Press, 1989).

Preziosi, Donald, 'Art History: Making the Visible Legible', in Donald Preziosi (ed.), *The Art of Art History: A Critical Anthology* (Oxford: Oxford University Press, 1998).

Pringle, M., 'The People Versus Technology', *Art Libraries Journal*, 31/3 (2006): 16–20.

Rasmussen, Steen Eiler, *Experiencing Architecture* (Cambridge: MIT Press, 1982).

Rellie, Jemima, 'The Disruptive Decade (1995–2005): The Impact on Museums', Personal Visions – Inspire, OMNi, Open Media Network, http://www.openmedianetwork.org.uk/contentandvision/inspire.htm (London 2007).

Renfrew, C. and Bahn, P., *Archaeology, Theories, Methods and Practice* (London: Thames and Hudson, 1991).

Resource Description Framework (RDF)/W3C Semantic Web Activity, http://www.w3.org/RDF/.

Ricoeur, Paul, *The Conflict of Interpretations* (London: Continuum, 2004).

Rogoff, Irit, 'Smuggling – An Embodied Criticality' (2006), http://eipcp.net/dlfiles/rogoff-smuggling.

Rorty, R., *Philosophy and the Mirror of Nature* (Princeton, NJ, 1980), p. 45.

Rubinstein, Daniel and Sluis, Katrina, 'A Life More Photographic: Mapping the Networked Image', *Photographies*, 1/1 (2008): 9–28.

Saeed, John I., *Semantics* (Malden, MA and Oxford: Blackwell, 2003).

Sandberg, M. 'Effigy and Narrative: Looking at the Nineteenth Century Folk Museum', in L. Charney and V.R. Schwartz (eds), *Cinema and the Invention of Modern Life* (Berkeley, 1995).

schraefel, mc, Smith, Daniel A., Owens, Alisdair, Russell et al., 'The Evolving mSpace Platform: Leveraging the Semantic Web on the Trail of the Memex', in *Proceedings of the sixteenth ACM Conference on Hypertext and Hypermedia. Salzburg, Austria* (ACM, 2005).

Sekula, Allan, 'Reading an Archive: Photography Between Labour and Capital', in Jessica Evans and Stuart Hall (eds), *Visual Culture: The Reader* (London: SAGE/Open University Press, 1999), pp. 181–92.

Semantic Web roadmap, http://www.w3.org/DesignIssues/Semantic.html.

Shadbolt, Nigel, Berners-Lee, Tim and Hall, Wendy, 'The Semantic Web Revisited', *IEEE Intelligent Systems*, 21/3 (2006).

Shneiderman, B. and Aris, A., 'Network Visualization by Semantic Substrates', *IEEE Transactions on Visualization and Computer Graphics*, 12/5 (2006), pp. 733–744.

Shneiderman, Ben and Plaisant, Catherine, *Designing the User Interface: Strategies for Effective Human-Computer Interaction* (Boston: Addison Wesley, 2005).

SIMILE Project, http://simile.mit.edu/.

Sirbu, Daniela, 'Digital Exploration of Unbuilt Architecture: A Non-Photorealistic Approach', in Kevin R. Klinger (ed.), *Connecting: Crossroads of Digital Discourse, ACADIA 2003 Conference Proceedings*, Indianapolis, USA (2003), pp. 234–45.

Sirbu, Daniela, 'Virtual Exploration of Teatro Olimpico', in Xavier Perrot (ed.), *Digital Culture and Heritage. Proceedings of ICHIM05* (Paris: Archives and Museum Informatics, 2005), http://www.archimuse.com/publishing/ichim05/Daniela_Sirbu.pdf.

Smeulders, Arnold W.M., Worring, Marcel, Santini, Simone et al., 'Content-Based Image Retrieval at the End of the Early Years', *IEEE Transactions on Pattern Analysis and Machine Intelligence* 22/12 (December 2000): 1349–80.

SPARQL Query Language for RDF, http://www.w3.org/TR/rdf-sparql-query/.

Stallabrass, Julian, *Internet Art: The Online Clash of Culture and Commerce* (London: Tate Press, 2003).

Stanney, Kay M. (ed.), *Handbook of Virtual Environments: Design, Implementation, and Applications* (Mahwah: Lawrence Erlbaum Associates, 2002).

STAR Project, http://hypermedia.research.glam.ac.uk/kos/STAR/.

Stewart, Kathleen, 'Nostalgia: A Polemic', *Cultural Anthropology*, 3/3 (August 1988): 227–41.

Stiegler, Bernard, *Technics and Time, 1: The Fault of Epimetheus*, trans. Richard Beardsworth, and George Collins (Stanford: Stanford University Press, 1998).

Stiegler, Bernard, 'The Discrete Image', in Jacques Derrida and Bernard Stiegler, *Echographies of Television* (Cambridge and Malden, MA: Polity, 2002).

Sullivan, G., *Art Practice as Research: Inquiry in the Visual Arts*, Thousand Oaks, CA: Sage Publications, Inc., 2005, pp. xxii, 265.

Surowiecki, James, *The Wisdom of Crowds* (London: Random House, 2004).

Trant, Jennifer, et al., 'The Eye of the Beholder: steve.museum and Social Tagging of Museum Collections', in J. Trant and D. Bearman (eds), *International Cultural Heritage Informatics Meeting (ICHIM07): Proceedings* (Toronto: Archives and Museum Informatics, 2007).

Tribe, Mark and Jana, Reena, *New Media Art* (Cologne: Taschen, 2006).

Turing, Alan, 'Computing Machinery and Intelligence', in Noah Wardrip-Fruin and Nick Montfort (eds), *The New Media Reader* (Cambridge, MA and London: MIT Press, 2004), pp. 50–64.

UK Museums and the Semantic Web, http://culturalsemanticweb.wordpress.com/.

Web Naming and Addressing Overview, http://www.w3.org/Addressing/.

Weibel, Peter and Druckrey, Timothy (eds), *net_condition: Art and Global Media* (Cambridge, MA: MIT Press, 2001).

Weinberger, David, *Everything is Miscellaneous: The Power of the New Digital Disorder* (New York: Times Books, 2007).

What Is Web 2.0, http://www.oreillynet.com/pub/a/oreilly/tim/news/2005/09/30/what-is-web-20.html.

White, C., 'John Arthur Giles Gere 1921–1995', in *Proceedings of the British Academy, 90: 1995 Lectures and Memoirs* (London, 1996), p. 373.

White, R.W., Kules, B., and Bederson, B., *Exploratory Search Interfaces: Categorization, Clustering and Beyond*, Report on the XSI 2005 Workshop at the Human-Computer Interaction Laboratory, University of Maryland, 2005, Communications of the ACM, volume 49, number 4 (2006), pp. 36–39.

Wilson, A. et al., *AHDS Moving Images and Sound Archiving Study* (London: AHDS, 2006).

Wolstencroft, Katy, Brass, Andy, Horrocks, Ian et al., 'A Little Semantic Web Goes a Long Way in Biology', in *The Semantic Web – ISWC 2005:4th International Semantic Web Conference, ISWC 2005, Galway, Ireland, November 6–10, 2005. Proceedings*, (Berlin: Springer, 2005).

Ze Wang, J., Li, J., Wiederhold, G. and Firschein, O., 'Classifying Objectionable Websites Based on Image Content', in Interactive Distributed Multimedia Systems and Telecommunication Services, *Lecture Notes in Computer Science*, vol. 1483 (Berlin/Heidelberg: Springer, 1998), p. 113.

Websites

http://amsterdam.nettime.org
http://artport. whitney.org
http://en.wikipedia.org/wiki/semantic_Web
http://gallery9. walkerart.org
http://jayanthr.wordpress.com/2008/06/18/software-bottleneck-and-itsresolution/
http://sympa.anart.no/sympa/info/syndicate
http://www.chart.ac.uk http://www.doc.ic.ac.uk/~mml/feast2/papers/pdf/556.pdf
http://www.discordia.us/scoop
http://www.flickr.com/photos/88 4 149@N00/2000000000/
http://www.furtherfield.org
http://www.hell.com
http://www.hero.ac.uk/uk/reference_and_subject_resources/subject_oriented_ directories3810.cfm
http://www.low-fi.org.uk
http://www.phrases.org.uk/meanings/a-picture-is-worth-a-thousand-words.html
http://www.rhizome.org
http://www.tate.org.uk/collection/carousel/index.htm
http://www.tate.org.uk/netart
http://www.tate.org.uk/netart/mongrel
http://www.thing.net

Index